DATE DUE

MR 11 '98			
MD 3 00			
DS 5 05			

STOPPARD:
THE PLAYS FOR RADIO 1964–1991

STOPPARD:
THE PLAYS FOR
RADIO
1964–1991

TOM STOPPARD

faber and faber

LONDON · BOSTON

d in 1990
nited
CIN 3AU
e) first published 1994

Printed in England by Clays Ltd, St Ives plc

2 4 6 8 10 9 7 5 3 1

CONTENTS

Introduction   vii

Six of these eight plays for radio were directed by John Tydeman, whom I first met when he was a trainee producer. Now he has just retired from the position of the BBC's Head of Radio Drama. This collection of all my work to date for 'Portland Place' is, therefore, a timely opportunity to pay my respects to a friend who has been a sympathetic and patient collaborator since Radio Three and Four were Third and Home.

The Dissolution of Dominic Boot and *'M' is for Moon Among Other Things* – reduced to 'Boot' and 'Moon' in my affections – were written for *Just Before Midnight*, a series of 15-minute plays which went out in 1964. The peg for 'Boot' – a man riding around in a taxi trying to raise the money to pay the cabbie – was the first and last self-propelled idea I ever had, and I think I wrote the play in a day. 'Moon' started off as a short story which never got into print, and was commissioned, or perhaps only encouraged, on the strength of 'Boot'.

If You're Glad I'll Be Frank ('Glad/Frank' ever after) came out of a conversation in a corridor at Portland Place with Richard Imison. John and Richard, Script Editor then and afterwards until his sadly early death last year, represented BBC Radio Drama to me for thirty years. Richard pounced on me Tigger-like with news of a series of short plays about people in imaginary jobs. There and then I proposed the Speaking Clock. I named her Gladys and gave her a propensity towards interior monologue in free verse, so she went out on the Third.

The next play – about a man painting the Forth Bridge solo – may have started life as another candidate for that series, but by this time I wanted to spread my wings and go solo myself; to write without regard to series or given lengths. *Albert's Bridge* was my first more-or-less full scale radio play, and Albert's interior monologues were longer than Glad's.

Where Are They Now? was written for Schools Radio. For the occasion I went against my principles, or at least my practice, and dropped a leaky bucket into the well of personal experience. Not that I was taught French by a Welsh sadist – *au contraire*, remembering kindly Miss Stokes who drove a pre-war Morris coupé – but no doubt many who have been at an English boarding school might suppose we were at the same one.

Artist Descending a Staircase, *The Dog It Was That Died* and *In the Native State* were separated by, roughly, ten-year intervals, a matter of circumstance rather than a conscious withdrawal from radio. Even so, ten years is an embarrassing gap for a writer who is enthusiastic for BBC Radio Drama and in debt to it. The existence of these three plays owed itself to John's and Richard's persistent letters and postcards. In each case the play grew from nothing other than the accumulating discomfort of failing to deliver.

John Tydeman was the director of 'Moon', 'Glad/Frank', *Where Are They Now?* (in its second production; the director for Schools was Dickon Reed), *Artist Descending A Staircase*, *The Dog It Was That Died* and *In the Native State*. 'Boot' was directed by Michael Bakewell, and *Albert's Bridge* by Charles Lefeaux.

TOM STOPPARD
May 1994

THE DISSOLUTION OF DOMINIC BOOT

CHARACTERS

DOMINIC
VIVIAN
TAXI DRIVER
SHEPTON
MOTHER
FATHER
GIRL CLERK
MAN CLERK
MISS BLIGH
CARTWRIGHT

Fade in street—traffic.

VIVIAN: Well, thanks for the lunch—oh golly, it's raining.

DOMINIC: Better run for it.

VIVIAN: Don't be silly . . . . (*Up*) Hey, taxi!

DOMINIC: I say, Viv . . .

VIVIAN: Come on, you can drop me off. (*To driver*) Just round the corner, Derby Street Library.

(*They get in—taxi drives.*)

DOMINIC: Look, Vivian, I haven't got . . .

VIVIAN: Dash it—that's taken about ten shillings out of my two-guinea hairdo—honestly, I'm furious. Don't you ever have an umbrella?

DOMINIC: Not when it's raining.

VIVIAN: Didn't I give you one for your birthday?

DOMINIC: No, it was your birthday.

VIVIAN: Why did I give it to you on *my* birthday?

DOMINIC: No, it was *I* who gave it to *you* on my birthday. *Your* birthday. Vivian, please stop talking about umbrellas. The thing is . . .

VIVIAN: If we're going out tonight, I'll have to have some repairs on my hair, it's beginning to straggle. Another pound down the drain.

DOMINIC: I'm afraid I can't tonight, Vivian, I promised to see my mother.

VIVIAN: What about?

DOMINIC: Um, about my father.

VIVIAN: What about him?

DOMINIC: Nothing. Just keeping her in touch.

VIVIAN: You never see your father.

DOMINIC: Well, we just sort of—talk about him.

VIVIAN: I thought you may be seeing her about us getting married.

DOMINIC: Oh, no.

VIVIAN: What do you mean by that?

DOMINIC: I mean, yes.

VIVIAN: Will we have enough by Christmas, or spring at the latest? After all, you've been saving now for months.

DOMINIC: Incidentally, Vivian . . .

VIVIAN: Oh, no! It's half-past two—Dominic, we'll have to start eating somewhere with quicker service. Anyway, I'm fed up with Italian. I don't know why we always go to Marcello's, do you?

DOMINIC: No. Only . . .

VIVIAN: (*Up*) Just there, next lamppost on the right. (*Down*) By the way, you're on the black list—you've had those six books overdue for weeks—what do you do with them? (*Up*) Thank you. (*Down*) Well, I'll see you tonight.
(*Opens door.*)

DOMINIC: I told you . . .

VIVIAN: Oh yes—tomorrow then, I'll see you in Marcello's. Goodbye darling. Oh no, not Marcello's. Oh, I don't know— phone me, will you?

DOMINIC: (*Slightly desperate*) Vivian—
(*She's gone.*)
(*Thinks:*) One and ninepence. Extras sixpence.
(*Coin counting:*) Sixpence, shilling, one and a penny, one and two, three, threepence halfpenny . . . threepence halfpenny . . .

DRIVER: Waiting till the rain stops?

DOMINIC: No, um, the Metropolitan Bank, Blackfriars, please.

Cut. Bank.

DOMINIC: In ones, please.

GIRL CLERK: Oh, Mr Boot, would you mind stepping down to the end of the counter there . . .

DOMINIC: What for? Oh ah, righto. (*Humming.*)
(*Walking.*)
Hello, Mr Honeydew.

SHEPTON: I'm Mr Shepton.
DOMINIC: Oh really? I thought you were the manager.
SHEPTON: The manager is Mr Bartlett.
DOMINIC: Oh yes, I'm always getting it wrong.
SHEPTON: Well . . . yes, well, Mr Bartlett has asked me . . .
DOMINIC: Over the top, am I?
SHEPTON: You're forty-three pounds beyond your limit, Mr Boot.
    I'm afraid that we have had to pass back two cheques
    received today from ah Marsello's er Markello's . . .
DOMINIC: Marchello's, Mr Sheppard.
SHEPTON: Shepton.

Cut. Taxi moving.
DOMINIC: (*Thinks:*) Three and three . . . three and six . . .
DRIVER: The Irish Widows' International Bank—is that on the
    left here?
DOMINIC: No, other side. Thanks. (*Thinks:*) Three and six, plus
    six, four bob . . .

Cut. Bank.
DOMINIC: In ones, please.
CLERK: Oh, good afternoon, Mr Boot. Would you have a word
    with Mr Honeydew?

Cut. DOMINIC *slamming taxi door.*
DOMINIC: Co-operative Wool and Synthetic Trust Bank in High
    Street, Ken, please.
DRIVER: You a bank robber, are you?
DOMINIC: In a modest way. Please hurry, I've got to cash a cheque
    before they close.
    (*Taxi starts moving.*)

Cut to traffic.
DRIVER: I did my best.
DOMINIC: Dammit.
DRIVER: Six and nine.
DOMINIC: Ah, would you mind taking a cheque?

Cut. A door is flung open.

MISS BLIGH: (*Very remote, quite detached*) Good afternoon, Mr Boot. Mr Cartwright has been asking . . .

DOMINIC: In a minute—can you lend me ten bob—I've got a taxi . . .

MISS BLIGH: Oh Mr Boot, what a pity you didn't come earlier. I've just spent it all on stamps—five pounds' worth, Mr Boot.

DOMINIC: Hang on.

(*Out door—cross pavement.*)

I say, do you take stamps?

DRIVER: Yes, if you like. Green Stamps, are they?

DOMINIC: All colours. I mean they're stamps. I don't know what colour they are. *Stamps!*

DRIVER: Do you mean like for letters?

DOMINIC: That's right, and parcels. Stamps.

DRIVER: Do me a favour.

(*Back across pavement through door.*)

DOMINIC: No good . . .

MISS BLIGH: Oh, what isn't, Mr Boot? Oh, you're terribly wet, is it raining?

(DOMINIC *through another door.*)

DOMINIC: I'm sorry to trouble you, Mr Cartwright. . .

CARTWRIGHT: I've been waiting forty-five minutes to trouble you, Mr Boot. Now look here, I'm going out for the rest of the afternoon, but I want to pick up the Lexington figures to take home, so please have them ready by six. Well, look to it.

DOMINIC: Mr Cartwright—could you lend me ten shillings. . .

Cut to taxi moving.

DRIVER: Nice area. What number are you?

DOMINIC: Forty-eight. On the left.

DRIVER: You use taxis a lot, don't you?

DOMINIC: Yes, hardly ever. I mean no, I do . . . . . (*thinks:*) Fourteen shillings . . . and six . . .

(*Taxi pulls up.*)

Thanks, I'll be out in a minute.

DOMINIC: (*Panting, muttering*) Fourteen and six, fourteen and six . . . property of the North Thames Gas Board . . . oh well . . . where's that poker . . . wardrobe, wardrobe—ah!—North Thames, here goes, uh . . . .
(*Breaks open gas meter—coins.*)
One, two four, five six seven, ten, ten and six, ten and six . . . oh no, damn . . . oh God . . . .

Cut. In taxi—moving.
DOMINIC: First left, second right. Oh, would you like ten bob to be going on with, here.
(*Coins.*)
DRIVER: You been robbing the gas meter?
DOMINIC: No, no, I just collect them. (*Thinks:*) Twenty-one and six—plus sixpence, minus ten bob I gave him, minus one and threepence halfpenny, that makes—twenty-two bob, plus sixpence, minus ten bob I gave him.
DRIVER: (*Pulling up*) Here we are, 73, Mansion Lane.
MOTHER: (*On pavement*) Taxi!
DOMINIC: Hello, Mother. I was just coming to see you.
MOTHER: Dominic! You always pick the wrong time. Never mind we can talk in the taxi. (*To driver*) Bond Street.
DOMINIC: Going shopping?
MOTHER: Hair-do. They always ruin it, but I don't trust anyone else. I'm thinking of going blue. And piled on top. Well, what's with Vivian?
DOMINIC: A bit straggly—the rain, you know.
MOTHER: What are you talking about? Why are you so wet? Don't you use Vivian's umbrella?
DOMINIC: No, why should I? She doesn't even use the one I gave her.
MOTHER: I mean the one she told me she gave you, for Christmas.
DOMINIC: (*Is everyone mad?*) She–never–gave–me–an–umbrella!
MOTHER: I like that girl. Have you seen anything of your father?
DOMINIC: No.
MOTHER: I'm told he's thinking of getting married again.
DOMINIC: Who'd have him?

MOTHER: God knows. I think you ought to go and see him. I
    think it's quite wrong not to keep in touch with one's father.
DOMINIC: Righto. (*Thinks:*) Twenty-four, minus ten, plus . . .
MOTHER: And if you find out anything about her, give me a ring
    at once. Why aren't you at the office?
DOMINIC: Well, things are a bit slack, and I'm my own boss now
    really, so I thought I'd take an hour off and have tea with
    you.
MOTHER: Well, it seems to be the first job you're any good at. I
    hope you're being sensible about it. I bet you're not saving.
DOMINIC: Oh, I am.
MOTHER: I was getting quite tired of you always coming to see me
    for money. Good God—twenty-five shillings—Dominic . . .
DOMINIC: (*Trapped*) It's all right—it's all on the office—I've been
    making some calls for them, you see, old Cartwright. . . .
    (*Thinks*) Oh God. . . .

Cut—DRIVER *driving*.
DRIVER: You know who used to cut my mum's hair? My dad.
DOMINIC: He was a hairdresser, was he?
DRIVER: No, he was a grocer. Corner shop off the Angel.
DOMINIC: (*Thinks:*) Thirty-one minus ten plus . . .
DRIVER: And guess who cut *his* hair. My mum.
DOMINIC: (*Thinks:*) Thirty-nine, and sixpence for Vivian and
    sixpence for Mother, minus ten, plus, no minus . . . . (*Up*)
    Can you lend me four pennies?

Cut—DOMINIC *dialling*—*phone*.
DOMINIC: (*On phone*) Hello, Charlie. Dom. Dominic. Is that
    Charles Monkton? Well, it's Dom. Dominic Boot. Yes—
    listen, Charles I'm in a bit of a fix—you know that two
    pounds I lent you? Yes, now. I'll come over. Where's your
    place? What? I'm not coming by train—I'm in a taxi. No,
    that's WHY I'm broke, Charlie—what? All right. Past East
    Croydon station, first left, 18B. Right.
    (*Down phone.*)

Cut.

DRIVER: You ever been to Croydon?

DOMINIC: No, Why?

DRIVER: It's over the six-mile limit.

DOMINIC: Limit?

DRIVER: Yes. You see, if you stop me, then I've got to take you wherever you want, that's the law. But if it's over six miles the meter doesn't count so I'm allowed to fix a price. That's the system.

DOMINIC: That's ridiculous.

DRIVER: Well, I lose on tips, you see. I can take you there, well in that time I can have four other fares and a tip on each. So I'm allowed to strike a bargain with you. Two pounds.

DOMINIC: A pound.

DRIVER: Right, you can pay me off now.

DOMINIC: Twenty-five bob.

DRIVER: Doesn't pay.

DOMINIC: Thirty with tip.

DRIVER: Thirty-two and six.

DOMINIC: Done!

Cut. In taxi—stationary.

DOMINIC: (*Thinks:*) Seventy-one in all. Minus ten I gave him. Sixty-one. Three pounds one. One and threepence halfpenny in change. About three pounds, then. Minus two of Charlie's. One pound. Minus, minus nothing. One pound, one pound. Who? Please God, who? Plus fourpence he lent me. One pound and fourpence. *Who?*

DRIVER: Well have you made up your mind? Can't sit in Croydon for ever. There's a fellow there who's looking like mad for a taxi. Looks like a town fare. If you don't want to go, say so quick.

(*Door opens—*DOMINIC *in street.*)

DOMINIC: Excuse me, you seem to be rather desperate for a taxi.

MAN: I am—I've got an important meeting . . . why?

DOMINIC: I think I can help you. Please take my taxi.

MAN: How very kind of you. Are you sure?

DOMINIC: Certainly. I'm in the business.

MAN: Business?

DOMINIC: I'm a taxi agent. That'll be twenty-five shillings.

MAN: I'll call a policeman.

DOMINIC: Very well, one pound and fourpence, and you pay the tip.

Cut—DRIVER *driving.*

DRIVER: What did that copper want?

DOMINIC: Little misunderstanding. (*Thinks:*) A hundred and eight, minus ten, minus two pounds . . . (*Up*) You must make a fortune.

DRIVER: Shilling a mile I have to give the company for this cab. And there's my fuel. I'd never keep body and soul together without the shop.

DOMINIC: Grocer's?

DRIVER: Clothes, furniture, stuff, second-hand. I've got a staff. My brother. He cuts my hair. Well, my mum and dad have passed on.

Cut.

DOMINIC: Father! Oh dear Father who art in Windsor . . .

FATHER: Good Lord, what brings you here?

DOMINIC: Well, I was missing you, Father.

FATHER: Don't be absurd. Still, good to see you. How's your mother?

DOMINIC: Very well, Father. Sends you her love.

FATHER: Nonsense. For goodness' sake sit down. Whisky?

DOMINIC: Fine. Oh, Father, by the way—I've got a cab outside . . .

FATHER: Can't you even walk ten minutes from the station? You people. (*Up*) Bates! Give this half crown to the taxi driver and bring us some whisky. Well now, Dominic, how's the job?

Cut.

DRIVER: Who was that?

DOMINIC: My father.

DRIVER: He seemed angry about something.

DOMINIC: He'd just had some bad news. Derby Street Library, please.

Cut.

DOMINIC: (*A desperate man*) Vivian!

VIVIAN: Sssssh . . . . (*Whispering*) For goodness' sake, what's the matter?

DOMINIC: (*A desperate man whispering*) Oh sorry. I say Vivian . . .

VIVIAN: Have you brought the books at last?

DOMINIC: Books? Oh—look, Vivian, please help me, you get paid today don't you? I've got to pay off that taxi, you see . . .

VIVIAN: Oh, Dominic—I'm very cross with you—we're saving to get married and you keep taking taxis everywhere. It's not fair, Dominic. Now you come running to me. Honestly.

DOMINIC: (*The desperate man, cracked and yelling*) OH, YOU STUPID COW, SHUT UP AND GIVE ME TEN POUNDS FOR THE LOVE OF GOD!

Cut. Interior.

DRIVER: Well, frankly, you couldn't have paid much for it, could you?

DOMINIC: It's a very fine engagement ring. Ten guineas.

DRIVER: See that? Scratched. Four pound ten.

DOMINIC: It's a diamond. Six pounds.

DRIVER: Five and I'm taking a chance.

DOMINIC: Done. What about the rest of the stuff?

DRIVER: Well it's a bit of a mess isn't it? I don't know how you can live like this, I don't really. I mean, it's really junk, isn't it? I'll give you ten bob for the desk, and another ten for the mirror. The bed's had it really—I mean six books isn't the same as a castor, is it? Thirty bob with the mattress. Now over here. Not a bad wardrobe—fifteen bob—gas stove— couple of pounds if you like. That's about it, isn't it? OK, Dom? Look, someone's bust up your gas meter.

DOMINIC: What about the clothes? There's some good stuff there.

DRIVER: Can't move it, you see. I'll give you ten bob to take it away, and that makes us square, doesn't it?
(*Doorbell.*)
Oh, that'll be my brother with the van.

DOMINIC: Mr Melon.

DRIVER: Lemon.

DOMINIC: Mr Lemon, I've got to get back to the office before six.
You couldn't throw that in, could you?

DRIVER: Can't do it, Dom. Company checks the mileage, you see.
That's a seven and a tanner drive, that is. Tell you what, I'll
cut my throat and do it for the suit.

DOMINIC: What suit?

DRIVER: That one you got on.

DOMINIC: But that only leaves me with a pair of pyjamas and a
raincoat. I can't go to the office like that. Can I?—*Can I?*

Cut. Door flung open.

DOMINIC: Is he back yet?

MISS BLIGH: Hello, Mr Boot. Is it still raining? Oh, you are wet. I
do like your pyjamas Mr Boot. What's the matter Mr Boot,
you seem awfully upset. Mr Cartwright seems upset too.
(*Door opens.*)

CARTWRIGHT: Well, Mr Boot—Good God, man, what are you
wearing? Have you gone mad?

DOMINIC: I don't think so, Mr Cartwright.

CARTWRIGHT: Get out of here. I'm giving you a week's notice.
And stop crying.

DOMINIC: Yes, Mr Cartwright.
(*Door slams.*)

MISS BLIGH: (*Always tender, soft, remote*) Come on, Mr Boot. I
think you ought to go home. Come on . . . I'm going your
way, Mr Boot.

DOMINIC: (*Weeping*) Oh . . . oh . . .
(*They go through door into street.*)

MISS BLIGH: It's raining again. Haven't you got an umbrella, Mr
Boot? Don't cry, Mr Boot. Your pyjamas are getting awfully
wet . . . I should do up your front, Mr Boot, you'll catch
cold. . . . Pull your socks up, Mr Boot. (*Up*)
Taxi! . . . come on, Mr Boot. Come on, you can drop me
off. . . .

'M' IS FOR MOON AMONG OTHER THINGS

CHARACTERS

CONSTANCE
ALFRED

Silence—a man grunts and shakes his paper—a woman flips over the pages of a book and sighs.

NB A married couple, ALFRED *and* CONSTANCE—*middle class, childless, aged 45 and 42.*

CONSTANCE: (*Sighs—thinks:*) Macbeth . . .

> (*Flip.*)
> Macedonia . . .
> (*Flip.*)
> Machine-gun . . .
> (*Flip.*)
> Magna Carta . . .
> (*Flip.*)
> Measles . . .
> (*Flip.*)
> Molluscs . . . molluscs . . .

ALFRED: (*Grunts—thinks:*) ' . . . the girl, wearing a red skirt and black sweater, asked the court that her name should not be continued in column five, continued in column five . . . '
(*Shakes paper.*)

CONSTANCE: (*Thinks:*) . . . Invertebrate animal . . . discovered that marine varieties . . .
(*Slams book shut.*)
I think enough for tonight—I wish the print wasn't so small . . . Have you seen my pills anywhere?

ALFRED: Mmmm . . . (*Thinks:*) ' . . . "anything like it in my thirty years on the Bench," he added. "While young louts like you are roaming the streets no girl is safe from . . . "'
(*Impatiently*) Oh . . .
(*Turns page.*)

CONSTANCE: (*Thinks:*) February the fifth, March the fifth, April, May, June, July, August . . . six.

ALFRED: (*Thinks:*) 'A Smooth-as-Silk Beauty as Fast as they Come!'

CONSTANCE: (*Thinks:*) The Friday before last must have been the twenty-seventh, that's right, because the Gilberts came to dinner and that was a Friday because of Mrs Gilbert not eating the meat, and the Encyclopaedia always comes on the twenty-seventh, and it was just when the M to N came when I phoned Alfred at the office about what to give the Gilberts, so it must have been Friday the twenty-seventh. So last Sunday was the twenty-ninth, so today is twenty-nine plus seven makes thirty-six, so it must be the sixth, unless July has thirty-one, in which case it's the seventh, no, the fifth. Thirty days hath April, June, is it? Wait a minute, the Friday before last was the twenty-seventh . . .

ALFRED: (*Thinks:*) 'I found her to be a smooth-as-silk beauty with the classic lines of thrust of . . . '

CONSTANCE: Alfred, is it the fifth or the sixth?

ALFRED: Mmm? (*Thinks:*) ' . . . surging to sixty mph in nine seconds . . . '

CONSTANCE: Fifth?

ALFRED: Fifth what?

CONSTANCE: What's today?

ALFRED: Sunday . . . (*Thinks:*) ' . . . the handbrake a touch stiff and I'd like to see an extra ashtray for the passenger but otherwise . . . ' (*Up*) Oh for goodness' sake—you know I hate people looking over my shoulder.
(*Turns page.*)

CONSTANCE: (*Thinks:*) August the fifth, nineteen sixty-two. (*Up*) Alfred, in half an hour I'll be exactly forty-two-and-a-half years old. That's a thought, isn't it?

ALFRED: Mmmm . . . (*Thinks:*) 'Little old grey-haired Mrs Winifred Garters wept last night as . . . '

CONSTANCE: What time were you born, Alfred?

ALFRED: What?

CONSTANCE: I was born just as the clock struck half-past ten at night—what time were you born?

ALFRED: I can't remember.

CONSTANCE: Didn't anyone tell you?

ALFRED: That's what I can't remember.

(*Hall clock chiming ten.*)

Oh, what's that?—ten? We haven't had the news today. I think there's one now, isn't there? Turn on the box—hang on, where's the *Radio Times*?—ah—is this this week's?

CONSTANCE: Forty-two-and-a-half, and all I've got is a headache.

ALFRED: Is this the new one? 'August five to twelve'—what's today?

CONSTANCE: Sunday.

ALFRED: No–no–no—what's—oh never mind—yes, this is it— News at five-past ten.

(*Turns on TV.*)

'Dial M for Murder'—oh, that might have been good.

CONSTANCE: It's an awful thing, you know. When you start worrying about the halves. I mean there's no purpose to make sense of it, is there? Every time it's half-past ten, it's another day older, and all I've done with it is to get up and stay up. Where's it all going?

(*Bring in finish of 'Dial M for Murder'—hold it and fade it low.*)

(*Thinks:*) They used to call me Millie . . . my middle name was my favourite till I was—how old was I? 17? Happy Birthday Millie, it used to be . . . Then I went over to Constance, it sounded more grown-up. Seventeen from forty-two. Twenty-five. A quarter of a century, constant Constance. . . . (*Up*) If I had a choice, perhaps I'd choose what I'm doing now. I don't care about that. But I want the choice. I don't want the moon, Alfred, all I want is the possibility of an alternative, so that I know I'm doing this because I want to instead of because there's nothing else.

ALFRED: Sshssh—hang on, Constance, let me hear the News . . . (*Bring in opening of tape (if there is one) of the 10.05 pm News—5 August 1962.*)

NEWS: The News . . . Marilyn Monroe, the actress, was found dead in her Los Angeles home today . . .

(*Fade out.*)

ALFRED: (*Fading in with 'oh's' used as a sort of dirge—thinks:*) Oh . . . oh . . . oh . . . oh . . . oh . . . poor Marilyn . . . poor poor thing . . . What have they done? . . . God, poor little thing . . . She must have been so unhappy. Oh Marilyn . . .

CONSTANCE: She seemed so full of life, didn't she?

ALFRED: (*Thinks:*) Abandoned . . . no love . . . like a child . . .

CONSTANCE: Poor thing, it's awful.

ALFRED: (*Thinks:*) Marilyn . . . you shouldn't have trusted them, they're all rotten . . .

CONSTANCE: Do you suppose she meant it? Oh, wasn't she lovely, I mean a lovely *person*, she made you feel it. Doesn't it go to show?

ALFRED: Oh, do shut up.

CONSTANCE: Alfred!

ALFRED: Oh, I'm sorry. I'm just tired . . . and upset.

CONSTANCE: It's all right, Alfred.

ALFRED: Of course she meant it. By God, you've only got to use your imagination. It's such a cold shallow world she was living in. No warmth or understanding—no one understood her, she was friendless.

CONSTANCE: Do you think so?

ALFRED: Of course. Hangers-on. People didn't appreciate her. Just using her. A girl like that. It's a crime . . .

CONSTANCE: Fate.

ALFRED: Fate! Don't be absurd!

CONSTANCE: Please don't shout, Alfred.

ALFRED: (*Wearily*) Oh damn them, dammit . . . Oh, let's go to bed. I'm tired.

CONSTANCE: Yes. I'm worn out—hope I'll be able to sleep.

ALFRED: I can never stay awake, and you can never get to sleep—what's the matter with you?

CONSTANCE: I don't know—can't sleep with this headache.

ALFRED: You know, you read too much, you're always complaining of eye strain and headaches, well it's no wonder.

CONSTANCE: The print's too small, really.

(*Flip flip flip of pages:*)

ALFRED: The Universal Treasury of People, Places and Things: Illustrated. M to N . . . A lot of useless knowledge.

CONSTANCE: I've got as far as Molluscs, but I'm skipping madly.

ALFRED: You forget it all anyway.

CONSTANCE: No I don't, not all of it.

ALFRED: Well, you forgot about Catholics, didn't you? There must have been *something* about them under C.

CONSTANCE: (*Unhappy, offensive-defensive, a little desperate*) Oh Alfred, *please*—not now again . . .

ALFRED: *Catholics*! Catholics-don't-eat-meat-on-Fridays. Or under M—*Meat*!, what-Catholics-don't eat-on-a-Friday. Or F—*Friday*!, the-day-Catholics-don't-eat-meat-on. Oh my God, you could probably have found it under G—*Mrs Gilbert*!, wife to Alfred's boss *Mr* Gilbert and a staunch Catholic who does not eat meat on a Friday! (*Pause.*) D is for Débâcle—that which occurs when Mrs Gilbert is offered meat by her husband's chief accountant's wife on a Friday!

CONSTANCE: (*Crying*) Well, I wouldn't have forgotten if you hadn't been so awful on the phone—I phoned you to ask you what to get for dinner and you wouldn't give me a chance—Alfred—you were—you behaved . . .

ALFRED: Oh, don't cry—I couldn't talk to you then . . . You had to call up just as Mr Gilbert, Anglican, was hovering round my neck with my monthly report . . . Oh, what does it matter anyway . . .

(*Pages turned.*)

M is for Money . . . Universal Treasury all right . . . Two guineas a volume, a guinea per letter of the alphabet. How can you get a guinea's worth out of X? Or Z?

CONSTANCE: It was a lovely birthday present.

ALFRED: Well, I'm sorry I haven't got as much money as your rich brother Stanley.

CONSTANCE: Oh, you know I didn't mean that. But it's lovely to know that every month there's another volume coming. That's the seventh, counting the A to B I got on the actual day. It's O to P this month. Oranges and Orang-utans. I don't know—it's just that the time isn't all a waste, somehow, do you know what I mean?

ALFRED: What's the capital of Mongolia?

CONSTANCE: The point isn't to know the capital of Mongolia, Alfred—the point is to . . . Alfred, at half-past ten I'll be forty-two-and-a-half years old and it's all slipping by.

ALFRED: Well, I'm blessed—do you know they haven't even got *her* in here.

CONSTANCE: Who?

ALFRED: 'Monroe Doctrine . . . Monroe, James, President of the United States . . . ' Universal ruddy Treasury.

CONSTANCE: Well, they can't have everything. I remember my first ABC book—everything was so simple then. I thought that each letter only stood for the one word they gave, you know? A is for Apple, B is for Baby, C is for Cat . . . M was for Moon. It was ages before I knew that M was for anything else . . . like Millie . . . She was 36, he said, didn't he?

ALFRED: Did he? Poor dear . . . What I meant was that it needn't have happened. That's why you can't call it fate.

CONSTANCE: It's all right, I wasn't thinking.

ALFRED: It was just that she had no one to recognize her needs, you see. No one to turn to, I mean. No wonder the poor girl got desperate. Those *actors*—people like that—they've got no humanity, no understanding—self, self, it's such a selfish society. A girl like that, dying with a telephone in her hand—who did she have to call who would have done her any good? No one. Perhaps that's fate.

CONSTANCE: Yes, I suppose so.

ALFRED: Well, let's go up. I'll lock up—you have the bathroom first.

CONSTANCE: I wonder who she was trying to phone, though . . . (*Fade out—sound of* CONSTANCE *getting into bed—or near offer.*)
Oooooh, bed. I feel quite worn out.

ALFRED: You got up too early again.

CONSTANCE: I couldn't drop off once I woke up. It's getting very tiresome.

ALFRED: Don't those pills work?

CONSTANCE: I suppose they must help. I think I'll take an extra one tonight.

ALFRED: Yes, I should.

CONSTANCE: Oh—Alfred—I forgot my glass of water. Do you mind, while you're still up.

ALFRED: Oh, gosh, where is it?

CONSTANCE: On the wash-stand. (*Thinks:*) Oh God, if I'd been in
   her place I would have eaten the bloody meat and gone to
   confession . . . Bitch . . . I shouldn't have phoned Alfred at
   the office, though . . .
ALFRED: Here you are. Got the pills?
   (*Clock chiming half-past ten*—ALFRED *getting into bed.*)
CONSTANCE: (*Thinks:*) Half-past ten, August the fifth, nineteen
   sixty-two. Well—Cheers! (*Gulps pill and drink.*) Happy
   anniversary, Millie.
   (*Puts glass down.*)
ALFRED: Should I turn the light off?
CONSTANCE: Yes.
   (*Click.*)
   (*Thinks:*) Maple tree, Mozambique . . . Mandragora . . .
   Marzipan . . . Mother . . . Moon . . . Melon . . .
   Menopause . . . Mongolia . . .
ALFRED: (*Thinks:*) Marilyn . . . don't worry, I'm glad you
   phoned, . . . Don't be unhappy, love, tell me all about it and
   I'm sure I'll think of something . . . Do you feel better
   already?—Well, it's nice to have someone you know you can
   count on any time, isn't it? . . . Don't cry, don't cry any
   more . . . I'll make it all right . . . (*Up—sigh*) Poor old
   thing . . .
CONSTANCE: Oh, you mustn't worry about me, Alfred, I'll be all
   right . . . (*Thinks:*) Marshmallow . . . Mickey
   Mouse . . . Marriage . . . Moravia . . . Mule . . .
   Market . . . Mumps . . .

IF YOU'RE GLAD I'LL BE FRANK

CHARACTERS

GLADYS
FRANK
1ST PORTER
MYRTLE TRELAWNEY
MR MORTIMER
MR COURTENAY-SMITH
SIR JOHN
LORD COOT
BERYL BLIGH
OPERATOR
IVY, A BUS CONDUCTRESS
2ND PORTER

From her first words it is apparent that GLADYS *is the* 'TIM'* *girl, and always has been.*

As such, she has two columns to herself.

The right-hand column is for the Speaking Clock, and as such it is ostensibly continuous. But of course we hear her voice direct, not through a telephone unless otherwise indicated.

The left-hand column is for her unspoken thoughts, and of course this one has the dominant value.

It should be obvious in the script when her 'TIM' *voice is needed in the background as counterpoint, and when it should be drowned altogether by the rising dominance of her thoughts.*

When her 'TIM' *voice intrudes again I have indicated this* not *by the actual words she uses, because the actual time she announces should be related to the number of minutes or seconds that have passed (i.e. depending on the pace of the broadcast) but by suggesting the space of time that her speaking voice should take up, and this appears in the script in this form: (3–4 seconds).*

GLADYS *operates the pips too, and these are indicated thus:* (PIP PIP PIP).

Some of GLADYS's *sustained passages fall into something half-way between prose and verse, and I have gone some way to indicate the rhythms by line-endings, but of course the effect should not be declamatory.*

*Until the introduction of STD in Britain the Speaking Clock was reached by dialling TIM.

SCENE I

FRANK, *who turns out to be a bus driver, is heard dialling* 'TIM'.

GLADYS (*through phone*): At the third stroke it will be eight fifty-nine precisely.

FRANK (*amazed disbelief*): It can't be. . . .

(PIP PIP PIP.)

. . . At the third stroke it will be eight fifty-nine and ten seconds. . . .

(*Fearful hope*): It's not. . . ?

(PIP PIP PIP.)

. . . At the third stroke it will be eight fifty-nine and twenty seconds. . . .

(*Joy.*) It is! . . . *Gladys!* It's my Gladys! (*Fade.*)

(PIP PIP PIP.)

SCENE 2

Exterior mid traffic, Big Ben begins its nine a.m. routine. Cut to interior: no traffic, Big Ben fainter.

PORTER (*murmurs*): Nine o'clock. Here we go.
   (*What happens is this:* MYRTLE, MORTIMER,
   COURTNAY-SMITH, SIR JOHN *and the* FIRST LORD OF
   THE POST OFFICE (LORD COOT) *enter from the street on the
   first, third, fifth, seventh and ninth strokes of Big Ben
   respectively* (*the second, fourth, sixth and eighth strokes being
   heard through the closed door.) Each opening of the door lets in
   traffic sound momentarily and amplifies Big Ben.*)

(*Street door.*)

PORTER: Morning, Mrs. Trelawney.

MYRTLE (*gay*): Hello, Tommy.

(*And out through door.*)

(*Street door.*)

PORTER: Morning, Mr. Mortimer.

MORTIMER (*tired*): Good morning, Tom.

(*And out through door.*)

(*Street door.*)

PORTER: Good morning, Mr. Courtenay-Smith.

C.-SMITH (*vague*): Morning, Mr. Thompson.

(*And out through door.*)

(*Street door.*)

PORTER: Good morning, Sir John.

SIR JOHN (*aloof*): Ah, Thompson. . . .

(*And out through door.*)

(*Street door.*)

PORTER: Good morning, my Lord.

1ST LORD: Morning, Tommy. (*Conspiratorial.*) Anything to report?

PORTER: All on schedule, my Lord.

1ST LORD: Jolly good.

(*Through door.*)

MYRTLE: Good morning, your Lordship.

1ST LORD: Good morning, Mrs. Trelawney.

(*Through door.*)

MORTIMER: Good morning, my Lord.

1ST LORD: Good morning, ah, Mortimer.

(*Through door.*)

C.-SMITH: Good morning, Lord Coot.

1ST LORD: Good morning, Mr. Courtenay-Smith.

(*Through door.*)

SIR JOHN: What ho, Cooty.

1ST LORD: Morning, Jack.

(*Through door.*)

BERYL: Good morning, sir.

1ST LORD (*startled*): Who are you?

BERYL: I'm new.
> (*Pause.*)

1ST LORD: I thought I couldn't account for you. . . . New what?

BERYL: New secretary, sir . . . Miss Bligh. They sent me over from Directory Enquiries last night.

1ST LORD: I see. What happened to my old—to Miss—er——

BERYL: Apparently she cracked, sir, at 1.53 a.m. I came at once.

1ST LORD: That's the ticket. The Post Office never sleeps. Do you know the form round here?

BERYL: Well. . . .

1ST LORD: Quite simple. I'm the First Lord of the Post Office, of course. I'm responsible for the lot, with special attention to the Telephone Services, which are as follows—write them down——
> UMP—dial-the-Test-score.
> SUN—dial-the-weather.
> POP—dial-a-pop.
> BET—dial-the-racing-results.
> GOD—dial-the-Bible-reading.
> EAT—dial-a-recipe.

And so on, with many others, including the most popular and important of them all—TIM, dial-the-speaking-clock. We can't afford to lose track of time, or we'd be lost. Now, you see, we must keep a continuous check on all of them, because if you don't keep an eye on them they slide back. The strain is appalling, and the staffing problems monumental.

Shall we start checking, then? To begin with, synchronize our watches, and then check with TIM—ready? I make it just coming up to nine two and forty seconds. . . .

SCENE 3

Follows straight on with the Time signal (PIP PIP PIP).
Heard direct, i.e. not through phone, as is GLADYS *now.*

GLADYS:

. . . At the third stroke it
will be nine two and fifty
seconds. . . .
(PIP PIP PIP.)
. . . At the third stroke it
will be nine three precisely.
(PIP PIP PIP.)

Or to put it another way,
three minutes past nine,
precisely, though which
nine in particular, I don't
say, so what's precise
about that? . . .

. . . nine three and ten
seconds. . . .
(PIP PIP PIP.)

The point is beginning to be
  lost on me.
Or rather it is becoming a
  different point.
Or rather I am beginning
  to see through it.
Because they think that
  time is something they
  invented,
for their own convenience,
and divided up into ticks
  and tocks
and sixties and twelves
and twenty-fours . . .
so that they'd know when
  the Olympic record has
  been broken

and when to stop serving
dinner in second-class
hotels,
when the season opens and
the betting closes,
when to retire;
when to leave the station,
renew their applications
when their subscriptions
have expired;
when time has run out.
So that they'd know how
long they lasted,
and pretend that it matters,
and how long they've got,
as if it mattered,
so that they'd know that we
know that they know.
That we know, that is.
That they know, of course.

And so on.

*(Faint time clock, 2–3
seconds.)*

Ad infinitum.

I used to say ad nauseum
but it goes on long after you
feel sick.
And I feel sick.
When you look down from
a great height
you become dizzy. Such
depth, such distance,
such disappearing tininess so
far away,
rushing away,

reducing the life-size to
   nothing—
it upsets the scale you live by.
Your eyes go first, followed
   by the head,
and if you can't look away
   you feel sick.
And that's my view of time;
and I can't look away.
Dizziness spirals up between
   my stomach and my head
corkscrewing out the stopper.
But I'm empty anyway.
I was emptied long ago.

Because it goes on,
this endless dividing up into
   equal parts,
this keeping track—
because time viewed from
   such distance
etcetera
rushing away
reducing the lifespan to
   nothing
and so on—
(*Pause.*)
The spirit goes first, followed
   by the mind.
And if you can't look away
   you go mad.

                                 (*Time clock, 2–3 seconds.*)

SCENE 4

FRANK *dialling; excited, intense. Ringing tone breaks off.*
OPERATOR *is heard through phone.*

OPERATOR: Number please.

FRANK: Listen, do all you people work in the same building?

OPERATOR: This is the operator—can I help you?

FRANK: I want to speak to Gladys Jenkins.

OPERATOR: What's the number, please?

FRANK: She works there—she's in the telephones, you see.

OPERATOR: Hello, sir—operator here——

FRANK: I want to be transferred to Mrs. Jenkins—this is her
husband.

OPERATOR: Mrs. Jenkins?

FRANK: Speaking clock.

OPERATOR: Do you want to know the time?

FRANK: No—I want my Gladys! What's her number?

OPERATOR: Speaking clock?

FRANK: Yes.

OPERATOR: TIM.

FRANK: Her *number*.

OPERATOR: T-I-M.

FRANK: I demand to speak to your superior——

OPERATOR: Just a moment, sir, putting you through.

GLADYS (*through the phone*): . . . At the third stroke it will be
nine twelve and forty seconds. . . .

FRANK: It's all right, Glad—it's me again—Frank!
(GLADY's *timespeak continues underneath.*)
Can you hear me now, Glad?—I've had a time of it I can
tell you—I must say, you gave me a turn! So that's where
you got to—Gladys? Give over a minute, love—it's
Frank—— Can you hear me, Gladys? Give me a sign?
(*Pause; timeclock.*)
I know your voice—it's you, isn't it, Gladys—are they
holding you?—I'll get you out of there, Gladys—I'll speak
to the top man—I'll get the wheels turning, Gladys! I'll pull

the strings, don't you worry, love—— But I've got to dash
now, love—I'm calling from the terminus and we're due
out——
(IVY, *a bus conductress breaks in.*)
IVY: Frank *Jenkins!* The passengers are looking at their watches!
FRANK (*to* IVY): Just coming. (*To* GLADYS.) That was Ivy, my
conductress—you don't know Ivy—I'm on a new route now,
the 52 to Acton—— Keep your chin up, Glad—you can hear
me, can't you? I'll be giving you another ring later——
Good-bye, Gladys—oh, Gladys—what's the time now?
GLADYS: Nine fourteen precisely——
FRANK: Thanks, Glad—oh, *thank* you, Gladys! (*He rings off.*)
IVY (*off*): Frank—it's nine fourteen—remember the schedule!
FRANK (*going*): Hey, Ivy—I've found her—I've found my
Gladys!

SCENE 5

GLADYS (*direct voice now*):

> . . . At the third stroke it
> will be nine fourteen and
> twenty seconds. . . .
> (ΓΙΓ ΓΙΓ ΓΙΓ.)

. . . At the third stroke . . .
I don't think I'll bother, I
don't think there's any point.
Let sleeping dogs and so on.
Because I wouldn't shake it off
by going back, I'd only be in
the middle of it,
with an inkling of infinity,
the only one who has seen both
  ends
rushing away from the middle.
You can't keep your balance

after that.
Because they don't know what
    time is.
They haven't experienced the
    silence
in which it passes
impartial disinterested
godlike.
Because they didn't invent it at all.
They only invented the clock.
And it doesn't go tick
and it doesn't go tock
and it doesn't go pip.
It doesn't go anything.
And it doesn't go anything for
    ever
It just goes,
before them, after them, without
them,
above all without them,
and their dialling fingers,
their routine-checking, schedule-
    setting time-keeping clockwork—
luminous, anti-magnetic,
fifteen-jewelled self-winding,
grandfather, cuckoo, electric
shock-, dust- and waterproofed,
    chiming;
it counts for nothing against the
    scale of time,
and makes them tiny, bound and
    gagged to the minute-hand
as though across a railway line—
struggling without hope, eyes busy
    with silent-screen distress
as the hour approaches—the express
swings round the curve towards

them
(and the Golden Labrador who
  might have saved them
never turns up on time).

                       (2–3 seconds.)

And they count for nothing
  measured against
the moment in which a glacier
  forms and melts.
Which does not stop them from
  trying
to compete;
they synchronize their watches,
count the beats,
to get the most out of the little
  they've got,
clocking in, and out,
and speeding up,
keeping up with their time-tables,
and adjusting their tables to keep
  up with their speed,
and check one against the other
and congratulate each other—
a minute saved to make another
  minute possible somewhere else
to be spent another time.
Enough to soft-boil a third of an egg:
hard-boil a fifth.

                       Precisely. . . .
                       (PIP PIP PIP.)
                       (3–4 seconds.)

Of course, it's a service if you like.
They dial for twenty seconds' worth
  of time
and hurry off contained within it
until the next correction,
with no sense of its enormity, none,

no sense of their scurrying
    insignificance;
only the authority of my voice,
the voice of the sun itself,
more accurate than Switzerland—
definitive
divine.

(*2–3 seconds, very faint.*)

If it made a difference
I could refuse to play,
sabotage the whole illusion
a little every day if it made a
    difference,
as if it would, if I coughed or
    jumped a minute
(they'd correct their watches by my
    falter).
And if I stopped to explain
At the third stroke it will be   At the third stroke it
will be. . . . (*Continues
3–4 seconds.*)

too late to catch up, far
far too late, gentlemen. . . .
they'd complain, to the Post Office.
And if stopped altogether,
just stopped, gave up the pretence,
it would make no difference.
Silence is the sound of time passing.

(*1–2 seconds, faint.*)

Don't ask when the pendulum
    began to swing.
Because there is no pendulum.
It's only the clock that goes tick
    tock
and never the time that chimes.
It's never the time that stops.

(*1–2 seconds, quick fade.*)

SCENE 6

VOICE THROUGH PHONE: . . . thirty minutes in a Regulo
  5 oven until it is a honey coloured brown. . . . Serves six.
1ST LORD (*ringing off*): Well, that's that one. Next.
BERYL: That was the last one, sir.
1ST LORD: Then start again at the beginning—continuous
  attention, you see. You'll have to take over this
  afternoon—I have a board meeting.
BERYL: Very good, sir.
1ST LORD: You don't have to call me sir. Call me my Lord.
BERYL: Very good, my Lord.
  (*Phone rings.*)
  Hello?
FRANK (*through phone*): This is Frank Jenkins.
BERYL: Yes?
FRANK: It's about my wife.
BERYL: Yes?
FRANK: Is she there?
BERYL: This is the First Lord's office.
FRANK: I want the top man in speaking clocks.
BERYL: What name please?
FRANK: Jenkins—it's about my wife, Gladys. She's the speaking
  clock.
BERYL: Hold on, please.
  My Lord, it's a Mr. Jenkins—he says his wife is the
  speaking clock.
1ST LORD: How extraordinary. Tell him we don't know what
  he's talking about.

SCENE 7

GLADYS (*direct*):   . . . At the third
                                 stroke it will be eleven
                                 thirty precisely. . . .
                                 (PIP PIP PIP.)

Old Frank. . . .
Yes, we met dancing, I liked him
    from the first.
He said, 'If you're Glad
I'll be Frank. . . .'
There was time to laugh then
but while I laughed a bumblebee
fluttered its wings a million times.
How can one compete?
His bus passed my window twice a day,
on the route he had then,
every day, with a toot and a wave
    and was gone.
toot toot toot
everything the same
if only you didn't know,
which I didn't
which I do.
He took his timetable seriously,
    Frank.
You could set your clock by him.
But not *time*—it flies by
unrepeatable
and the moment after next the
    passengers are dead
and the bus scrap and the scrap dust,
caught by the wind, blown into the
    crevasse
as the earth splits and scatters
at the speed of bees wings.
Old Frank. He had all the time
in the world for me,
such as it was.

(PIP PIP PIP.)

Scene 8

In the street FRANK's *bus comes to a rather abrupt halt, the door of his cab opens, slams shut as he runs across the pavement and through a door. He is breathless and in a frantic hurry.*

FRANK: Hey, you—who's in charge here?

PORTER: I am. Is that your bus?

FRANK: Who's the top man—quick!

PORTER: You can't park there after seven if the month's got an R in it or before nine if it hasn't except on Christmas and the Chairman's birthday should it fall in Lent.

FRANK: I have an appointment with the chairman.

PORTER (*to the sound of horns*): Seems to be a bit of a traffic jam out there.

FRANK: What floor's he on?

PORTER: He's not on the floor this early. Is this your conductress?

(*As the door flies open.*)

IVY: Frank—what are you doing!

FRANK: All right, all right! (*To* PORTER.) Listen—I'll be passing your door again at one-fourteen. Tell him to be ready——

CONDUCTRESS: Frank—we'll get behind time!

FRANK (*leaving hurriedly*): It's all right, I got ninety seconds ahead going round the park. . . .

(*And out; and break.*)

Scene 9

In the street FRANK's *bus draws up once more; same slam, same feet, same door, same frenzy.*

FRANK: Where is he? I've got ninety-five seconds.

2ND PORTER: Who?

FRANK: Who are you?

2ND PORTER: What do you want?

FRANK: Where's the other porter?

2ND PORTER: Gone to lunch—it's one-fourteen.

FRANK: Never mind him—where's the chairman?

2ND PORTER: They eat together.

(*Door crashes open.*)

CONDUCTRESS: Frank *Jenkins!*

2ND PORTER: Like brothers.

CONDUCTRESS: What about the schedule!?

FRANK (*to* PORTER): Listen—I'll be back here at two forty-seven——

CONDUCTRESS (*almost in tears*): I ask you to remember the schedule!

2ND PORTER (*as the horns sound*): Hello—is that your bus out there?

FRANK (*leaving hurriedly*): Two forty-seven!—tell him it's about Gladys Jenkins!

SCENE 10

GLADYS (*through phone*): . . . three fourteen and twenty seconds. . . .

(PIP PIP PIP.)

1ST LORD (*ringing off*): Precisely! Next!

BERYL: God, my Lord.

GOD (*through phone*): In the beginning was the Heaven and the Earth. . . .

(*Fade.*)

SCENE 11

GLADYS (*direct*):
. . . At the third
stroke it will be three
fourteen and fifty
seconds. . .

Check, check, check. . . .
One day I'll give him something
to check up for . . .
tick tock
tick tock
check check
chick chock
tick
you can check
your click clock
by my pip pip pip
                                    (PIP PIP PIP.)
I never waver,
I'm reliable,
lord, lord,
I'm your servant,
trained,
precisely.
                                    . . . precisely.
(*With a click* FRANK *is on the line.*)
(*We hear him, as* GLADYS *does, through the phone.*)

FRANK: Hello, Gladys—it's Frank. I bet you wondered where
I'd got to. . . . Well, I've had a bit of trouble getting hold
of the right man, you see, but don't you worry because the
next trip will give me the time—I'll be bang outside his
door slap in the middle of the rush hour so I'll have a good
four minutes—can you hear me, Gladys? . . .
(*Breaks a little.*)
Oh, Gladys—talk to me—I want you back, I'll let you do
anything you like if you come back—I'll let you be a nun, if
that's what you really want . . . Gladys? I love you,
Gladys——

Hold on, love, hold on a bit, and I'll have you out of
there. . . .
Got to go now, Gladys, Ivy's calling me, we're due out. Bye
bye . . . bye bye. . . . (*Rings off.*)

GLADYS:

I can hear them all
though they do not know enough to
speak to me.
I can hear them breathe,
pause, listen,
sometimes the frogsong of clockwindings
and the muttered repetition to the
nearest minute . . .
but never a question of a question,
never spoken,
it remains open, permanent,
demanding a different answer
every ten seconds.

Until Frank.
Oh, Frank, you knew my voice,
but how can I reply?
I'd bring the whole thing down with a cough,
stun them with a sigh. . . .
(*Sobbing a little.*)
I was going to be a nun, but they wouldn't have me because
I didn't believe, I didn't believe *enough*, that is; most of it I
believed all right, or was willing to believe, but not enough
for their purposes, not about him being the son of God, for
instance, that's the part that put paid to my ambition, that's
where we didn't see eye to eye. No, that's one of the main
points, she said, without that you might as well believe in a
pair of old socks for all the good you are to us, or words to
that effect. I asked her to stretch a point but she wasn't
having any of it. I asked her to let me stay inside without
being a proper nun, it made no difference to me, it was the
serenity I was after, that and the clean linen, but she wasn't

having any of that.
(*Almost a wail.*)
But it's not the same thing at all!
I thought it would be—peace!
Oh, Frank—tell them—
I shan't go on, I'll let go
and sneeze the fear of God into
their alarm-setting, egg-timing,
train-catching, coffee-breaking
   faith in
an uncomprehended clockwork—

yes, if I let go,
lost track
changed the beat, went off the rails—
cracked——

	. . . At the third stroke
	it will be three eighteen
	and ten seconds. . . .
	(PIP PIP PIP.)
At the third stroke	At the third stroke
it will be	it will be
three eighteen and	three eighteen and
twenty seconds. . . .	twenty seconds. . . .
And so what?	(PIP PIP PIP.)
At the third stroke	At the third stroke
it will be	it will be
too late to do any good,	three eighteen and thirty
gentlemen——	seconds. . . .
	(PIP PIP PIP.)
At the third stroke	At the third stroke. . . .
Manchester City 2,	
Whores of Lancashire 43 for	
seven declared	
At the third stroke	
Sheffield Wednesday will be cloudy	

and so will Finisterre. . . .
(*The Queen.*) So a Merry Christmas
and God Bless you everywhere. . . .
And now the Prime Minister!:
Gentlemen, the jig is up—I have
given you tears. . . .
And now the First Lord!—
Don't lose your heads while all
about you on the burning deck. . . .
Oh—Frank! Help me! . . .

SCENE 12

FRANK's *bus stops abruptly. Same place, same slam, same feet, same door, same frenzy.*

FRANK: Right, let's not waste time—where is she?
PORTER: State your business.
FRANK: I'm looking for my wife.
PORTER: Name?
FRANK: Jenkins—you know me.
PORTER: *Her* name!
FRANK: Sorry—Jenkins.
PORTER: Better. Your name?
FRANK: Jenkins.
PORTER: Relative?
FRANK: Husband.
PORTER: Holds water so far.
FRANK: I demand to see your superior.
PORTER: Name?
FRANK: Jenkins!
PORTER: No one of that name here.
FRANK: I see your game—a conspiracy, is it?
PORTER (*as the horns sound*): Is that your bus out there?
FRANK: I demand to speak to the chief of speaking clocks.

PORTER (*as the door bursts open*): Here she comes.

IVY (*conductress*): I'm not covering up for you again, Frank Jenkins!

PORTER: Hey—you can't go in there!
(*Door.*)

MYRTLE: Hello.

FRANK: Where's the top man?

MYRTLE: Keep on as you're going.
(*Door.*)

MORTIMER: Who are you?

FRANK: I want my wife!

MORTIMER: Now, look here, old man, there's a time and place for everything——

FRANK: I want her back!

MORTIMER: My dear fellow, please don't make a scene in the office——

FRANK: You're holding her against her will——

MORTIMER: I think that's for her to say. The fact is Myrtle and I are in love——

FRANK: I want my Gladys.

MORTIMER: Gladys? Isn't your name Trelawney?

FRANK: Jenkins—where's my Gladys?

MORTIMER: Gladys?

FRANK: My wife——

MORTIMER: Are you suggesting that a man of my scrupulous morality——
(*Door.*)

MYRTLE: Darling, there's a bus conductress outside——

MORTIMER: Thank you, Mrs. Trelawney——

IVY (*desperate*): Frank!—the traffic is beginning to move!

FRANK: I demand to see your superior!

MORTIMER: You can't go in there!
(*Door.*)

C.-SMITH: Yes?

FRANK: Are you the top man?

MORTIMER: Excuse me, Mr. Courtenay-Smith, this man just burst into——

IVY: Frank—I ask you to think of your schedule!

FRANK: Shut up! You there, are you the top man?

C.-SMITH: In my field, or do you speak hierarchically?

FRANK: I speak of Gladys Jenkins.

C.-SMITH: Not my field——

FRANK: You've got my wife——

MORTIMER: How dare you suggest that a man of Mr. Courtenay-Smith's scrupulous morality——

IVY: Frank! the passengers have noticed!

(*Door.*)

C.-SMITH: Where's he gone?

MYRTLE: Darling, what's going on?

MORTIMER: Mrs. Trelawney, I must ask you to address me——

C.-SMITH: My God—the time-and-motion system won't take the strain!

IVY (*fading*): Fra-a-a-nk. . . !

SCENE 13

GLADYS (*breaking down slowly but surely*):

At the third stroke
I'm going to give it up,
yes, yes . . . it's asking too much,
for one person to be in the know
of so much, for so many . . .
and at the third stroke
Frank will come
. . . Frank. . . .
I'm going to drop it now,
it can go on without me,
and it will,
time doesn't need me—
they think I'm time, but I'm
not—
I'm Gladys Jenkins and at the

At the third stroke it
will be four twenty-
three and ten
seconds. . . .

third stroke
I'm going to cough,
sneeze
whisper an obscenity that will leave
ten thousand coronaries sprawled
across their telephone tables,
and the trains will run half empty
and all the bloody eggs will turn to
volcanic rock smoking in dry
    cracked saucepans
as soon as I shout—
Ship!
(a vessel)
*Pis*cine!
(pertaining to fishes)
*Fruc!*tuate
(fruit-bearing)
(*She giggles hysterically.*)
oh yes I will
and then they'll let me go
they'll have to
because Frank knows I'm here—
come on, please Frank, I love you
and at the third stroke I will
yes I will yes at the third stroke I
    will. . . .

SCENE 14

1ST LORD: Well, gentlemen, in bringing this board meeting to a
    close, and I'm sure you're all as bored as I am,
    (*Chuckle chuckle, hear hear.*)
    I think we must congratulate ourselves on the variety and
    consistency of the services which we in the telephone office
    have maintained for the public in the face of the most

difficult problems. I believe I'm right in saying that if the last Test Match had not been abandoned because of the rain, UMP would barely have lasted the five days, but all was well as it happened, though the same rainy conditions did put an extra strain on SUN our weather forecast service. . . . I don't know if you have anything to add, Sir John?

SIR JOHN: Well, Cooty—my Lord, that is—only to join with the rest of the Board in heartily congratulating you on the excellent report——

(*Hear hear hear hear.*)

1ST LORD: Thank you. Now is there any other business?

(*Door.*)

FRANK (*out of breath*): Where's Gladys Jenkins?!

1ST LORD: There you have me, gentlemen.

SIR JOHN: Point of order, my Lord.

1ST LORD: Yes, Jack?

SIR JOHN: I don't think this man——

FRANK: I'm not taking any more of this—where've you got my Glad——

(*Door.*)

C.-SMITH: Forgive me, my Lord—this man is quite unauthorized——

IVY: Frank, the passengers are rioting! All is lost!

MORTIMER: Now look here——

MYRTLE: Darling, do shut up!

FRANK: Damn you. What have you done with my wife?

SIR JOHN: Don't you come here with your nasty little innuendoes, Trelawney—whatever you may have heard about the Bournemouth conference, Myrtle and I——

IVY: The passengers are coming!

(FIRST LORD *gets quiet by banging his gavel.*)

(*Pause.*)

(*Noise of rioting passengers.*)

1ST LORD: Gentlemen—please! (*Pause.*) Now what's all the row about?

IVY: It's the passengers, sir.

FRANK: Are you the top man?

1ST LORD: Certainly.

FRANK: What have you done with my Gladys?

MORTIMER: How dare you suggest that a man of the First Lord's scrupulous morality——

1ST LORD: Please, Mr. Mortimer, let him finish.

FRANK: She's the speaking clock.

1ST LORD: What do you mean? *TIM?*

FRANK: Gladys. Yes.

1ST LORD (*chuckling*): My dear fellow—there's no Gladys—we wouldn't trust your wife with the *time*—it's a machine, I thought everyone knew that. . . .

FRANK: A machine?

1ST LORD: He thought it was his wife!
(*General chuckles.*)
Wife . . . thought it was his wife! . . .

FRANK: It was her voice——

IVY: Oh, Frank—they wouldn't use your Glad for that. It's just the speaking clock——

FRANK: She was educated——

IVY: Oh Frank—come on, come on now, we'll be in awful trouble with the Inspector.

FRANK: But Ivy—she *talked* to me . . .

IVY: She couldn't have done——

1ST LORD: She *talked* to you, my dear fellow?

FRANK: Well, not exactly. . . .

IVY: Of course she didn't. Come on, now. . . .

1ST LORD: That's it—back to your offices gentlemen. We must all make up for lost time.
(*General movement out.*)

FRANK: But she sounded like my Gladys. . . .

IVY: You'll have to go on looking, Frank. . . .
(FIRST LORD *alone.*)

1ST LORD: Dear me, dear me. . . .
(*Door.*)

BERYL (*urgent*): Sir!

1ST LORD: What is it, Miss Bligh?

BERYL: It's the speaking clock—I was just checking it and——

1ST LORD: All right—get me TIM, I'll see to it.

BERYL: Yes, my Lord. (*Dialling.*) She's on now, my Lord.

GLADYS (*through phone. Sobbing hysterically*): At the third stroke it will be five thirty five and fifty seconds. . . .
   (PIP PIP PIP.)

1ST LORD: Mrs. Jenkins. . . . This is the First Lord speaking.

GLADYS: At the third stroke it will be five thirty-six precisely. . . .

1ST LORD: Mrs. Jenkins—pull yourself together, stop crying. And you've lost forty seconds somewhere by my watch——

GLADYS: At the third stroke I don't know what time it is and I don't care, because it doesn't go tick tock at all, it just goes and I have seen—I have seen infinity!

1ST LORD: *Mrs. Jenkins!*

GLADYS (*sniffing*): I can't go on!

1ST LORD: Come on now, this isn't like you at all. Let's get things back on the rails, hm? Think of the public, Mrs. Jenkins. . . . Come on now . . . at the third stroke. . . .

GLADYS: At the third stroke. . . .

1ST LORD: It will be five thirty seven and forty seconds.
   (PIP PIP PIP.)
   Carry on from there. . . .

GLADYS: At the third stroke it will be five thirty-seven and fifty seconds. . . .

1ST LORD: That's it—spot on, Mrs. Jenkins. Control your voice now.
   (PIP PIP PIP.)

GLADYS: At the third stroke it will be five thirty-eight precisely.

1ST LORD: Well done, Mrs. Jenkins. Well done—I'll check you again within the hour, as usual. (*Rings off.*)

GLADYS (*direct now*):

He thinks he's God. . . .

At the third stroke it will be five thirty-eight and ten seconds. . . .
(PIP PIP PIP.)
At the third stroke. . . .
(*Fading out.*)

ALBERT'S BRIDGE

CHARACTERS

BOB
CHARLIE
DAD
ALBERT
CHAIRMAN
DAVE
GEORGE
FITCH
MOTHER
FATHER
KATE
FRASER

Fade up bridge, with painting on mike. Four men are painting a big girdered railway bridge. They are spaced vertically, in ascending order: BOB, CHARLIE, DAD, ALBERT. *To begin with, the mike is at* ALBERT'*s level, the top.*

BOB (*the most distant*): Char-lee!
CHARLIE (*less distant*): Hel-lo!
BOB: Right, Charlie?
CHARLIE: Right! Comin' down! . . . Hey, Dad!
DAD (*an older man, not very distant*): Hel-lo!
CHARLIE: Bob 'n' me is done down here!
DAD: Right!
CHARLIE: Have you done?
DAD: Comin' down! . . . Albert! Al-bert!
CHARLIE (*more distant*): Albert!
BOB (*more distant*): Al-bert!
ALBERT (*very close, crooning softly, tunelessly amid various tunes while painting*):
    How high the moon in June?
    how blue the moon when it's high noon
    and the turtle doves above
    croon out of tune in love
    saying please above the trees
    which when there's thunder you don't run under
    —those trees—

'cos there'll be pennies fall on Alabama
and you'll drown in foggy London town
the sun was shi-ning . . . on my Yiddisher Mama.

BOB (*more distant*): Albert!

CHARLIE (*less distant*): Albert!

DAD (*off*): Albert!

ALBERT: Hel-lo!

DAD: Bob 'n' me 'n' Charlie's done!

ALBERT: Right!

Dip-brush-slap-slide-slick, and once again, dip, brush,
slap—oh, it goes on so nicely . . . tickle it into the corner,
there, behind the rivet. . . . No one will see that from the
ground; I could cheat up here. But I'd know; so dip, brush,
slap, slide and once again for the last time till the next
time—every surface sleek, renewed—dip, brush, slap,
slick, tickle and wipe—right in there with the old rust-proof
rust-brown—all glossed and even, end to end—the last
touch—perfection! (*Painting stops.*) Oh my! I could stand
back to admire it and fall three hundred feet into the sea.
Mind your heads! (*Laughs. Climbing down.*) Mind your
head, Dad!

DAD: I'm not your dad. Keep off the wet—work down the slope
to the middle—and watch your feet.
(*Everyone climbing down, the distance between them closing.*)
Going down for good, oh yes, I'm not facing that again.
Ten coats I've done, end to end, and now I'm done all
right. I had ambitions, you know. . . .

CHARLIE (*nearer*): Mind my head, Dad.

DAD: Watch my feet, Charlie—comin' down——

CHARLIE: I'll watch your feet—you mind my head. Watch your
head, Bob——

BOB (*nearer*): Watch your feet, Charlie——

CHARLIE: Mind my feet, Bob—watch my head, Dad. . . .

DAD: I'm not your dad, and mind my feet—that's my head,
Albert.

ALBERT: Comin' down. . . . Doesn't she look beautiful?

DAD: Looks the same as always. There's no progress. Twenty

years, twenty thousand pots of paint . . . yes, I had plans.

CHARLIE: I thought we'd never see the end of it.

BOB: It's not the bleeding end.

CHARLIE: There's no end to it.

DAD: Ten coats non-stop, one after the other, and it's no improvement, no change even, just holding its own against the weather—that's a long time, that's a lot of paint. I could have made my mark.

ALBERT: Continuity—that's hard to come by.

DAD: I've spread my life over those girders, and in five minutes I could scrape down to the iron, I could scratch down to my prime.

ALBERT: Simplicity—so . . . contained; neat; your bargain with the world, your wages, your time, your energy, your property, everything you took out and everything you put in, the bargain that has carried you this far—all contained there in ten layers of paint, accounted for. Now that's something; to keep track of everything you put into the kitty, to have it lie there, under your eye, fixed and immediate—there are no consequences to a coat of paint. That's more than you can say for a factory man; his bits and pieces scatter, grow wheels, disintegrate, change colour, join up in new forms, which he doesn't know anything about. In short, he doesn't know what he's done, to whom.

DAD: Watch your feet, Albert. Mind your head, Charlie.

CHARLIE: You mind my head. Take care my feet, Bob——

BOB: Watch your feet, Charlie——

CHARLIE: Mind your feet, Dad——

DAD: That's my head, Albert——

ALBERT: Coming down. . . .

Ah, look at it up there criss-crossed and infinite, you can't see where it ends—I could take off and swing through its branches screaming like a gibbon!

DAD: Mind where you're putting your feet, Albert.

CHARLIE: Watch my head, Dad.

BOB: Train coming, Charlie.

(*Distant train coming.*)

CHARLIE: I've seen it.

BOB (*jumping down on to gravel*): And down.

CHARLIE: Mind where you jump, Dad.

DAD: Seen it.

CHARLIE (*jumping down*): None too soon.

DAD: Train coming, Albert.

ALBERT: I'm with you.

DAD (*jumps down*): Finished.

CHARLIE: Like hell.

BOB: Well, that's another two years behind you.

DAD: A feller once offered me a half share in a very nice trading station in the China Seas. I had it in me.

ALBERT: Mind your toes.

(*He jumps. Climbing down ends. All are now on mike.*)
Now that's a good way to end a day—ending so much else.

CHARLIE: All right for some. Students.

BOB: Slummers.

CHARLIE: Pocket-money holiday lads, oh yes.

ALBERT: One bridge—freshly painted—a million tons of iron thrown across the bay—rust brown and even to the last lick—spick and span, rust-proofed, weather-resistant— perfect!

DAD: Other end needs painting now. A man could go mad.

(*The train arrives and goes screaming past.*)

(*Set CHAIRMAN over end of train, cutting bridge.*)

CHAIRMAN: Let us not forget, gentlemen, that Clufton Bay Bridge is the fourth biggest single-span double-track shore-to-shore railway bridge in the world bar none——

DAVE: Hear, hear, Mr. Chairman——

CHAIRMAN: Thank you, Dave——

GEORGE: I've been studying these figures, Mr. Chairman——

CHAIRMAN: Just a moment, George. We've got an amenity here in Clufton, that bridge stands for the whole town, quite apart from the money earned in railway dues——

DAVE: Hear, hear, Mr. Chairman——

CHAIRMAN: Thank you, Dave.

GEORGE: According to the City Engineer's figures, Mr. Chairman——

CHAIRMAN: Just a moment, George. When my grandfather built this bridge he didn't spare the brass—and I for one, as chairman of the Clufton Bay Bridge Sub-Committee— entrusted as we are with the upkeep and responsibility of what is a symbol of Clufton's prosperity—I for one do not begrudge the spending of a few extra quid on a lick of paint.

DAVE: Hear, hear, Mr. Chairman.

CHAIRMAN: Thank you, Dave.

GEORGE: I know it's a symbol of your prosperity, Mr. Chairman, but——

CHAIRMAN: That's a highly improper remark, George. Clufton's prosperity is what I said.

DAVE: Hear, hear, Mr. Chairman.

CHAIRMAN: Thank you, Dave.

GEORGE: My mistake, Mr. Chairman—but if Mr. Fitch's figures are correct——

FITCH (*distinctive voice; clipped, confident; rimless spectacles*): My figures are always correct, Mr. Chairman.

CHAIRMAN: Hear that, George? The City Engineer's figures are a model of correctitude.

DAVE: Hear, hear, Mr. Chairman.

CHAIRMAN: Thank you, Dave.

GEORGE: Then this new paint he's recommending is going to cost us four times as much as the paint we've been using up to now.

(*Pause.*)

CHAIRMAN: Four times as much? Money?

DAVE: Hear, hear, Mr. Chairman.

CHAIRMAN: Just a moment, Dave. I don't think your figures are correct, George. Mr. Fitch knows his business.

GEORGE: What business is he in—paint?

CHAIRMAN: That's a highly improper remark, George—er, you're not in the paint business, are you, Mr. Fitch?

FITCH: No, Mr. Chairman.

CHAIRMAN: No, no, of course you're not. You should be ashamed, George.

DAVE: Hear, hear, Mr. Chairman.

CHAIRMAN: Shut up, Dave. Now what about it, Mr. Fitch—is this right what George says?

FITCH: Well, up to a point, Mr. Chairman, yes. But in the long run, no.

CHAIRMAN: Don't fiddle-faddle with me, Fitch. Does this new-fangled paint of yours cost four times as much as the paint we've got, and if so, what's in it for you?

GEORGE: Hear, hear, Mr. Chairman.

CHAIRMAN: Thank you, George.

FITCH: To put the matter at its simplest, Mr. Chairman, the new paint costs four times as much and lasts four times as long.

CHAIRMAN: Well, there's your answer, George. It costs four times as much but it lasts four times as long. Very neat, Fitch—I thought we'd got you there.

GEORGE: What's the point, then?

FITCH: Apart from its silvery colour, Mr. Chairman, which would be a pleasanter effect than the present rusty brown, the new paint would also afford a considerable saving, as you can no doubt see.

CHAIRMAN: Everybody see that? Well, I don't.

GEORGE: Nor do I.

DAVE: Hear, hear, George.

GEORGE: Shut up, Dave.

FITCH: If I might explain, gentlemen. As you know, in common with other great bridges of its kind, the painting of Clufton Bay Bridge is a continuous operation. That is to say, by the time the painters have reached the far end, the end they started at needs painting again.

DAVE: I never knew that!

CHAIRMAN AND GEORGE: Shut up, Dave.

FITCH: This cycle is not a fortuitous one. It is contrived by relating the area of the surfaces to be painted—call it A—to

the rate of the painting—B—and the durability of the
paint—C. The resultant equation determines the variable
factor X—i.e. the number of painters required to paint
surfaces A at speed B within time C. For example——

CHAIRMAN: E.g.

FITCH: Quite. Er, e.g. with X plus one painters the work would
proceed at a higher rate—i.e. B, plus, e.g. Q. However, the
factors A and C, the surface area and the lasting quality of
the paint remain, of course, constant. The result would be
that the painters would be ready to begin painting the
bridge for the second time strictly speaking before it needed
re-painting. This creates the co-efficient—Waste.

CHAIRMAN: W.

FITCH: If you like. This co-efficient belies efficiency, you see.

CHAIRMAN: U.C. You see, George?

GEORGE: OK, I see.

FITCH: To continue. Furthermore, the value of the
co-efficient—Waste—is progressive. Let me put it like this,
gentlemen. Because the rate of painting is constant, i.e. too
fast to allow the paintwork to deteriorate, each bit the men
come to requires re-painting even less than the bit before it.
You see, they are all the time catching up on themselves
progressively, until there'll come a point where they'll be
re-painting the bridge while it's still wet! (*Pause*.) No that
can't be right. . . .

CHAIRMAN: Come to the point Fitch. Wake up, Dave.

DAVE (*waking up*): Hear, hear, Mr. Chairman.

FITCH: To put it another way, gentlemen, that is to say,
conversely. With one too few painters—X minus one—the
rate of progress goes down to let us say, B minus Q. So
what is the result? By the time the painters are ready to
start re-painting, the end they started at has deteriorated
into unsightly and damaged rust—a co-efficient
representing the converse inefficiency.

CHAIRMAN: Pull yourself together, Fitch—I don't know what
you're drivellin' about.

GEORGE: In a nutshell, Fitch—the new paint costs four times as

much and lasts four times as long. Where's the money
saved?

FITCH: We sack three painters.

(*Pause.*)

CHAIRMAN: Ah. . . .

FITCH: You see, to date we have achieved your optimum
efficiency by employing four men. It takes them two years
to paint the bridge, which is the length of time the paint
lasts. This new paint will last eight years, so we only need
one painter to paint the bridge by himself. After eight
years, the end he started at will be just ready for
re-painting. The saving to the ratepayers would be £3,529
15s. 9d. per annum.

GEORGE: Excuse me, Mr. Chairman——

CHAIRMAN: Just a moment, George. I congratulate you, Mr.
Fitch. An inspired stroke. We'll put it up to the meeting of
the full council.

GEORGE: Excuse me——

CHAIRMAN: Shut up, George.

DAVE: Hear, hear, Mr. Chairman.

FITCH: Thank you, Mr. Chairman.

CHAIRMAN: Thank you, Mr. Fitch.

(*Fade.*)

MOTHER: Aren't you getting up, Albert? It's gone eleven. . . .
Are you listening to me, Albert?

ALBERT (*in bed*): What?

MOTHER: I'm talking to you, Albert.

ALBERT: Yes?

MOTHER: Yes-what?

ALBERT: Yes, Mother.

MOTHER: That's better. Oh dear, what was I saying?

ALBERT: I don't know, Mother.

MOTHER (*sighs*): I was against that university from the start.

ALBERT: The country needs universities.

MOTHER: I mean it's changed you, Albert. You're thinking all
the time. It's not like you, Albert.

ALBERT: Thinking?

MOTHER: You don't talk to me. Or your father. Well, I'm glad it's all behind you, I hope it starts to wear off.

ALBERT: I wanted to stay on after my degree, but they wouldn't have me.

MOTHER: I don't know what you want to know about philosophy for. Your father didn't have to study philosophy, and look where he is, Chairman of Metal Alloys and Allied Metals. It's not as if you were going to be a philosopher or something. . . . Yes, you could have been a trainee executive by now. As it is you'll have to do your stint on the factory floor, philosophy or no philosophy. That university has held you back.

ALBERT: I'll have to get myself articled to a philosopher. . . . Start at the bottom. Of course, a philosopher's clerk wouldn't get the really interesting work straight off, I know that. It'll be a matter of filing the generalizations, tidying up paradoxes, laying out the premises before the boss gets in—that kind of thing; but after I've learned the ropes I might get a half share in a dialectic, perhaps, and work up towards a treatise. . . . Yes, I could have my own thriving little philosopher's office in a few years.

(*Pause.*)

MOTHER: Would you like to have some coffee downstairs?

ALBERT: Yes.

MOTHER: Yes-what?

ALBERT: Yes please.

(*Pause.*)

MOTHER: I still think it was mean of you not to let us know you had a summer vacation.

ALBERT: I thought you knew. I've had one every year.

MOTHER: You know I've no head for dates. You could have come home to see us.

ALBERT: I'm sorry—there was this temporary job going. . . .

MOTHER: Your father would have given you some money if you'd asked him.

ALBERT: I thought I'd have a go myself.

MOTHER: You'll have to get up now.

ALBERT: It was fantastic up there. The scale of it. From the ground it looks just like a cat's cradle, from a distance you can take it all in, and then up there in the middle of it the thinnest threads are as thick as your body and you could play tennis on the main girders.

MOTHER: Kate will be up in a minute to make the beds.

ALBERT: It's absurd, really, being up there, looking down on the university lying under you like a couple of bricks, full of dots studying philosophy——

MOTHER: I don't want you getting in Kate's way—she's got to clean.

ALBERT: What could they possibly know? I saw more up there in three weeks than those dots did in three years. I saw the context. It reduced philosophy and everything else. I got a perspective. Because that bridge was—separate—complete—removed, defined by principles of engineering which makes it stop at a certain point, which compels a certain shape, certain joints—the whole thing utterly fixed by the rules that make it stay up. It's complete, and a man can give his life to its maintenance, a very fine bargain.

MOTHER: Do you love me, Albert?

ALBERT: Yes.

MOTHER: Yes-what?

ALBERT: Yes please.

(*Cut to a gavel banged on table.*)

MAYORAL VOICE: Number 43 on the order paper, proposal from Bridge sub-committee. . . .

VOICE 1: Move. . . .

VOICE 2: Second.

MAYORAL VOICE: All in favour.
(*Absent-minded murmur of fifty 'Ayes'.*)
Against. (*Pause.*) Carried. Number 44 on the order paper. (*Fade.*)

(*Fade up knock on door off. Door opens.*)

KATE: Oh, I'm sorry, Mr. Albert.

ALBERT: Hello, I was just thinking of getting up.

(*Cut to.*)

BOB: What—by myself? It would take years.

FITCH: Eight years, yes.

BOB: No. I demand a transfer.

FITCH: I thought I'd give you first refusal.

BOB: I want to go back to painting the Corporation crest on the dustcarts.

FITCH: I could fit you in on the magenta.

BOB: On the what?

FITCH: It's one man to a colour nowadays. Efficiency.

(*Cut.*)

CHARLIE: You must be joking.

FITCH: It's an opportunity for you.

CHARLIE: I'd go mad. What's it all about?

FITCH: Efficiency.

CHARLIE: I'm not doing that bridge on me tod.

FITCH: It's no more work than before.

CHARLIE: I'd jump off within a month.

FITCH: Oh. Well, we couldn't have that. That would be only one ninety-sixth of it done.

(*Cut.*)

DAD: You mean it's a cheaper way of doing it.

FITCH: More efficient.

DAD: We've been doing a good job.

FITCH: Efficiency isn't a matter of good and bad, entirely. It's a matter of the optimum use of resources—time, money, manpower.

DAD: You mean it's cheaper. I'm an old man.

FITCH: You've got eight years in you.

DAD: It might be my last eight. I haven't done anything yet— I've got a future.

FITCH: Well, I could put you on yellow no-parking lines.

DAD: Yes, all right.
   (*Cut.*)

FITCH: . . . But do you have any qualifications?
ALBERT: I've got a degree in philosophy, Mr. Fitch.
FITCH: That's a little unusual.
ALBERT: I wouldn't say that. There were lots of us doing it.
FITCH: That's all very well if you're going to be a philosopher,
   but what we're talking about is painting bridges.
ALBERT: Yes, yes, I can see what you're driving at, of course,
   but I don't suppose it did me any harm. Almost everyone
   who didn't know what to do, did philosophy. Well, that's
   logical.
FITCH: You're an educated man.
ALBERT: Thank you.
FITCH: What I mean is, you're not the run-of-the-mill bridge
   painter, not the raw material I'm looking for.
ALBERT: Well, I did it in the vacation.
FITCH: Yes . . . yes, I did have reports of you. But surely. . . .
ALBERT: I know what you mean, but that's what I want to do. I
   liked it. I don't want to work in a factory or an office.
FITCH: Is it the open air life that attracts you?
ALBERT: No. It's the work, the whole thing—crawling round
   that great basket, so high up, being responsible for so much
   that is visible. Actually I don't know if that's why I like it. I
   like it because I was happy up there, doing something
   simple but so grand, without end. It doesn't get away from
   you.
FITCH: The intellectual rather than the practical—that's it, is it?
ALBERT: Probably.
FITCH: I'm the same. It's poetry to me—a perfect equation of
   space, time and energy——
ALBERT: Yes——
FITCH: It's not just slapping paint on a girder——
ALBERT: No——
FITCH: It's continuity—control—mathematics.
ALBERT: Poetry.

FITCH: Yes, I should have known it was a job for a university
man. . . .

ALBERT: Like me and you——

FITCH: Well, I went to night school myself.

ALBERT: Same thing, different time.

FITCH: That's what I say.

ALBERT: I'm your man, Mr. Fitch.

FITCH: You'll stick to it for eight years, will you?

ALBERT: Oh, I'll paint it more than once.

(*Cut.*)

(*Breakfast in background.*)

FATHER: Now then, Albert, you've had your fun. When I was
your age I'd got six years of work behind me.

ALBERT: Well, I'm starting work now, Father.

FATHER: Quite so, but don't think you're going to start at the
top. You'll get there all right in time but you've got to learn
the business first. Is there any more tea, Mother?

MOTHER: Ring for Kate, would you, Albert?

ALBERT (*going*): Yes, mother.

MOTHER: That reminds me.

FATHER: You'll start where I started. On the shop floor.

ALBERT (*approach*): Well, actually, Father——

MOTHER: I don't want to sound Victorian, but one can't just
turn a blind eye.

ALBERT: What?

FATHER: Yes, I never went in for books and philosophy and
look at me now.

MOTHER: I suppose that's the penance one pays for having
servants nowadays.

ALBERT: What?

FATHER: I started Metal Alloys and Allied Metals—built it up
from a biscuit-tin furnace in the back garden, small
smelting jobs for the cycle-repair shop.

MOTHER: I've suspected her for some time and now one can't
ignore it. Even with her corset.

ALBERT: Who?

FATHER: You can come in on Monday and I'll hand you over to the plant foreman.

ALBERT: I've already got a job. Actually.

FATHER: You haven't got a job till I give you one.

ALBERT: I'm going to paint Clufton Bay Bridge, starting Monday.

MOTHER: What colour?

ALBERT: Silver.

FATHER: Just a minute——

KATE (*off*): You rang, madam?

MOTHER: More tea, Kate, please.

KATE: Yes, madam.

MOTHER: And a word.

KATE: Yes, madam.

MOTHER: Are you ill?

KATE: No, madam.

MOTHER: I believe I heard you being ill in the bathroom, this morning.

KATE: Yes, madam.

MOTHER: And yesterday?

KATE: Yes, madam.

ALBERT: What's the matter, Kate?

KATE: Nothing, Mr. Albert.

MOTHER: Leave this to me. Cook tells me you fainted in the kitchen last week.

KATE: I came over funny.

ALBERT: Kate. . . .

MOTHER: Let's not beat about the bush. Is it the gardener's boy?

KATE: No, madam.

MOTHER: Then who is it?

ALBERT: Who's what?

MOTHER: Well, I'm sorry. You can have a month's wages, of course. You'd better make sure that the young man does the right thing by you.
(*Cut.*)

KATE: I never thought you'd do the right thing by me, Albert.

ALBERT: We'll be all right. It's a nice room.

KATE: Your mum didn't like it.

ALBERT: My mother's got no taste. I'll make a fire.

KATE: And wrap up warm when you go out—it'll be freezing up there.

ALBERT: Only a breeze.

KATE: It'll be ice in a month. If you fell I'd die, Albert.

ALBERT: So would I.

KATE: Don't you ever fall. They shouldn't make it a year-round job. It's dangerous.

ALBERT: No—you don't know how big it is—the threads are like ladders and the cross-pieces are like piers into the sky.

KATE: You hold on tight, for the spring, and the baby.

(*Cut in bridge and painting.*)

ALBERT: Slip, slap, brush, dip, slop, slide, slick and wipe. . . .
In eight years I'll be pushing thirty, and the Clufton Bay
Bridge will be a silver bridge—dip-brush, slick, slide, slap
without end, I'm the bridge man,
web-spinning silvering spiderman
crawling between heaven and earth on a
cantilevered span,
cat's cradled in the sky . . .
look down at the toy ships
where the sea pounds under toy trains to
toy towns
under my hand.
Am I the spider or the fly?
I'm the bridge man. . . .

The downstairs maid went upstairs to make a bed that I was
in—and suddenly——
(*Cut out bridge. Cut in crying baby.*)

I name this child Albert.

KATE: You can't.

ALBERT: Very well. I name this child Kate.

KATE: Katherine.

ALBERT: Tomorrow wheel her along to the bridge so I can see you.

KATE: All right. But don't wave, Albert. Don't wave. If you waved and fell——

ALBERT: I shan't wave.

> (*Cut in bridge and painting.*)
> Dip brush, dip brush
> without end, come rain or shine;
> A fine way to spend my time.
> My life is set out for me,
> the future traced in brown,
> my past measured in silver;
> how absurd, how sublime
> (don't look down)
> to climb and clamber in a giant frame;
> dip brush, dip brush, slick, slide wipe
> and again.
> (*Painting stops.*)
> I straddle a sort of overflowing gutter on which bathtub boats push up and down. . . . The banks are littered with various bricks, kiddiblocks with windows; dinky toys move through the gaps, dodged by moving dots that have no colour; under my feet the Triang train thunders across the Meccano, and the minibrick estates straggle up over the hill in neat rows with paintbox gardens. It's the most expensive toytown in the store—the detail is remarkable. But fragile. I tremble for it, half expecting some petulant pampered child to step over the hill and kick the whole thing to bits with her Startrite sandals.
> (*Painting.*)
> Don't look down,
> the dots are looking up.
> Don't wave, don't fall, tumbling down a
> telescope, diminishing to a dot.
> In eight years who will I be?
> Not me.

I'll be assimilated then,
the honest working man, father of three—
you've seen him around,
content in his obscurity, come to terms with public truths,
digging the garden of a council house
in what is now my Sunday suit.
I'm okay for fifty years, with any luck;
I can see me climb
up a silver bridge to paint it for the seventh time,
keeping track of my life spent in painting in the colour of
    my track:
above it all.
How sublime
(dip brush, dip brush) silvering the brown.
Which dot is mine?
Don't wave, don't look down.
Don't fall.
(*Cut bridge.*)

KATE: I saw you today.

ALBERT: What was I doing?

KATE: Painting, I suppose. Crawling backwards along a
    cross-piece.

ALBERT: Pulling silver after me. I didn't see you. Or I didn't
    see which one was you.

KATE: Coming out of the hairdressers. Six and six, I had it cut.

ALBERT: Just goes to show—if you get far enough away, six and
    sixpence doesn't show, and nor does anything, at a
    distance.

KATE: Well, life is all close up, isn't it?

ALBERT: Yes, it hits you, when you come back down. How
    close it all is. You can't stand back to look at it.

KATE: Do you like my hair like this?

ALBERT: Like what? Oh—yes. Do you like mine?

KATE: I got whistled at in the street.

ALBERT: It's always happening to me.

KATE: A lorry driver, at the traffic lights.

ALBERT: They're the worst, I find.

KATE: Oh, Albert. I had the pram with me too.

ALBERT: You look too young for it. Big sister.

KATE: And I cook very nice, don't I?

ALBERT: I'd whistle at you.

KATE: I'd come, if you whistled. I'd give you a wink and say, 'Cheeky!'

ALBERT: Oh, yes—you'd get off with me. No trouble at all. I'd take you down by the canal after the pictures.

KATE: What do you know about it—with your education and all?

ALBERT: Me? I'm a working man.

KATE: You don't have regrets, do you, Albert?

ALBERT: No.

KATE: It wasn't a good bargain, on the face of it.

ALBERT: It depends on what you want.

KATE: Me and the baby. Two rooms and a forty-five hour week, hard work and no advancement.

ALBERT: I'm not ambitious.

KATE: You could have had so much—a white wedding, nice house, an office job with real prospects, the country club . . . tennis. . . . Yes, you could have had Metal Alloys and Allied Metals—the top job, responsibility, your own office with telephones. . . .

ALBERT: Yes, I'm well out of that.

(*Cut in bridge and painting.*)

Progress. Two lines of silver meeting in an angle bracket—and tickle in there behind the rivet—slip slop and wipe and on we go up the slope.

Does the town look up? Do they all gawp and say to each other, look at him! How ridiculous he looks up there, so small, how laughably inadequate. Or do they say, How brave! One man against the elements! Pitted against so much!

The lone explorer feeling his way between the iron crevasses, tacked against the sky by his boots and fingers.

Dots, bricks and beetles.
I could drown them in my spit.

(*Cut bridge, cut in baby's rattle in background.*)

KATE: That isn't nice, Albert.

ALBERT: Spitting?

KATE: Talking like that.

ALBERT: It doesn't represent desire. I'll let them live. I'm only trying to tell you what it's like.

KATE: I know what it's like. It's painting a girder. There's other jobs.

ALBERT: It's my bridge—I wish you'd stop her rattling, it's getting on my nerves.

KATE: That's very advanced for six months.

ALBERT: I'm not doubting her progress. If she played the trumpet it would be even more advanced but it would still be sending me round the twist. Here, give——
(*He dispossesses the rattler, who bawls.*)

KATE: Now you've set her off. She doesn't *understand.*
(*Comforting.*) Come on, then. . . .

ALBERT: Well, see you later.

KATE: Where are you going?

ALBERT: Work.

KATE: It's your Saturday off.

ALBERT: No, it's my Saturday on.

KATE: Last Saturday was your Saturday on.

ALBERT: Well, I'll take two off in a row.

(*Cut in bridge.*)
Listen . . .
The hot sun makes you think of insects,
but this insect hum is the whole city
caught in a seashell. . . .
All conversation is hidden there,
among motors, coughing fits, applause,
screams, laughter, feet on the stairs,
secretaries typing to dictation,

radios delivering the cricket scores,
tapes running, wheels turning, mills grinding,
chips frying, lavatories flushing, lovers sighing,
the mayor blowing his nose.
All audible life in the vibration
of a hairdryer in the room below.
(*Painting.*)
Dip brush, slide, stroke,
it goes on as smooth and shiny
as my sweat. I itch.
Paint on my arm,
silver paint on my brown arm;
it could be part of the bridge.
(*Painting stops.*)
Listen. The note of Clufton is B flat.
The whole world could be the same.
Look down. Is it a fact
that all the dots have names?
(*Cut bridge.*)

KATE: Jack Morris is taking Maureen and little Leslie to Paris.
ALBERT: Who's Jack Morris?
KATE: Next door, Albert.
ALBERT: Oh yes. Who's Maureen?
KATE: Mrs. Morris.
ALBERT: So little Leslie would be their little girl.
KATE: It's a little boy.
ALBERT: Ah. Why are we talking about them?
KATE: They're going to Paris for a holiday. Where are we going?
ALBERT: When?
KATE: That's what I'd like to know.
ALBERT: What?
KATE: Don't you have a holiday?
ALBERT: Oh. I suppose I must. Everybody does. Yes, I expect
   Fitch took that into account.
KATE: You're not going to dodge your holiday—I know what
   you're up to, you're already working full Saturdays, don't

think I'm such a fool that I don't know. . . . And you're
working till dark.

ALBERT: Overtime. I lose time in the winter.

KATE (*sniffing*): It's because you don't like it here, being at
home.

ALBERT: Oh, Kate . . . I've got a schedule, you see.

KATE: You're miles ahead of it.

ALBERT: I've got to have some in hand in case of accidents.

KATE: I told you! You'll fall off, and me and Katherine will be
alone.

ALBERT: No, no, no . . . stop crying. We'll have a holiday. I'll
take a week.

KATE: A fortnight.

ALBERT: All right, I don't mind.

KATE: Can we go to Paris?

ALBERT: I've been to Paris. There's nothing there, believe me.
We could go to Scotland.

KATE: Touring?

ALBERT: Certainly. The Firth of Forth.

KATE: We haven't got a car. Maureen said we could go with
them.

ALBERT: But they're going to Paris.

KATE: We could afford it. It wouldn't be hard, it's easier with
two children and joined forces. . . . It would be lovely, I've
always wanted to see the Champs Elysée and the Arc de
Triumph and the Seine and the Eiffel Tower. . . .
(*Cliché French accordion music. Cross-fade to Eiffel Tower.
It's the same as Clufton Bridge.*)
(*Distant. Shouting up.*) Albert! A-a-albert! (*Repeated, fading,
despairing.*) Come down! Please come down!

ALBERT: I thought as much. Dots, bricks, beetles . . . in B flat.
Still, I'm glad I came. The pointlessness takes one's breath
away—a tower connects nothing, it stands only so that one
can go up and look down. Bridge-builders have none of this
audacity, compromise themselves with function. Monsieur
Eiffel, poet and philosopher, every eight years I'll scratch
your name in the silver of Clufton Bay Bridge.

KATE (*distant, despairing*): Al-bert!
ALBERT (*quiet*): Coming down.

> (*Cut Eiffel Tower.*)
> (*Crockery smashes, flung against wall.*)

KATE: What's her name?
ALBERT: Kate. . . .
KATE: What a bloody coincidence!
ALBERT: You've got it all wrong, Kate, there's no woman——
KATE (*crying*): I can smell her on your coat!
ALBERT: It's paint—I tell you I was up on the bridge.
KATE: All night!
ALBERT: I just thought I would. It was nice up there.
KATE: You're barmy if you expect me to believe that, you're
  round the twist——
ALBERT: It's true——
KATE: And I believe it, I *am* round the twist! I'm as barmy as
  you are, but I believe it——
ALBERT: That's better——

> (*Another cup smashes.*)

KATE: No it isn't—it's worse! A woman would be normal.
  (*Breaking down.*) You don't talk to me, you don't talk to
  Katherine, you can't wait to get out of the house and up
  your favourite girder. (*Quieter, sobbing.*) You don't like me
  any more, I know you don't—I'm boring for you, I haven't
  got what you want, and you don't want to hear the things I
  tell you because I've got nothing to tell you, nothing
  happens. . . .
ALBERT: I like a quiet life, that's all.
KATE: Gutless. You'll spend your whole life painting that
  bridge. . . .
ALBERT: It's a good job.
KATE: You know damn well it's a stupid job which any thick
  idiot could do—but you're educated, Albert. You had
  opportunities. There was Metal Alloys and Allied
  Metals—you could have gone right up the ladder—we'd
  have a house, and friends, and we'd entertain and

Katherine would have nice friends—you could have been an executive!

ALBERT: I was lying in bed one day when the maid came in to make it. . . . She was all starchy. When she moved, her skirt sort of crackled against her nylons. . . . I never had any regrets, but I did want her to be happy too.

KATE (*sobbing*): I've begun talking to myself, over the sink and stove. . . . I talk to myself because nobody else listens, and you won't talk to me, so I talk to the sink and the stove and the baby, and maybe one day one of them will answer me. (*Baby gurgles, almost a word.*)

(*Cut to bridge and painting.*)

ALBERT (*crooning flatly amid and around the tune of 'Night and Day'*):
Night and day, I am the one . . .
day and night, I'm really a part of me . . .
I've got me under my skin.
So why
don't I take all of me.
When I begin the beguine. . . .
I get accustomed to my face,
The thought of me makes me stop
before I begin.
Yes, I've got me under my skin,
and I get a kick out of me. . . .
Day and night, night and day. . . .
Shall I compare me to a summer's day,
'Cos I can't get me out of my mind
I saw me in Monterey . . .
and I'm all right by me,
yes I'm all right, I'm all right,
I'm all right by me. . . .
(*Applause, two-handed, from quite close. Painting stops.*)
Who's there? Who's that?

FRASER (*applauding*): Very nice, very nice. The egotist school of songwriting.

ALBERT: Who are you?

FRASER: You mean my name?

ALBERT: I suppose so.

FRASER: Fraser.

ALBERT: What are you doing on my bridge?

FRASER: Yours?

ALBERT: I'm painting it. I'm authorized.

FRASER: You've got a big job ahead of you.

ALBERT: I've got the time.

FRASER: You've got the time perhaps, but I'd say that time is against you. The condition of the paintwork is very shoddy.

ALBERT: Well, it hasn't been done for a fair while.

FRASER: Yes, it's beginning to look definitely tatty.

ALBERT: I'm getting through it bit by bit.

FRASER: Too slow. The old paint isn't lasting. People have noticed, you know. There's been talk.

ALBERT: Look here—are you the bridge inspector or something?

FRASER: What?

ALBERT: Did Mr. Fitch send you?

FRASER: Who?

ALBERT: What's it all about then?

FRASER: Look down there. I came up because up was the only direction left. The rest has been filled up and is still filling. The city is a hold in which blind prisoners are packed wall to wall. Motor-cars nose each other down every street, and they are beginning to breed, spread, they press the people to the walls by their knees, pinning them by their knees, and there's no end to it, because if you stopped making them, thousands of people would be thrown out of work, and they'd have no money to spend, the shopkeepers would get caught up in it, and the farms and factories, and all the people dependent on them, with their children and all. There's too much of everything, but the space for it is constant. So the shell of human existence is filling out, expanding, and it's going to go bang.

ALBERT: You're frightened of traffic?

FRASER: We are at the mercy of a vast complex of moving parts, any of which might fail. Civilization is in decline, and the white rhino is being wiped out for the racket in bogus aphrodisiacs.

ALBERT: An animal lover——

FRASER: That was merely a trifle I snatched at in my inability to express the whole. I have never been able to understand, for instance, why anyone should want to be a dentist. I cannot pin down the divinity which ensures that just so many people take up dentistry and just so many agree to milk the cows which would otherwise scream in pain just as children would scream if there were no dentists.

ALBERT: I see. A lunatic, in fact.

FRASER: Not certifiably so. By no means certified. I am simply open, wide open, to certain insights. I do not believe that there is anyone in control. There is the semblance of pattern—supply meeting demand, one-way streets, give and take, the presumption of return tickets, promises to pay the bearer on demand, etcetera—but there's nothing really holding it together. One is forced to recognize the arbitrariness of what we claim to be order. Somewhere there is a lynch pin, which, when removed, will collapse the whole monkey-puzzle. And I'm not staying there till it happens.

ALBERT: I see. Well, we all have our problems, but I don't see how that justifies you climbing about council property. So would you kindly descend——

FRASER: That's what I came up for.

ALBERT: To descend?

FRASER: It never occurred to me to stay.

ALBERT: You came up to go down?

FRASER: To jump.

ALBERT: Jump?

FRASER: Off.

ALBERT: Jump off? You'd kill yourself. Ah.

FRASER: Yes.

ALBERT: I see. All right, then.

FRASER: My mind was made up——

ALBERT: I see your point.

FRASER: It seemed the easiest thing to do.

ALBERT: I agree. Well then, time is hurrying by, waiting for no man. Or is that tide?

FRASER: I see you're trying to humour me. Well, I expected that. You'll be sending for a priest next.

ALBERT: Come, come, don't procrastinate.

FRASER: Me?

ALBERT: You said you were going to jump.

FRASER: Well?

ALBERT: Well, jump.

FRASER: Aren't you going to try to talk me out of it?

ALBERT: You know your own mind. And you're holding me up. I've got to paint where you're standing.

FRASER: You wouldn't just stand there without lifting a finger?

ALBERT: I knew it. You're just a talker. Those ones never do it.

FRASER: I can't believe it. You wouldn't just stand there and watch me kill myself.

ALBERT: I thought that's what you wanted.

FRASER: Well, I did. I couldn't bear the noise, and the chaos. I couldn't get free of it, the enormity of that disorder, so dependent on a chance sequence of action and reaction. So I started to climb, to get some height, you know, enough height to drop from, to be sure, and the higher I climbed, the more I saw and the less I heard. And look now. I've been up here for hours, looking down and all it is, is dots and bricks, giving out a gentle hum. Quite safe. Quite small after all. Quite ordered, seen from above. Laid out in squares, each square a function, each dot a functionary. I really think it might work. Yes, from a vantage point like this, the idea of society is just about tenable.

ALBERT: Funked it. Well, mind how you go. Don't fall.

(*Cut bridge.*)

CHAIRMAN: Gentlemen. This special emergency meeting of the Clufton Bay Bridge Sub-Committee has been called as a result of public representations, both direct and via the press, concerning the unsightly condition of what is the symbol of Clufton's prosperity. My grandfather, who was loved by the public, and owed everything to them, must be turning in his grave. It is a salutary reminder that we are all servants of the public, Mr. Fitch.

DAVE: Hear, hear, Mr. Chairman.

CHAIRMAN: Shut up, Dave. As chairman, I, of course, take full responsibility. That is the duty of the chairman, regardless of where that responsibility actually lies, Mr. Fitch.

GEORGE: Hear, hear, Mr. Chairman.

CHAIRMAN: It is no smiling matter, George. The city publicity officer has been on to me, the Parks and Amenities have been on to me, British Railways have been on to me and the *Clufton Chronicle* has been doing its damndest to get on to me. This committee is the shame and the laughing stock of the Clufton Council, and as the future—as a possible future Mayor—I am gravely embarrassed by having to carry the can for a lack of foresight and watchfulness on the part of committee members whose names I will not mention, George. I have issued a statement to the effect that the squalid state of disrepair of Clufton's highly-respected bridge is the result of a miscalculation by a senior public official, for which I, as chairman, take full responsibility, Mr. Fitch.

FITCH (*a broken man*): I can only say in mitigation that I have been under pressure—a sick man—domestic and financial worries——

CHAIRMAN: Quite, quite. Let's stick to essentials. Two years ago, at your insistence and against my better judgement, which I left unspoken in deference to your professional capacity, we arranged to switch to improved paint lasting eight years, and through a reasoning which I never pretended to follow, to sack three of the four painters. Today, two years later, we are left with a bridge that is only one quarter painted while the other three-quarters is in a condition ranging from the sub-standard to the decrepit.

Now then—what happened?

FITCH: Mr. Chairman, gentlemen, I have served Clufton man and boy for five years. . . . Clufton is the repository of my dreams and boyhood memories, the temple of my hopes to transform the running of a living community to a thing of precision and efficiency, a cybernetic poem—a programmed machine as perfect as a rose——

CHAIRMAN: For God's sake, Fitch, pull yourself together.

FITCH: Gentlemen, let us take as our starting point the proposition that X painters painting at the rate of Y would take Z years to paint surface ABC. We found that when X equalled four, Z equalled two, Y and ABC remaining constant. Then along came factor P, a paint lasting eight years——

CHAIRMAN: I can't stand it.

GEORGE: I think what Mr. Fitch is getting at, Mr. Chairman, is that the brown paint on the bridge was only supposed to last two years, the time that it took four painters to finish the job and start again. Well, of course, when we cut down to one painter using eight-year paint, it was obvious that in two years' time he'd only be a quarter of the way along, so the old paint would be ready for another coat.

CHAIRMAN: If it was obvious why didn't you say so?

GEORGE: I couldn't catch the eye of the chairman. Of course, if we could hang on for another six years, Mr. Fitch would emerge triumphantly vindicated as the poet of precision and efficiency.

CHAIRMAN: I might be dead in six years.

DAVE: Hear, hear, Mr. Chairman.

CHAIRMAN: Thank you, Dave. So what are we going to do about it? Fitch?

FITCH: Er. . . . If we hired extra painters, one to start at the far end, one in the middle going one way, another going the opposite way, no . . . er, the progressive element intercedes—if we have two painters back to back at a point nine-sixteenths from the far end—no——

CHAIRMAN: We'd better go back to the old system and hire

three more painters. Carry on from there.

FITCH: You can't do that! They wouldn't be quick enough on the one hand and they'd finish too soon on the other—you see, the bridge won't need re-painting for another six years, and the resultant co-efficient—waste and unsightliness—the entire system would disintegrate and cost thousands——

CHAIRMAN: Money? (*Appalled.*) My grandfather——

GEORGE: I think I see a way out, Mr. Chairman. From the points of view of efficiency and expediency, I think we can get the whole thing resolved with just a bit of organization.

FITCH: Every day counts.

GEORGE: One day is all we'll need.

(*Cut.*)

ALBERT: Met a feller up on the bridge the other day.

KATE (*strained*): Oh yes?

ALBERT: Yes. Climbed up to chuck himself off.

KATE: Did he?

ALBERT: No. Once he got up there, the mood passed.

KATE: Albert. . . .

ALBERT (*going*): Just off.

KATE: You used to say good-bye.

(*Cut to bridge.*)

FRASER: Hello.

ALBERT: Who's that?

FRASER: Me again.

ALBERT: Did you forget something?

FRASER: No, it all came back to me. After I went down, it all started again. So I came back up.

ALBERT: To jump?

FRASER: Yes.

ALBERT: Go on then.

FRASER: I'm all right again now. I don't want to.

ALBERT: Now look here, this isn't a public right of way. I'll report you.

FRASER: I can't help it. I'm forced up and coaxed down. I'm a victim of perspective.

ALBERT (*shouts*): Get down!

FRASER: All right, I'm going.

(*Cut bridge.*)

ALBERT: I'm not a complaining man. I let people get on with
their own lives, I'm sympathetic to problems, but a line
must be drawn. I've found him up there four times now,
Mr. Fitch, and each time it's the same story—he doesn't
want to jump after all. I've given him every chance.

FITCH: Yes yes, but that isn't what I've asked to see you about
at all. You haven't been listening to me.

ALBERT: It's unnerving me, finding company up there. Well,
it's changing the character of the job, and playing hell with
my schedule—simply on the level of efficiency I protest.

FITCH: Well, as I say, for the reasons given, the matter is to be
resolved. We have to get the bridge finished by the end of
the week.

ALBERT: What?

FITCH: We can't allow further deterioration. The public is
roused.

ALBERT: Wait a minute—I can't possibly finish by the end of
the week.

FITCH: I realize, of course, you'll need help. I have made
arrangements.

ALBERT: What arrangements?

FITCH: Eighteen-hundred painters will report for work at seven
o'clock tomorrow morning. By nightfall the job will be
done. I have personally worked it out, and my department
has taken care of the logistics.

ALBERT: Eighteen-hundred?

FITCH: Seventeen-hundred-and-ninety-nine. I kept a place for
you. I thought you'd like that.

(*Cut to door slam.*)

ALBERT (*breathless*): They're moving in on me, the dots are
ganging up. I'll need food and spare clothes, a couple of
blankets. What are you doing?

KATE (*off*): Packing, Albert. I'm going.

ALBERT: Kate, they've got it in for me. They're trying to move
me off—and I've earned my position. I've worked for it.

KATE (*approach*): I've got a position—a housemaid, living in.
With Katherine. I'll let you know my days off, for visiting.
(*Pause.*)

ALBERT: Kate . . . I'm sorry. . . . Will you come and see me
sometimes. . . . ? Will you come along and wave?

(*Cut in bridge and painting.*)
(*More rapid than before.*)
Dip brush, dip brush—slap it on, slide silver
over the iron, glide like mercury—slick, wipe,
tickle it wet, swish, slop, sweep and wipe the
silver slime, it's all I can do—
in eight years I'll be pushing thirty-two
a manic painter coming through for the second time.
Dip brush, dip brush—

FRASER: What's the rush?
(*Painting stops.*)

ALBERT: Fraser.

FRASER: You're going at it.

ALBERT (*shouting*): Get down! Get down!

FRASER: This isn't like you at all.

ALBERT: I'm not having you up here.

FRASER: There's room for both of us.

ALBERT: You're just the first, and I'm not going to have it. If
you're going to jump—jump.

FRASER: That's why I came, again.

ALBERT (*closer and quieter*): You're going to jump?

FRASER: No. Not today.

ALBERT (*furious*): Up and down like a yo-yo!

FRASER: I agree that it is ludicrous. Down there I am assailed
by the flying splinters of a world breaking up at the speed
of procreation without end. The centre cannot hold and the
outside edge is filling out like a balloon, without the
assurance of infinity. More men are hungry than honest,

and more eat than produce. The apocalypse cannot be long delayed.

ALBERT: You'd be better out of it. I'll tell them why you did it, if that's what's worrying you.

FRASER: . . . So I climb up again and prepare to cast myself off, without faith in angels to catch me—or desire that they should—and lo! I look down at it all and find that the proportions have been re-established. My confidence is restored, by perspective.

ALBERT: But it's my bridge——

FRASER: You think only of yourself—you see yourself as the centre, whereas I know that I am not placed at all——

ALBERT: There are other bridges—bigger——

FRASER (*listening*): What's that?

ALBERT: San Francisco—Sydney——

FRASER: Listen.

ALBERT: Brooklyn—there's a place for you——

FRASER: Listen!

ALBERT: —but I was here first—this is mine——
   (*He tails off as there is the faintest sound of 1,800 men marching, whistling 'Colonel Bogey'.*)

FRASER: There's an army on the march. . . .

ALBERT: So they're coming. . . .

FRASER: A solid phalanx moving squarely up the road, an officer at the head. . . .

ALBERT: Fitch.

FRASER: But they're not soldiers.

ALBERT: He's mad.

FRASER (*appalled*): They're just—people.

ALBERT (*shouts—to the people*): Go away!

FRASER: Coming here.

ALBERT: Halt! About turn!

FRASER: They've lined up hundreds and hundreds of ordinary people—the overflow—all the fit men in the prime of life—they're always the ones on the list—preference is given to the old and the sick, the women and children—when it comes to the point, it's the young and able-bodied who go first——

ALBERT: Can't you see—they're taking over!

FRASER: Ten abreast—sixty deep—and another phalanx
behind—and another—successive waves——
(*The whistling is getting louder.*)
—so it has come to this.

ALBERT: They're going to come up!

FRASER: It was the only direction left.

ALBERT: They're going to wheel right——

FITCH (*distant*): Right—wheel!

ALBERT: Off the road and through the gate——

FITCH: Straighten up there!

ALBERT: Up to the end of the bridge, on to the tracks——

FRASER: That's it, then—they have finally run out of space, the
edges have all filled out and now there is only up.

ALBERT: Eighteen-hundred men—flung against me by a
madman! Was I so important? Here they come.
(*This is difficult; as the front rank reaches the bridge, the
tramp-tramp of the march should start to ring hollow,
progressively, as more and more leave terra firma and reach the
bridge.*)
(*From now, approaching tears.*) I could have done it, given
time——

FRASER: There will be more behind them—the concrete mixers
churn and churn until only a single row of corn grows
between two cities, and is finally ground between their
walls. . . .

ALBERT: They didn't give me a fair chance—I would have
worked nights——

FRASER: They'll all come following—women and children
too—and those that are at the top will be pushed off like
disgraced legionaires——

ALBERT: I had it under control—ahead of schedule——

FRASER: Ah well. But they should be breaking step.
(*Tramp tramp*).
Like soldiers do when they come to a bridge——

ALBERT: I was all right—I was doing well——

FRASER: For the very good reason—
   (*Tramp tramp.*)
   that if they don't—
ALBERT: I was still young—fit—
FRASER: —the pressures cannot bounce—but build and have to
   break out—
   (*The rivets are starting to pop.*)
ALBERT: —good head for heights——
FRASER: —they don't know, or don't believe it, but the physical
   laws are inviolable—
   (*Cracking and wrenching.*)
ALBERT: What's happening?
FRASER: —and if you carry on like that, a bridge will shiver, the
   girders tensed and trembling for the release of the energy
   being driven through them—
ALBERT: —it's breaking up!
FRASER: —until the rivets pop—
ALBERT (*screams*): What are they doing to my bridge!
FRASER: —and a forty-foot girder moans like a Jew's harp—
   (*Twang.*)
   —and one's enough—
ALBERT: To go to such lengths! I didn't do them any harm!
   What did I have that they wanted?
   (*The bridge collapses.*)

WHERE ARE THEY NOW?

1945

DOBSON	late 40s
GROUCHO	
CHICO	
HARPO	13 years old
ANDERSON	

1969

MARKS	
BRINDLEY	late 30s
GALE	
CRAWFORD	18 years old
JENKINS	70 years old
HEADMASTER	in his 60s
YOUNG MARKS	11 years old
BELLAMY	11 years old

DOBSON reappears

In addition, a small group of 13-year-olds is required to chorus one line; and a large number of Old Boys are heard singing the School Song with a piano accompaniment.

NOTE: The play is set entirely in two inter-cut locations, School Dinner (1945) and Old Boys' Dinner (1969). Part of the idea is to move between the two without using any of the familiar grammar of fading down and fading up; the action is continuous. For the sake of absolute clarity I have scored a line across the page at the points where the location changes but the hope is that these points are in fact self-evident, both on the page and on the air.

The OLD BOYS *are heard taking their places at the tables. The scrapes and murmurs die down to an expectant silence.*

HEADMASTER: For what we are about to receive may the Lord make us truly thankful.
OLD BOYS: Amen.
(*The* OLD BOYS *take their seats.*)

GROUCHO: Eurgh!
DOBSON: Pass it along, boy, and be your age.
GROUCHO: I don't like dogfish, sir.
DOBSON: It is not dogfish, it is salmon, *rock* salmon, *finest* rock salmon, caught, quite possibly, off the rocky coasts of our Canadian allies, what is it, Chico?
CHICO: Rock salmon, sir.
DOBSON: Exactly. Why is Harpo weeping?
GROUCHO: He's not weeping, he's praying. It's double French today, isn't it, Harpo?
DOBSON: That will do, boy.
CHICO: Can I have yours, Groucho? You can have some of my strawberry jam at tea.
GROUCHO: I don't want your rotten turnip jam, Brindley, I've got Mexican honey my mother sent from Mexico.
DOBSON: Enough! Who's on tucker today?
CHORUS: Harpo, sir!
DOBSON: Serve the Pom, then, Harpo, and do cheer up. Eat your salmon, boy.

GROUCHO: It's what we had in biology yesterday—fried in
    batter.
DOBSON: Four C's by tomorrow morning.
GROUCHO: Oh, *sir*!
DOBSON: Even with your parents in Mexico it cannot have
    escaped your attention for the last five years that there's a
    war on.
GROUCHO: I think it's off, sir.
DOBSON: You mean the Germans have surrendered?
GROUCHO: The dog salmon, sir.
DOBSON: *Rock* salmon.
GROUCHO: It's off.
DOBSON: Two helpings for you then, Groucho.
GROUCHO: Ugh!
CHICO: He's right, sir.
DOBSON: None for you then, Chico.
CHICO: Oh *sir*!
GROUCHO: That'll teach you, Brindley.
DOBSON: I may look old but I'm not senile. *Root, boy!*
CHICO: Senex—senis—old man!

DOBSON: Splendid, Brindley, old man! Splendid to see
    you! Can I help you to wine—ah, waiter!
    (*A gavel bangs. The hubbub is dying down.* BRINDLEY *speaks
    quietly.*)
BRINDLEY: Oh, thank you, Mr. Dobson.
    (*Gavel.* DOBSON *is, apparently, a little deaf now.*)
DOBSON: Does everybody know everybody? What—Oh!—Ah!
    Headmaster . . .
    (*The* HEADMASTER *is some way off mike, at first.*)
HEADMASTER: Gentlemen, it would not be appropriate to let
    the whole evening pass before bidding you welcome, and
    yet I would not wish to belabour you with that welcome
    while your salmon lies untasted on the plate—so for the
    moment I will restrict my remarks to expressing my

pleasure at seeing so many Old Boys here tonight, and later while you are digesting not only the smoked salmon but also the turkey and the apple pie, I shall have more to tell you of the School and the events of the past year. Until then, as Monsieur Leblanc would wish me to say, bon appetit!

(*He desists amid dutiful chuckles, and the murmur re-establishes itself.*)

MARKS: Leave the bottle, waiter, we'll look after that, there's a good fellow. Pretty unimaginative menu, what, Brindley?

BRINDLEY: Do you think so, Marks?

DOBSON: I don't suppose you know Leblanc, do you?

BRINDLEY: No—Mr. Jenkins taught French in my day.

DOBSON: Leblanc *is* French, of course. I don't really see the point of that. After all I have taught Latin adequately for fifty years without so much as crossing the Rubicon, eh-eh . . . ? Still, Leblanc looks better on the prospectus than Jenkins. The boys call him Chalky, so he must have taught them *something*.

MARKS: We used to call Jenkins Paddy.

BRINDLEY: Taffy.

MARKS: I mean Taffy. Taffy Jenkins.

DOBSON: Yes, you were an inspired lot.

MARKS: Good of you to say so, sir. I thought we were a cut above the average. I think most of us have done pretty well—except Reverend Brindley here, of course—no offence, old chap—some things are worth more than gold, eh?

BRINDLEY: The correct usage is *Mr.* Brindley. I do wish you would get these things right. You may refer to me in full, if you like, as 'the Reverend Jonathan Brindley', or 'The Reverend Mr. Brindley' but to say Reverend Brindley is as silly as saying Corpulent Marks. Besides, your assumption may be premature—after all, the Archbishop of Canterbury gets seven and a half thousand a year.

MARKS: Did you look that up?

BRINDLEY: Certainly not! It's . . . it's common knowledge, isn't it?

DOBSON: And what about Mr. Gale here? I've often wondered what became of you.

BRINDLEY: What! You don't read the right paper! Our friend Gale is a journalist of considerable repute—a crusading journalist, I think one might call you, eh Gale?

DOBSON: Oh, I'm very sorry. But your failure to contribute to the Magazine's 'Where Are They Now?' page does not leave you entirely blameless, Gale. Nevertheless, it is very good to see you after so many years. And what do you crusade for?

(*Small pause.*)

BRINDLEY: Mr. Gale has lately returned from Lagos.

DOBSON: Really? How very interesting! What is happening on the Ivory Coast nowadays?

(*A small embarrassed silence.*)

MARKS (*jovially*): I say, are you going to keep that bottle to yourself, Gale? It's pretty poor chablis but I'll have another crack at it. Thanks very much . . . Talking of Jenkins, do you remember his famous Bruiser?

BRINDLEY: My goodness yes, the fearsome Jenkins and his Bruiser—I hope that sort of thing no longer exists, Mr. Dobson?

MARKS: Nonsense, Brindley—never did us any harm—a few thumps with the end of a rope to keep us up to scratch. No good sending a bunch of ninnies into the world, what say you, Gale?

JENKINS: *My* name's Jenkins, as a matter of fact.

DOBSON: Ah, that explains it.

JENKINS: Explains what?

DOBSON: That chair you are sitting in was meant for Jenkins the French, as I understood it—indeed Mr. Gale wrote to ask that he might sit at the same table—but then it transpired that Jenkins the French had in point of fact died——

MARKS: Died?

DOBSON: Quite so. Every master dies in the twelve months

preceding one Old Boys' Dinner or another—except for that appalling man Grimes who actually died during one. I shall be no exception. Where was I?

MARKS: Poor chap.

BRINDLEY: Yes indeed. He seemed indestructible. It was part of his fearsomeness.

MARKS: I don't think I was actually *afraid* of him . . .

JENKINS: It does say Jenkins on this place-card.

DOBSON: Exactly. Everything is explained. The chair was not for Jenkins the French, it was for you. What year did you leave, boy?

JENKINS: 1918.

DOBSON: What! You were *below* me! What house?

JENKINS: I wasn't in any particular house as such.

DOBSON: Nonsense! Everyone was in a house. I was in Routledge, as it was then.

JENKINS: Oh. I can't honestly remember now. I was only a weekday boarder, wetlegs they called us, I forget why.

DOBSON: Weekday boarder? No such thing.

JENKINS: There was then. The war, I expect.

DOBSON: I remember the war perfectly well. I was in Routledge.

JENKINS (*helpfully*): I remember I had a colour.

DOBSON: Got your pink? Batting or bowling?

JENKINS: No, no—we were all split up into colours. I was maroon.

DOBSON (*forgetting himself*): You're mad! I may be senile but I'm not completely loco!

JENKINS (*stiffly*): Just as you like. As a matter of fact, I don't remember you either.

DOBSON: Don't remember *me*?! I've been at the School man and boy longer than anyone alive! Did you subscribe to my clock?

JENKINS: Clock?

DOBSON: Obviously not!

JENKINS: I'm afraid I've been out East more or less since I was twenty one . . . Ever been to Malaya, by any chance?

DOBSON (*witheringly*): You mean in the summer holidays? I see they've sewn the slices of lemon into little muslin bags this year. Why do you suppose that is?

MARKS: It's to stop it squirting in your eye.

DOBSON: We've never had muslin bags at the Royal Derby Hotel before. Perhaps there were cases of temporary blindness after last year's dinner.

BRINDLEY: I believe that Mr. Marks was temporarily blind after last year's dinner.

(*The table laughs loudly at this, until* CRAWFORD, *to his embarrassment, is left laughing all by himself.*)

DOBSON: Oh—I don't suppose you know Mr. Crawford, do you?

CRAWFORD: How do you do?

DOBSON: Crawford, on your left, round the table, that's Mr. Gale, Mr. Jenkins, Mr. Brindley, and this is Mr. Marks on my right.

MARKS: You're an *Old* Boy, Mr. Crawford?

CRAWFORD: Yes, sir.

DOBSON: Mr. Crawford left school last term. He was head boy.

MARKS: Good lord!—sorry, Crawford, it's just that in my day the top cap was always a swaggering young blood with a five o'clock shadow and a world-weary manner. How old *are* you?

CRAWFORD: Eighteen, sir.

MARKS: Children! The Upper Henty must be full of children!

CRAWFORD: Yes, sir.

BRINDLEY: Mr. Marks is being heavily ironic, old chap.

CRAWFORD: Sorry, sir.

MARKS: Yes, sir—sorry, sir . . . Do you remember Runcible? And Grant-Menzies? They were kings? Grant-Menzies used a cane with a silver knob and kept a pre-war Lagonda garaged in town. They could reduce the lockers to trembling silence with one look.

DOBSON: Runcible is here—at the Headmaster's table. Do you approve of the new seating arrangements? We've always had the Old Boys' Dinner at long tables in the past, Gale, in

the Chatsworth Room downstairs, but we managed to
arrange a swap.

MARKS: Speaking for myself I think the change was long
overdue. Let the lower decks have the long tables, say I. I
like a round table, we've always had a round table at home.
I suppose you have a rectory table, Brindley.

BRINDLEY: I think you mean refectory.

MARKS: Long tables always remind me of school. (*jocularly*)
Who's on tucker today, eh?

CHORUS: Harpo, sir!

DOBSON: So you are—well, jump to it, lad, let's have the
pudding in—Oh! Why haven't you been eating? Do you
hear me, boy? . . . What did he say?

CHICO: He says he's not feeling well.

DOBSON: Not feeling well? Why should anybody expect to feel
well? Has he got a mog chit?

GROUCHO: He's just got the frits, haven't you, Harpo?

CHICO: It's all right for you, Groucho—he got as far as you this
morning.

DOBSON: All right, all right—do stop crying and take your plate
away. You really shouldn't get into such a state over Mr.
Jenkins. He no doubt has a thankless task trying to educate
you in a subject that will prove invaluable to you in later life
should you join the Foreign Legion, which most of you
will probably have to . . . No, you can't leave yours,
Anderson; I'm not having any more waste.

ANDERSON: I don't feel well, sir.

DOBSON: If you don't feel well why didn't you go to Staggers
this morning?

ANDERSON: I don't know, sir.

DOBSON: Oh, don't be stupid, boy! I will not tolerate stupid
replies. Very well, go to matron immediately after lunch,
and if she can't find anything wrong with you I'm going to
put you on tunky for the whole weekend—*Have you been
reading at table?!*

ANDERSON: No, sir.

DOBSON: No?—what do you mean, no? Is that a book or isn't it?

ANDERSON: Yes, sir. I wasn't actually reading, sir.

DOBSON: Give it to me at once . . . What's this? Ah! Very well, since you find this so fascinating, let me have page sixteen translated into Latin by the morning, as far as 'dit le boulanger'.

ANDERSON (*dumbfounded*): French into *Latin*?

DOBSON: Now isn't that interesting? It has never occurred to Anderson that one foreign language can be translated into another. He assumes that every strange tongue exists only by virtue of its not being English. Ah—milk pudding!

CHICO: Dried milk.

GROUCHO: Frogspawn.

DOBSON: Put it down then. Thank you.

HARPO: Yes, sir.

DOBSON: Ah! Harpo speaks! You're not mute after all. You just have nothing to say.

GROUCHO: You can have mine, Brindley.

CHICO: No, thanks, Groucho. It's not milk, it's Klim, I bet you.

DOBSON: Nothing wrong with Klim. Fresh from the Ministry of Food's prize herd of Jersey wocs. I have just said something extremely risible—Root, boy!

CHICO: Rido—ridere—risi, I laugh!

(CRAWFORD *laughing solo, slightly inebriated*.)

CRAWFORD: Very good! Very good!

DOBSON (*reprovingly*): It wasn't *that* funny, Crawford.

CRAWFORD (*stops laughing*): Oh, sorry, sir.

DOBSON: Perhaps you had better pass the wine on.

CRAWFORD: Yes, sir, sorry, sir.

MARKS: There you are, Brindley.

BRINDLEY: Oh, I don't think I should have any more . . .

MARKS: Can't say I blame you, old man. I only care for French wines, myself.

BRINDLEY: It does say Burgundy on the bottle.

MARKS: It's the old wine ramp, vicar! Cheapish, reddish and

Spanish, marks my word or my name's not Mark—or
rather—

(BRINDLEY *giggles*.)

I say, Brindley, you've had enough!

BRINDLEY: Gale has imbibed most of it, with respect——

MARKS: You're welcome to it, Gale, and as for the turkey, I
wouldn't give it to my chow.

DOBSON: Your char?

MARKS: No, my *chow*—an absolute brute, he is, but one needs
to have a guard dog about the place—got a bit of decent
silver, you know . . .

JENKINS (*quietly, under* MARKS): I hope that fellow Marks isn't
the typical Old Boy nowadays, eh Gale? I'll tell you one
thing, he wouldn't have lasted long up country, certainly
not in the old days. The Christmas turkey came out of a tin,
if you were lucky, my goodness yes. Suited me, though. I'll
tell you quite frankly, Gale, after the war I didn't bother
with home leave at all. It wasn't home any more, you see,
not as I knew it. Spent my leaves in K.L. or Singapore.
Mind you, here I am again, and for good. I'll tell you what
it was, Gale. Once I'd retired and life was *all* leave, well I
began to feel I was *abroad* again. Dammit, I was homesick.
(*Chuckles*.) Or schoolsick. I think I came back just to attend
this dinner, for the first time. Like you, I believe. Perhaps
your reasons were similar? I gather you have been working
in foreign climes . . . ? The old school *was* my England,
you see; at least it was the part I knew best and thought
about, and missed. I had a fine time . . . good friends. We
all seemed to belong to each other, you know. Do you know
what I mean?

GALE (*quietly*): No.

JENKINS (*unhearing*): I was hoping I might see one or two
survivors . . . Bunny Sullivan especially, he was a close
friend. And the younger Robertson—his brother was killed
in my last year, he was in destroyers. But I don't think I
know anybody . . . Mr. Dobson! What happened to Bunny
Sullivan, do you know?

DOBSON: You mean *Bunty* Sullivan—and anyway, it wasn't Sullivan. I forget his name but it wasn't Sullivan. I expect you've got mixed up with Seligman.

JENKINS: He was captain of squash.

DOBSON: Fives, you mean.

JENKINS: Was it?

DOBSON: We have never been a squash school. (*Quietly*, to MARKS) You realize, Marks, that that fellow isn't really Jenkins at all?

MARKS (*a quarter drunk*): 'Course not. Jenkins is dead, God rest his soul. (*Piously*.) I'll never forget you, Tommy Jenkins, here's to you, old chap!

DOBSON: No—no—I mean he isn't even the Jenkins he claims to be. There may have *been* a Jenkins, but I don't know this chap.

MARKS: Well, it must be fifty years . . .

DOBSON: I never forget a boy. Besides, he's made several elementary mistakes. I don't know what his game is but he's an imposter.

JENKINS (*to* GALE): He must have been a complete nonentity. If he was there at all. I mean, there's something damned odd about the man—what is he trying to prove with this rigmarole? Dammit, I *played* squash. Personally, I think the old boy is just past it, he's obviously mixing up this school with some other school he was at. His mind's gone. I should know—I had my first cigarette in the squash court! Bunty and I were sick as dogs. Bunny. Oh yes . . . where are they now, the snows of yesteryear? Life was simpler then. And England was such a *pretty* place. I swear people were nicer. I don't remember such desperation over . . . winning the next trick. Yes, the old school was damned good to me. And it was all pasture-land then, you know. On long summer evenings when we were all in bed and almost asleep, we'd hear the farmer's boy on the hill, calling the cattle home, singing them home . . . God, yes.

MARKS (*loudly, independently*): Happiest days of my life, to coin a phrase!

BRINDLEY: Yes, indeed.

MARKS: Love to have them all over again. Still, I've done the next best thing.

BRINDLEY: What's that?

MARKS: Sent the boy, of course. How's Gerald buckling down, Crawford? Well-liked lad, is he?

CRAWFORD: Gerald, sir?

MARKS: My boy.

DOBSON (*quietly*): Marks, Crawford.

CRAWFORD: Oh—yes, sir. We don't call him Gerald, sir.

MARKS: 'Course not. Has he got a nickname? Little beggar tells me nothing.

CRAWFORD: Er, I'm not sure. He's in Junior School, sir.

MARKS: He's got to have a nickname. You haven't been accepted till you've got a nickname—isn't that right, Chico?

BRINDLEY: Goodness!—I'd quite forgotten!

DOBSON: Oh, yes!—Yes, yes—Gale, Brindley and Marks, we used to call you the—what was it?—the Three Musketeers, Chico . . . no, that can't be right . . .

JENKINS (*quietly*): I told you he's past it.

BRINDLEY (*laughing*): No, no—it was the Three Marx Brothers —Groucho, Chico and . . .

DOBSON: Harpo. Exactly.

MARKS: That was it. Those were the days, eh?

BRINDLEY: Yes, indeed. Did you have a nickname, Crawford?

CRAWFORD: Well, not really, sir.

DOBSON: I regret to say that I am referred to as Dobbin.

MARKS: Dobbin!

DOBSON: Crawford seems embarrassed. Perhaps he thinks I didn't know? I can't think why—after all, Crawford, you were aware, were you not, that you were sometimes known as Crackers?

MARKS: Crackers!

CRAWFORD (*viciously*): *Who said that?*

(*Silence.*)

Marks?!

YOUNG MARKS (*scared*): It wasn't me, Crawford.

CRAWFORD: Come on, I want to know which of you said that!
Bellamy?

BELLAMY: Said what?

CRAWFORD: *My name is Crawford!* Come here.

BELLAMY: We didn't mean anything, Crawford!

CRAWFORD: And you, Marks.

YOUNG MARKS: I didn't do anything, Crawford!

CRAWFORD: You stink, Marks. You stink and you're a wet. I do
not like wet, stinky boys. Do you hear me, Marks? I will
not abide wetness and stinkiness on any account. Why are
you so wet? Don't go away, Bellamy! Now then, Marks, tell
me why are you so wet. How dare you be wet in my
presence? Do you like being wet? Answer me, you moronic
little tick, don't you know that failure to answer a question
offends me, Marks? Take off your shoe, go on take it off,
I'll teach you to be wet——

YOUNG MARKS: You can't, please Crawford, I've got a mog
from matron, I'm excused football, and everything——

CRAWFORD: How dare you answer me back! My God, you're so
wet, Marks, wetness must be beaten out of you—I'm
watching you, Bellamy, don't leave us—bend over,
Marks—(*grabbing him*) *bend over*!

YOUNG MARKS: Please, Crawford! (*Thump.* MARKS *cries out.*)

(*Thump. Thump. The* HEADMASTER's *gavel. Silence
overtakes the* OLD BOYS' *Dinner.*)

HEADMASTER: The traditional order of programme will be
slightly different this evening, owing to a very sad
circumstance.

DOBSON (*quietly*): I deplore this. Anybody would think that no
one had ever died before.

HEADMASTER: I have to inform you that a few days ago, Mr. R.
L. Jenkins died in hospital after a short illness. Many of
you will remember him with affection and respect.

MARKS: Hear, hear.

HEADMASTER: He was a master for twenty years, and ever since

his retirement ten years ago, he has been one of us, a
familiar figure at these dinners, and even more behind the
scenes, a tireless and selfless worker for the school. It is
sad—indeed it is very difficult—to realize that his dapper
figure, with gown billowing and moustache bristling, will
no more be seen hurrying from Monk's Pond to Chapel,
and indeed Chapel will not be the same without his baritone
shaming younger men.

DOBSON: Ridiculous fuss.

HEADMASTER: He could be a stern man, but he always had a
twinkle in his eye, and I think everyone who was taught by
him learned to respect his demanding standards. Like all
the best teachers, he had a passion for his subject and the
absolute conviction that if it was not necessarily the most
important subject, it was the most rewarding. I think it
would be fitting, therefore, if before we said Grace, we were
to stand for a minute or two in silence and think of Mr.
Jenkins, who is now lost to us.

(*After a short pause, the company gets to its feet.*)

JENKINS (*quietly*): I say—Gale! Are you asleep?

GALE (*flatly*): Good-bye, Mr. Jenkins! Or rather, au revoir.

JENKINS: Mr. Gale—we've got to stand for Jenkins.

GALE: I'm sitting down for Jenkins. We stood for Jenkins long
enough.

(GALE *is speaking very quietly, but not whispering.*)

DOBSON: Hush!

GALE: And anyway Jenkins has stood me up.

DOBSON: Gale!

GALE: Jenkins, where are you now, now that I really need you?

MARKS: What's the matter with you, man?

GALE: Oh, shut up, Marks. He never taught you anything
either. He made us afraid.

MARKS: Speak for yourself.

GALE: We walked into French like condemned men. We were
too afraid to *learn*. All our energy went into ingratiating
ourselves and deflecting his sadism on to our friends. We
brought him lumps of French to propitiate him until the

bell went, and some of it stuck, that's all—right, Brindley?

BRINDLEY: Gale, I beg you—this is not the time.

GALE: Once when I was ill—itself an admission of some obscure
failure, you will remember—I spent my time in the San
feverishly keeping up with the French I had missed, using
my brother's exercise book—he used to lend me it. One day
he forgot to pick it up and found himself in a French lesson
without any prep to hand in. Jenkins slapped him around
for five minutes. (*Gavel.*) . . . What a *stupid* man! I think
we would have liked French. It is not, after all, a complex
language.

(*The gavel sounds again.*)

HEADMASTER: I can hardly believe my ears. I apologize to those
who have had to endure that muttering. I do not know the
reason for it but I am profoundly shocked. I will say no
more at present. Please be seated, gentlemen, for
Announcements, which will be followed as usual by Grace
and then the School Song, with our music master, Signor
Luzzato, at the pianoforte.

(*The* OLD BOYS *sit down.*)

MARKS: Trust Groucho to make a scene.

HEADMASTER (*barks*): Silence!

(*Sounds subside.*)

First of all I want to draw attention to the deplorable state of
the lockers. In future boys who omit to put away their
Wellingtons *properly* will be punished. Prefects, please see to
it. Next—it has been drawn to my attention that, after last
Saturday's away match at Bridlington, certain members of
the Second Eleven were seen in the town without their caps
and in the company of girls. I must say that I am profoundly
shocked by this misuse of trust. The boys have already been
punished, and it is only for the sake of the school and the
team as a whole that I have been prevailed upon not to bar
them from playing in future matches. However, if there is
any repetition of this street-corner behaviour, I shall without
demur have the Bridlington fixture cancelled.

HEADMASTER: But now for some happier news. It is with great
pride and pleasure that I am able to announce to you an
item of news that has brought great honour to the
School—namely that for services to national industry,
Geoffrey Carson has been honoured by her Majesty the
Queen with the Order of the British Empire. Congratula-
tions, Carson Minor!
(*Laughter and applause from the* OLD BOYS. *The* HEADMAS-
TER'S *voice and occasional light applause continues under the
following.*)

DOBSON: Why did you come?

GALE: I wanted to see if I'd got him right—if he had any other
existence which might explain him . . . As it is, he'll have
to go to my grave as I remember him. Still, perhaps he
remembered me as a minor bully and a prig, which I was.

JENKINS: Some of us have happier memories.

GALE: Oh yes, the snows of yesteryear . . . (*Agonized.*) Where
were they *then*? Oh, where the Fat Owl of the Remove,
where the incorruptible Steerforth? Where the Harrow
match and your best friend's beribboned sister? Whither
Mr. Chips? Oh no, it's farewell to the radiators and the
punishable whisper, cheerio to the uncomprehending
trudge through *Macbeth* and sunbeams defined by chalk-
dust, the sense of loss in the fruitcake sent from home, the
counted days, the hollow fear of inconsiderable matters, the
hand raised in bluff—*Sir, sir, me sir!*——

MARKS: It wasn't all like that, Groucho. We had good times.

GALE: And Marks has sent his son. God, I wish there was a way
to let small boys know that it doesn't really matter. I wish I
could give them the scorn to ride them out—those
momentous trivialities and tiny desolations. I suppose it's
not very important, but at least we would have been
happier children, and childhood is Last Chance Gulch for
happiness. After that, you know too much. I remember
once—I was seven, my first term at prep school—I
remember walking down one of the corridors, trailing my

finger along a raised edge along the wall, and I was suddenly totally happy, not elated or particularly pleased, or anything like that—I mean I experienced happiness as a state of being: everywhere I looked, in my mind, *nothing was wrong*. You never get that back when you grow up; it's a condition of maturity that almost *everything* is wrong, *all the time*, and happiness is a borrowed word for something else—a passing change of emphasis.

(*The* HEADMASTER *ceases, the* OLD BOYS *stand up*.)

GALE: Maturity is a high price to pay for growing up.

HEADMASTER: Let us say Grace.

(*There is a general clearing of throats*.)

HEADMASTER: For what we have received may the Lord make us truly thankful.

OLD BOYS: Amen.

(*General easing movement but all remain standing*. MARKS *giggles*.)

BRINDLEY: What are you laughing at?

MARKS: Just thinking—for ten years of my life, three times a day, I thanked the Lord for what I was about to receive and thanked him again for what I had just received, and then we lost touch—and I suddenly thought, *where is He now?*

BRINDLEY (*giggling*): I say, that's not at all funny, Harpo . . . Er, do you intend to drink your wine?

MARKS: No, no—have it by all means. The brandy's quite tolerable.

(*A piano chord is sounded. The piano continues to play a couple of bars of introduction, but* JENKINS *has already accepted the first chord as his cue to start singing, to the tune of 'Men of Harlech'*.)

JENKINS: Sons of Oakleigh, oaken-hearted
          Are we ever broken-hearted?
          No! . . .

(*The piano falters and dies*. JENKINS' *solo also dies*.)

I say, have they changed the Song?

DOBSON: What school were you *at*, Mr. Jenkins?

JENKINS: Oakleigh, of course. Oakleigh House for the Sons of

Merchant Seamen's Widows.

BRINDLEY: Oh dear. I think that's the lot having dinner
downstairs, in the Chatsworth Room.

(*The piano has re-started, from scratch. Now—to the tune of*
'Onward Christian Soldiers'.)

OLD BOYS: Onward fellow Hovians,
       Onward into life!
       Never mind the struggle,
       Never shun the strife!
       Spread the flag of Britain
       All around the globe!
       And the lesson we have learned
       In happy days at Hove!

       Be the scourge of cruelty
       Of heathen be the bane!
       It's not so much the runs we score
       As how we play the game!
       Onward fellow Hovians,
       Play it by the rules!
       Up for Queen and Country,
       Up the dear old school!

       Onward fellow Hovians,
       Onward into life!
       Never mind the struggle,
       Never shun the strife!
       Spread the flag of Britain
       All around the globe!
       And the lesson we have learned
       In happy days at Hove!

(*During this, for the first time, there is a cross-fade into the past:*
on an open windy field, GALE *is playing some sort of game with*
a few other boys. He is shouting and laughing, calling for the
ball, and being called—'Here, Gale! Gale, Gale!'—the voices
distant and almost snatched away by the wind. It is a day he
has forgotten, but clearly he was very happy.)

ARTIST DESCENDING
A STAIRCASE

CHARACTERS

MARTELLO (SENIOR)
BEAUCHAMP (SENIOR)
DONNER (SENIOR)
SOPHIE
MARTELLO (JUNIOR)
BEAUCHAMP (JUNIOR)
DONNER (JUNIOR)

NOTE: There are eleven scenes. The play begins in the here-and now; the next five scenes are each a flashback from the previous scene; the seventh, eighth, ninth, tenth and eleventh scenes are, respectively, continuations of the fifth, fourth, third, second and first. So the play is set temporally in six parts, in the sequence ABCDEFEDCBA

A = here and now
B = a couple of hours ago
C = Last week
D = 1922
E = 1920
F = 1914

*We hear, on a continuous loop of tape, a sequence of sounds which is
to be interpreted by* MARTELLO *and* BEAUCHAMP *thus:*

    (*a*) DONNER *dozing: an irregular droning noise.*

    (*b*) *Careful footsteps approach. The effect is stealthy. A board
         creaks.*

    (*c*) *This wakes* DONNER, *i.e. the droning stops in mid-beat.*

    (*d*) *The footsteps freeze.*

    (*e*) DONNER'*s voice, unalarmed: 'Ah! There you are . . .'*

    (*f*) *Two more quick steps, and then Thump!*

    (*g*) DONNER *cries out.*

    (*h*) *Wood cracks as he falls through a balustrade.*

    (*i*) *He falls heavily down the stairs, with a final sickening thump
        when he hits the bottom. Silence.*

*After a pause, this entire sequence begins again . . . Droning . . .
Footsteps . . . (as before).*

MARTELLO: I think this is where I came in.

    (TAPE: '*Ah! There you are . . .*')

BEAUCHAMP: And this is where you hit him.

    (TAPE: *Thump!*)

MARTELLO: I *mean*, it's going round again. The tape is going
    round in a *loop*.

BEAUCHAMP: Well, of course. I record in loops, lassoing my
    material—no, like trawling—no, like—no matter.

    (TAPE: DONNER *reaches the bottom of the stairs.*)

MARTELLO: Poor Donner.

    (MARTELLO *and* BEAUCHAMP *are old men, as was* DONNER.

(*The* TAPE *starts off again as before.*)

BEAUCHAMP (*over* TAPE): Round and round, recording layer
    upon layer of silence while Donner dozed after a heavy
    lunch, the spools quietly folding silence upon itself, yes like
    packing linen into trunks . . . Fold, fold until the footsteps
    broke it . . . and woke him——
    (TAPE: '*Ah! There you are* . . .')
    How peaceful it was, in the afternoon in the great houses
    before the Great War, to doze after luncheon with only a fly
    buzzing in the stuffy room and a sense of the maids
    somewhere quietly folding the linen into pine chests . . .
    (TAPE: DONNER *reaches the bottom of the stairs.*)
    Donner knew the post-prandial nap. His people were
    excellently connected. With mine, in fact.
    (TAPE: *re-continues under.*)
    I suppose we should let someone know, though not
    necessarily the entire circumstances. I'm not one to tell tales
    if no good can come of it.

MARTELLO: I will stand by you, Beauchamp. We have been
    together a long time.

BEAUCHAMP: You may rely on me, Martello. I shall not cast the
    first stone.

MARTELLO: You *have* cast it, Beauchamp, but I do not prejudge
    you.

BEAUCHAMP: My feelings precisely, but there seems to be some
    confusion in your mind——

MARTELLO: My very thought. Turn off your machine, it seems
    to be disturbing your concentration——
    (TAPE: '*Ah!*——' *and is switched off.*)

BEAUCHAMP: There you are.

MARTELLO: On the contrary, Beauchamp, there *you* are. Unless
    we can agree on *that*, I can't even begin to help you clear up
    this mess.

BEAUCHAMP: Don't touch him, Martello.

MARTELLO: I don't mean clear up *Donner!*—honestly,
    Beauchamp, you buffoon!

BEAUCHAMP: Cynic!

MARTELLO: Geriatric!

BEAUCHAMP: Murderer!

(*Pause.*)

MARTELLO: As I was saying, I shall help you so far as I can to get through the difficult days ahead, whether in duplicity or in the police courts, depending on how you intend to face the situation; but I shall do so only on the condition that we drop this farce of accusation and counter-accusation. You had only two friends in the world, and having killed one you can't afford to irritate the other.

BEAUCHAMP: Very well!—I gave you your chance, and now I'm going to get the police.

MARTELLO: A very sensible decision. You are too feeble to run, and too forgetful to tell lies consistent with each other. Furthermore, you are too old to make the gain worth the trouble. Be absolutely frank with them, but do not plead insanity. That would reflect undeserved credit on three generations of art critics.

BEAUCHAMP: I must say, Martello, I have to admire your gall.

MARTELLO: Stress all mitigating factors, such as Donner's refusal to clean the bath after use, and his infuriating mannerisms any of which might have got him murdered years ago. Remember how John used to say, 'If Donner whistles the opening of Beethoven's Fifth in six/eight time once more I'll *kill him*!'?

BEAUCHAMP: John who?

MARTELLO: Augustus John.

BEAUCHAMP: No, no, it was Edith Sitwell.

MARTELLO: Rubbish!—you're getting old, Beauchamp.

BEAUCHAMP: I am two years younger than you, Martello.

MARTELLO: Anybody who is two years younger than me is *senile*. It is only by a great effort of will that my body has not decomposed. Which reminds me, you can't leave Donner lying there at the bottom of the stairs for very long in this weather, and that is only the practical argument; how long can you *ethically* leave him?

BEAUCHAMP: It is nothing to do with me.

MARTELLO: Beauchamp, I am shocked. You were at school together. You signed his first manifesto, as he signed yours. You have conjured with his name and travelled on his ticket; shared his roof, his prejudices, his occasional grant; eaten his bread and drunk his health (God forgive my *brain*!—it is so attuned to the ironic tone it has become ironical in repose; I have to whip sincerity out of it as one whips responses from a mule!)—to put it plain, you have been friends for over sixty years.

BEAUCHAMP: Well, the same goes for you.

MARTELLO: Yes, but you killed him.

BEAUCHAMP: I did no such thing! And you have good reason to know it! I am thoroughly disillusioned in you, Martello. I was willing to bend over backwards to see your side of it, but I can't stand a chap who won't come clean when he's found out.

MARTELLO: I, on the other hand, admire your hopeless persistence. But the tape recorder speaks for itself. That is, of course, the point about tape recorders. In this case it is eloquent, grandiloquent, not to say Grundigloquent—Oh God, if only I could turn it *off*!—no wonder I have achieved nothing with my life!—my brain is on a flying trapeze that outstrips all the possibilities of action. Mental acrobatics, Beauchamp—I have achieved nothing but mental acrobatics—*nothing!*—whereas you, however wrongly and for whatever reason, came to grips with life at least this once, and killed Donner.

BEAUCHAMP: It's not true, Martello!

MARTELLO: Yes, yes, I tell you, *nothing!*—Niente! Nada! Nichts!—Oh, a few pieces here and there, a few scandals—Zurich—Paris—Buenos Aires—but, all in all, nothing, not even among the nihilists! (*Pause.*) I tell you, Beauchamp, it's no secret between us that I never saw much point in your tonal art. I remember saying to Sophie, in the early days when you were still using gramophone discs, Beauchamp is wasting his time, I said, there'll be no revelations coming out of *that*; no truth. And the critics

won't listen either. And they didn't. But this time you've
got them by the ears. It has the impact of newsreel. In my
opinion it's a *tour de force*.

BEAUCHAMP: You are clearly deranged. It is probably the first
time a murderer has tried to justify himself on artistic
grounds. As it happens, you are also misguided. Far from
creating a *tour de force*, you ruined what would have been a
strand in my masterwork of accumulated silence, and left in
its place a melodramatic fragment whose point will not be
lost on a jury.
(*He presses* TAPE *switch:* '—*There you are*——' *etc.*)
There indeed he is, ladies and gentlemen, caught by the
fortuitous presence of a recording machine that had been
left running in the room where Mr. Donner was quietly
working on a portrait from memory, a portrait fated to be
unfinished.

MARTELLO: Poor Donner, he never had much luck with
Sophie.

BEAUCHAMP: For the existence of this recording we have to
thank Mr. Beauchamp, a fact which argues his innocence,
were it ever in doubt. Mr. Beauchamp, an artist who may
be familiar to some of you——

MARTELLO: If you are extremely old and collect trivia——

BEAUCHAMP: —and his friends, Mr. Donner and the man
Martello, lived and worked together in a single large attic
studio approached by a staircase, which led upwards from
the landing, and was guarded at the top by an insubstantial
rail, through which, as you will hear, Mr. Donner fell.

MARTELLO: An accident, really.

BEAUCHAMP: If you say so.

MARTELLO: You didn't mean to *kill* him. It was manslaughter.

BEAUCHAMP: You will hear how Mr. Donner, while working,
dozed off in his chair . . .
(TAPE: *Droning.*)
Footsteps approach.
(TAPE: *Footsteps.*)
Someone has entered quietly. Who? No visitors came to

this place. Martello and Mr. Beauchamp met their
acquaintances outside, formerly at the Savage, latterly in
public houses. And Mr. Donner, who was somewhat
reclusive, not to say misanthropic, had no friends at all—
except the other two, *a fact whose importance speaks for
itself*——
(TAPE: '*Ah! There you are* . . .'—*and is switched off.*)
Not, 'Who the devil are you?', or 'Good Lord, what are you
doing here, I haven't seen you for donkey's years!'—no.
'Ah. There you are.' The footsteps can only have belonged
to the man Martello.

MARTELLO: Or, of course, the man Beauchamp. I don't see
where this is getting us—we already know perfectly well
that it was *one* of us, and it is absurd that you should
prevaricate in this way when there is no third party to
impress. I came home to find Donner dead, and you at the
top of the stairs, fiddling with your tape-recorder. It is quite
clear that I arrived just in time to stop you wiping out the
evidence.

BEAUCHAMP: But it was *I* who came home and found Donner
dead—with your footsteps on the machine. My first thought
was to preserve any evidence it had picked up, so I very
quietly ascended——

MARTELLO: Beauchamp, why are you bothering to lie to *me*?
You are like a man on a desert island refusing to admit to
his only companion that he ate the last coconut.

BEAUCHAMP: For the very good reason that while my back was
turned you shinned up the tree and guzzled it. And
incidentally—I see that you have discovered where I keep
my special marmalade. That's *stealing*, Martello, common
theft. That marmalade does *not* come out of the housekeeping——

MARTELLO: It must have been Donner.

BEAUCHAMP: It was not Donner. Donner never cleaned the tub
and he always helped himself to cheese in such a way as to
leave all the rind, but he never stole my marmalade because
he didn't *like* marmalade. He did steal my *honey*, I know

that for a fact. And he had the nerve to accuse me of taking the top off the milk.

MARTELLO: Well, you do.

BEAUCHAMP (*furiously*): Because I have paid the milkman four weeks running! It's *my milk*!

MARTELLO: I suppose we should leave a note for him. Two pints a day will be enough now.

BEAUCHAMP: Since you will be in jail, one pint will be ample. Poor Donner. He was not so easy to get on with in recent years, but I shall always regret that my last conversation with him was not more friendly.

MARTELLO: Were you rowing about the housekeeping again?

BEAUCHAMP: No, no. He was rather unfeeling about my work in progress, as a matter of fact.

MARTELLO: He was rude about mine the other day. He attacked it.

BEAUCHAMP: He said mine was rubbish.

MARTELLO: Did he attack you? Was that it?

BEAUCHAMP: Why did he resent me? He seemed embittered, lately . . .

MARTELLO: He'd been brooding about Sophie.

BEAUCHAMP: And that ridiculous painting. What was the matter with the man?

MARTELLO: I think I was rather at fault . . .

BEAUCHAMP: I paid him the compliment of letting him hear how my master-tape was progressing . . .

Flashback

(BEAUCHAMP's '*master-tape*' *is a bubbling cauldron of squeaks, gurgles, crackles, and other unharmonious noises. He allows it to play for longer than one would reasonably hope.*)

BEAUCHAMP: Well, what do you think of it, Donner? Take your time, choose your words carefully.

DONNER: I think it's rubbish.

BEAUCHAMP: Oh. You mean, a sort of tonal debris, as it were?

DONNER: No, rubbish, general rubbish. In the sense of being

worthless, without value; rot, nonsense. Rubbish, in fact.

BEAUCHAMP: Ah. The detritus of audible existence, a sort of refuse heap of sound . . .

DONNER: I mean, *rubbish*. I'm sorry, Beauchamp, but you must come to terms with the fact that our paths have diverged. I very much enjoyed my years in that child's garden of easy victories known as the avant garde, but I am now engaged in the infinitely more difficult task of painting what the eye sees.

BEAUCHAMP: Well, I've never seen a naked woman sitting about a garden with a unicorn eating the roses.

DONNER: Don't split hairs with *me*, Beauchamp. You don't know what art is. Those tape recordings of yours are the mechanical expression of a small intellectual idea, the kind of notion that might occur to a man in his bath and be forgotten in the business of drying between his toes. You can call it art if you like, but it is the commonplace of any ironic imagination, and there are thousands of clerks and shop assistants who would be astonished to be called artists on their bath night.

BEAUCHAMP: Wait a minute, Donner——

DONNER: And they, incidentally, would call your tapes——

BEAUCHAMP: Quiet!——

DONNER: —rubbish.

(*Smack!*)

BEAUCHAMP: Missed him! I don't want that fly buzzing around the microphone—I'm starting up a new loop.

DONNER: I see I'm wasting my breath.

BEAUCHAMP: I heard you. Clerks—bath-night—rubbish, and so on. But my tapes are not for clerks. They are for initiates, as is all art.

DONNER: My kind is for Everyman.

BEAUCHAMP: Only because every man is an initiate of that particular mystery. But your painting is not for dogs, parrots, bicycles . . . You select your public. It is the same with me, but my tapes have greater mystery—they elude dogs, parrots, clerks and the greater part of mankind. If you played my tape on the radio, it would seem a meaningless noise, because it fulfils no expectations: people have been taught to expect certain kinds of insight but not others. The first duty of the artist is to capture the radio station.

DONNER: It was Lewis who said that.

BEAUCHAMP: Lewis who?

DONNER: Wyndham Lewis.

BEAUCHAMP: It was Edith Sitwell, as a matter of fact.

DONNER: Rubbish.

BEAUCHAMP: She came out with it while we were dancing.

DONNER: You never danced with Edith Sitwell.

BEAUCHAMP: Oh yes I did.

DONNER: You're thinking of that American woman who sang negro spirituals at Nancy Cunard's coming-out ball.

BEAUCHAMP: It was Queen Mary's wedding, as a matter of fact.

DONNER: You're mad.

BEAUCHAMP: I don't mean wedding, I mean launching.

DONNER: I can understand your confusion but it was Nancy Cunard's coming-out.

BEAUCHAMP: Down at the docks?

DONNER: British boats are not launched to the sound of minstrel favourites.

BEAUCHAMP: I don't mean launching, I mean maiden voyage.

DONNER: I refuse to discuss it. Horrible noise, anyway.

BEAUCHAMP: Only because people have not been taught what to listen for, or how to listen.

DONNER: What are you talking about?

BEAUCHAMP: Really, Donner, your mind keeps wandering about in a senile chaos! My *tape*. If I had one good man placed high up in the BBC my tape would become art for millions, in time.

DONNER: It would not become art. It would become a mildly interesting noise instead of a totally meaningless noise. An artist is someone who is gifted in some way which enables him to do something more or less well which can only be done badly or not at all by someone who is not thus gifted.

To speak of an art which requires no gift is a contradiction
employed by people like yourself who have an artistic bent
but no particular skill.

(*Smack!*)

BEAUCHAMP: Missed!

DONNER: An artistic imagination coupled with skill is talent.

BEAUCHAMP: Where is he?—Ah——

(*Smack!*)

Damn!

DONNER: Skill without imagination is craftsmanship and gives
us many useful objects such as wickerwork picnic baskets.
Imagination without skill gives us modern art.

BEAUCHAMP: A perfectly reasonable summary.

(*Thump! fist on desk.*)

DONNER: Beauchamp!

BEAUCHAMP: Did you get him?

DONNER: I am trying to open your eyes to the nakedness of
your emperor.

BEAUCHAMP: But Donner, ever since I've known you you've
been running around asking for the name of his
tailor—symbolism, surrealism, imagism, vorticism,
fauvism, cubism—dada, drip-action, hard-edge, pop, found
objects and post-object—it's only a matter of days since you
spent the entire housekeeping on sugar to make an edible
Venus de Milo, and now you've discovered the fashions of
your childhood. What *happened* to you?

DONNER: I have returned to traditional values, that is where the
true history of art continues to lie, not in your small jokes. I
make no apology for the past, but precocity at our age is
faintly ludicrous, don't you think?

BEAUCHAMP: At our age, *any*thing we do is faintly ludicrous.
Our best hope as artists is to transcend our limitations and
become *utterly* ludicrous. Which you are proceeding to do
with your portrait of Sophie, for surely you can see that a
post-Pop pre-Raphaelite is pure dada brought up to
date——

(*Smack!*)

DONNER: Shut up, damn you!—how dare you talk of
her?!—how dare you——
(*And weeps*——)
—*and would you stop cleaning the bath with my face flannel!!!*
(*Pause.*) I'm sorry—please accept my apology——

BEAUCHAMP: I'm sorry, Donner . . . I had no idea you felt so
strongly about it.

DONNER: (*Sniffle.*) Well, I have to wash my face with it.

BEAUCHAMP: No, no, I mean about your new . . . Donner,
what *has* happened?—What happened between you and
Martello? You have not been yourself . . . since you
smashed your Venus and began your portrait . . . You have
. . . shunned me——

DONNER: I did not intend to.

BEAUCHAMP: Have I offended you? Is it about the milk?

DONNER: No. I have just been—sad.

BEAUCHAMP: Do you blame me for Sophie?

DONNER: I don't know. It was a long time ago now. It *is*
becoming a good likeness, isn't it?

BEAUCHAMP: Oh yes. She would have liked it. I mean if she
could have seen it. A real Academy picture . . . !

DONNER: Yes.

BEAUCHAMP: I don't know, Donner . . . before the war, in
Soho, you were always making plans to smuggle a live
ostrich into the Royal Academy; and now look at you. In
Zurich in 1915 you told Tarzan he was too conservative.

DONNER: Tarzan?

BEAUCHAMP: I don't mean Tarzan. Who do I mean? Similar
name, conservative, 1915 . . .

DONNER: Tsar Nicholas?

BEAUCHAMP: No, no, Zurich.

DONNER: I remember Zurich . . . after our walking tour. God,
what a walk! You were crazy, Beauchamp, you and your
horse.

BEAUCHAMP: I'll never forget it. That really was a walk. When
we got to Zurich, my boots were worn to paper. Sat in the
Café Rousseau and put my feet up, ordered a lemon squash.

DONNER: The Café Rousseau was Monte Carlo later.

BEAUCHAMP: Monte Carlo was the Café Russe.

DONNER: Was it?

BEAUCHAMP: Put my feet up and ordered a citron pressé in the Café Rousseau.

DONNER: Still doesn't sound right.

BEAUCHAMP: Couldn't have it—no lemons. The waiter was very apologetic. No lemons because of the war, he said. Good God, I said, is Switzerland at war?—things have come to a pretty pass, is it the St. Bernard?—Not a smile. Man at the next table laughed out loud and offered me a glass of squash made from lemon powder, remarking, 'If lemons don't exist, it is necessary to invent them.' It seemed wittier at the time, I don't know why.

DONNER: Voltaire!—of course, the Café Voltaire!

BEAUCHAMP: That was a rum bird.

DONNER: Voltaire?

BEAUCHAMP: No, Lenin.

DONNER: Oh yes. Very rum.

BEAUCHAMP: Very liberal with his lemon powder but a rum bird nevertheless. Edith saw through him right away. She said to him, 'I don't know what you're waiting for but it's not going to happen in Switzerland.' Of course, she was absolutely right.

DONNER: Edith was never in Switzerland. Your memory is playing you up again.

BEAUCHAMP: Oh yes she was.

DONNER: Not that time. That time was Hugo Ball and Hans Arp, Max, Kurt, André . . . Picabia . . . Tristan Tzara——

BEAUCHAMP: That was him!

DONNER: What was?

BEAUCHAMP: Conservative. But he had audacity. Wrote his name in the snow, and said, 'There! . . . I think I'll call it The Alps.'

DONNER: That was Marcel. He used to beat Lenin at chess. I think he had talent under all those jokes. He said to me, 'There are two ways of becoming an artist. The first way is to do things by which is meant art. The second way is to make art mean the things you do.' What a stroke of genius! It made anything possible and everything safe!—safe from criticism, since our art admitted no standards outside itself; safe from comparison, since it had no history; safe from evaluation, since it referred to no system of values beyond the currency it had invented. We were no longer accountable. We were artists by mutual agreement.

BEAUCHAMP: So was everyone from Praxiteles to Rodin. There's nothing divine about classical standards; it's just a bigger club.

DONNER: It seems there is something divine about modern art nonetheless, for it is only sustained by faith. That is why artist have become as complacent as priests. They do not have to demonstrate their truths. Like priests they demand our faith that something is more than it appears to be— bread, wine, a tin of soup, a twisted girder, a mauve square, a meaningless collection of sounds on a loop of tape . . .

(*This is said so bitterly that*——)

BEAUCHAMP: Donner . . . what happened?—what did Martello say to you?

DONNER: It really doesn't matter. And how do I know he wasn't lying, just getting his own back?—you see, I damaged his figure, slightly . . . He was working on it—I didn't know what it was—And I brought him a cup of tea——

Flashback

(MARTELLO *is scraping and chipping, and clicking his tongue, and scraping again. He sighs.*)

DONNER: That's it—help yourself to sugar.

MARTELLO: I'm not getting any. She's set too hard.

DONNER: Knock off one of her nipples.

MARTELLO: I'd need a chisel.

DONNER: Wait a minute. I'll tilt her over. Get the breast into your cup, and I'll stir her around a bit.

MARTELLO: What a ridiculous business. How am I going to sprinkle her on my cornflakes?

DONNER: Starving peasants don't have cornflakes. Good God, Martello, if they had any corn do you think they'd turn it into a sunshine breakfast for figure-conscious typists?

MARTELLO: What the hell are you talking about? What starving peasants? Honestly, Donner, you go from one extreme to the other. On the whole I preferred your ceramic sugar lumps.

DONNER: No, I got the whole thing back to front with my ceramic food. Of course, ceramic bread and steak and strawberries with plaster-of-paris cream defined the problem very neatly, but I was still avoiding the answer. The question remained: how can one justify a work of art to a man with an empty belly? The answer, like all great insights, was simple: make it edible.

MARTELLO: Brilliant.

DONNER: It came to me in my—incidentally, is it you who keeps using my face-cloth to clean the tub?

MARTELLO: No. It must be Beauchamp.

DONNER: That man has absolutely no respect for property.

MARTELLO: I know. And he's taken to hiding the marmalade. Do you happen to know where it is?

DONNER: In the pickle jar.

MARTELLO: Cunning devil! Thank you.

DONNER: The olive oil is really honey.

MARTELLO: Incredible. It probably came to him in his bath, while he was using your flannel.

DONNER: Where is he?

MARTELLO: He went out to get some more sugar, out of his own money. I wonder where he'll hide it.

DONNER: Let him. Sugar art is only the beginning.

MARTELLO: It will give cubism a new lease of life.

DONNER: Think of Le Penseur sculpted in . . .

MARTELLO: Cold rice pudding.

DONNER: Salt. Think of poor villages getting a month's supply of salt in the form of classical sculpture!

MARTELLO: And not just classical!—your own pieces,
  reproduced indelibly yet edibly——

DONNER: Think of pizza pies raised to the level of Van Gogh
  sunflowers!—think of a whole new range of pigments, from
  salt to liquorice!

MARTELLO: Your signed loaves of bread reproduced in sculpted
  dough, *baked* . . . your ceramic steaks carved from meat! It
  will give opinion back to the intellectuals and put taste
  where it belongs. From now on the artist's palate——

DONNER: Are you laughing at me, Martello?

MARTELLO: Certainly not, Donner. Let them eat art.

DONNER: Imagine my next exhibition, thrown open to the
  hungry . . . You know, Martello, for the first time I feel
  free of that small sense of shame which every artist lives
  with. I think, in a way, edible art is what we've all been
  looking for.

MARTELLO: Who?

DONNER: All of us!—Breton!—Ernst!—Marcel—Max—you—
  me—Remember how Pablo used to shout that the war had mad
  art irrelevant?—well——

MARTELLO: Which Pablo?

DONNER: What do you mean, which Pablo?—*Pablo!*

MARTELLO: What, that one-armed waiter at the Café Suisse?

DONNER: Yes—the Café Russe—the proprietor, lost a leg at
  Verdun——

MARTELLO: God, he was slow, that Pablo. But it's amazing how
  you remember all the people who gave you credit . . .

DONNER: He gave you credit because you had been at Verdun.

MARTELLO: That's true.

DONNER: It was a lie.

MARTELLO: Wasn't I? It must have been pretty close to
  Verdun, our route was right through that bit of country,
  remember it well.

DONNER: God yes, what a walk. You were crazy, Martello.

MARTELLO: I must have been, I suppose.

DONNER: Beauchamp was crazy too.

MARTELLO: Him and his horse.

DONNER: That was about the last really good time we had . . .

MARTELLO: You hated it.

DONNER: No.

MARTELLO: More than the war.

DONNER: That's what killed it for me. After that, being an artist made no sense. I should have stopped then. Art made no sense.

MARTELLO: Except for nonsense art. Pablo never understood the difference. He used to get so angry about his missing arm——

DONNER: (leg . . .)

MARTELLO: I can see him now—a tray in each hand, swearing . . . wait a minute——

DONNER: *Leg.*

MARTELLO: A tray in each leg—Are you deliberately trying to confuse me?

DONNER: He was right. He understood exactly. There *wasn't* any difference. We tried to make a distinction between the art that celebrated reason and history and logic and all assumptions, and our own dislocated anti-art of lost faith—but it was all the same insult to a one-legged soldier and the one-legged, one-armed, one-eyed regiment of the maimed. And here we are still at it, looking for another twist. Finally the only thing I can say in defence of my figure is that you can eat it.

MARTELLO: And of mine that you can smile at it. How do you like her?

DONNER: It looks like a scarecrow trying to be a tailor's dummy. Is it symbolic?

MARTELLO: Metaphorical.

DONNER: Why has she got straw on her head?

MARTELLO: Not straw—ripe corn. It's her hair. It was either ripe corn or spun gold, and I wouldn't know how to do that, it was bad enough getting the pearls for her teeth.

DONNER: They look like false teeth.

MARTELLO: Well of course they're artificial pearls. So are the rubies, of course. I know you'll appreciate her breasts.

DONNER: Oh yes. Are they edible?

MARTELLO: Well, you're not supposed to eat them—I'm only using real fruit for the moment, and real feathers for her swan-like neck. I don't know how to do her eyes: stars seem somehow inappropriate . . . Would you have described them as dark pools, perhaps?

DONNER: Who?

MARTELLO: Well, Sophie of course.

DONNER: Are you telling me that that *thing* is supposed to be Sophie?

MARTELLO: Metaphorically.

DONNER: You cad, Martello!

MARTELLO: I beg your pardon?

DONNER: You unspeakable rotter! Is nothing sacred to you?

MARTELLO: Hold on, Donner, no offence intended.

DONNER: What right have you to sneer at her memory?—I won't allow it, damn you! My God, she had a sad enough life without having her beauty mocked in death by your contemptible artistic presumptions——
  (*Thump! A pearl bounces . . .*)

MARTELLO: Now steady on, Donner, you've knocked out one of her teeth.

DONNER (*by now nearly weeping*): Oh Sophie . . . I cannot think of beauty without remembering your innocent grace, your hair like . . .

MARTELLO: Ripe corn——

DONNER: Gold. Your tragic gaze—eyes like——

MARTELLO: Stars——

DONNER: Bottomless pools, and when you laughed——

MARTELLO: Teeth like pearls——

DONNER: It was like a silver bell whose sound parted your pale ruby lips——

MARTELLO: *A silver bell!*—yes!—behind her breasts——

DONNER: —were like——

MARTELLO: —ripe pears——

DONNER: Firm young apples——

MARTELLO: Pears—For heaven's sake control yourself, Donner,

those are real artificial pearls——
(*Pearls bouncing*—DONNER *thumping, gasping* . . .)
DONNER: Oh Sophie . . . I try to shut out the memory but it
needs only . . . a ribbon . . . a flower . . . a phrase of music
. . . a river flowing beneath ancient bridges . . . the scent of
summertime . . .
(*Cliché Paris music, accordion* . . .)

Flashback

(*Keep music in. Fade.*)
SOPHIE: I must say I won't be entirely sorry to leave Lambeth
—the river smells like a dead cat, and the accordionist
downstairs is driving me insane . . .
(SOPHIE *is 22 and not at all bitter. Background is sound of
leather suitcase being snapped shut and strapped up by* YOUNG
BEAUCHAMP *who is in his mid-20s.*)
If only someone would give him a job, elsewhere, even for a
few minutes. Or perhaps we could employ him to take
down our suitcases. He'd have to put his accordion down
for that. But then he'd probably whistle through his teeth.
I'm sorry to be so useless, darling . . . Are the others
downstairs? . . . Yes . . . that's them: isn't it awful to know
voices, instantly and certainly, by their shouts to the
waggoner five floors down . . . I wish that yours was the
only voice I knew that well. I like them well enough—they
are both kind, and your oldest friends, which is enough to
endear them . . . But I think now—forgive me—but I think
now—before it is too late . . . I think we ought not to go
with them, I think we ought to remain, just you and I . . .
Darling—please—Please don't do up the strap—say what
you think—it's not too late—Please say quickly, I heard
Banjo's feet across the hall, he'll be up in a moment . . .
(*The strap-noise, surreptitious now, starts again.*)
Please don't do it up! . . . not even slowly . . .
(*Wan, affectionate, ironic.*) I can hear the clothes you put on
in the morning . . . Your serge today, hear it and smell
it—with a cornflower out of the vase: I caught that the

minute you put it in your buttonhole—do you sometimes
wonder whether I'm a witch . . . ? I'm only your good
fairy, if you let me, and I want to stay here with you. I'll be
all right, after all this time, I'm confident now, I won't be
frightened, ever, even when you leave me here—and of
course you will be going out—often—to visit Mouse and
Banjo in their new studio—Please *say*.
BEAUCHAMP: Sophie . . . How can I say . . . ?
(*Door*. YOUNG MARTELLO.)
MARTELLO: Hello . . . So—what news?
BEAUCHAMP: None.
(*Violently pulls strap tight*.)
I'll take this down. How's the waggon?
MARTELLO: All right, but I fear for the horse—bow-backed and
spindle-shanked.
BEAUCHAMP: I'll . . . come back.
(*Door*.)
SOPHIE: I'm sorry not to be helping. I have to sit by the
window and be look-out.
MARTELLO: (*laughs openly*): Oh, that's frightfully good. Always
making such good fun of yourself, Sophie . . .
(*Accordion*.)
SOPHIE: Perhaps there will be another accordionist waiting for
us across the river. And no doubt the smell will be much
the same on the left bank. But I shall like the Chelsea side
much better.
MARTELLO: It's a better class of people, of course. Even the
artists are desperately middle-class.
SOPHIE: I was thinking of the sunshine—we'll be facing south
on that bank, and we'll get the sun through our front
windows. I shall sit at my new post, with the sun on my
face, and imagine the view as Turner painted it. It probably
has not changed so very much, apart from the colours.
Don't you wish you could paint like Turner?—no, I'm
sorry, of course you don't, how stupid of me . . . Well, I
don't suppose Turner would have wished to paint like you.
He *could* have done, of course.

MARTELLO: Of course.

SOPHIE: But he would not have wished to.

MARTELLO: It would not have occurred to him to do so; I think that's really the point.

SOPHIE: Yes, I think it really is. What are you doing now?

MARTELLO: I'm not painting now. I'm making a figure.

SOPHIE: I really meant *now*—at this moment—what are you doing here?

MARTELLO: Oh. Well, I'm not actually doing anything now, just talking to you.

SOPHIE: Can you see a hamper anywhere?

MARTELLO: A hamper?—no.

SOPHIE: There ought to be one; for my shoes and handbags.

MARTELLO: Well, wait till Biscuit comes up—I think I can hear him on the stairs.

SOPHIE: No, that's Mouse. What silly schoolboy names. When will you stop using them?

MARTELLO: I suppose they are silly when you hear them—but we never hear them because they are merely our names . . . I expect we shall stop using them when we are very old and painting like Landseer.

SOPHIE: Not without lessons. I didn't mean to sound scornful, about your names. I'm nervous about moving.

MARTELLO: Yes. Of course.

SOPHIE: Nicknames are really very touching. Did you ever play the banjo?

MARTELLO: No. I was thought to be similarly shaped when young. Biscuit kept saying, 'Well, that takes the biscuit.'

SOPHIE: Yes, I know. And 'Mouse' because he enters quietly.

DONNER: Hello, Sophie.

(*Pause.*)

SOPHIE: What *is* going on? (*Pause.*) He told me about your figure.

MARTELLO: Did he?

SOPHIE: Only that you were doing one. What is it?

MARTELLO: Well, actually it's called 'The Cripple'. It's going to be a wooden man with a real leg.

SOPHIE: A sort of joke.

MARTELLO: Yes.

SOPHIE: And will you actually use a real leg?

MARTELLO: Well, no, of course not. I shall have to make it.

SOPHIE: What will you make it of?

MARTELLO: Well, wood . . . of course.
(*Pause.*)

SOPHIE: How about a black-patch-man with a real eye——

MARTELLO: Sophie——

SOPHIE (*breaks—bursts out*): He doesn't know what to do with me, does he?—Well, what's going to happen?—you're all *going*, aren't you?

MARTELLO (*quietly*): Mouse is going to stay. Excuse me . . .
(*Leaves, closes door.*)
(*Pause.*)

SOPHIE (*recovered*): You're staying?

DONNER: Yes.

SOPHIE: Why?

DONNER: Either way it's what I want to do.

SOPHIE: Either way?

DONNER: If you're going with them, I don't want to live so close to you any more.

SOPHIE: If I'm going . . . ?

DONNER: Sophie, you know I love you . . . how long I've loved you . . .

SOPHIE: He wants me to stay? With you?

DONNER (*cries out*): Why do you want to go? (*quietly*) He's stopped caring for you. He only hurts you now, and I can't bear it. When he made you happy I couldn't bear it, and now that he hurts you I . . . just can't bear it——

SOPHIE: Does he love someone else?

DONNER: He hasn't got anyone else.

SOPHIE: That isn't what I asked. Does he love that poet?—that educated Bohemian with the private income?—He read me her poems, and then he stopped reading me her poems. I thought he must be seeing her.

DONNER: Only in company. I'm sure she doesn't think twice about him——

SOPHIE: Is she going with him——?

DONNER: No—of course not! . . . It's not even a suitable place to share like that—it's just one large attic room, the beds all together and just cooking gear in the corner——

SOPHIE: He never intended that I should go.

DONNER: It really is most unsuitable. The bathroom is on the landing below, with steep unprotected stairs—you could fall—Sophie, you *must* stay here, you know it here—and I'll abide by any terms——

SOPHIE: When was he going to tell me?

DONNER: Every day.

SOPHIE: Perhaps he was going to leave a note on the mantelpiece. As a sort of joke.

DONNER: Sophie . . . I love you. I'll look after you.

SOPHIE: Yes, I know you would. But I can't love you back, Mouse. I'm sorry, but I can't. I have lost the capability of falling in love. The last image that I have of love is him larking about in that gallery where you had your first exhibition. 'Frontiers in Art'—what a lark you were, you three, with your paintings of barbed wire fences and signboards saying 'You are now entering Patagonia'—you were such cards, weren't you? all of you merry, not at all like artists but like three strapping schoolboy cricketers growing your first pale moustaches. I liked you all very much. I liked the way you roared with laughter at all your friends. I never heard anything any of you said, and you didn't take any notice of me at the back in my stiff frock and ribbons and my awful thick glasses, but I liked you all anyway, and bit by bit I couldn't stop looking at him, and thinking, which one is he?—Martello? Beauchamp? Donner? . . . It was quick: one moment the sick apprehension of something irrevocable which I had not chosen, and then he was the secret in the deep centre of my life. I wouldn't have called it love myself, but it seems to be the word that people use for it.

DONNER: And when you next saw us——
SOPHIE: ——I couldn't see you. But at least I no longer had to
wear those glasses, and I knew I looked quite pretty . . .
DONNER: You were beautiful.

Flashback

(MARTELLO *and* SOPHIE *are climbing stairs. Above them,
behind closed doors, the sound of a ping-pong game in progress.*)
MARTELLO: Quite a climb, I'm afraid . . . Five more steps up
now, and then turn left and that will be the top floor . . .
SOPHIE: It must be a lovely big room . . .
MARTELLO: We each have our own room, actually, but we share
the drawing room—Left—jolly good show.
SOPHIE: I hear that ping-pong is quite the fad.
MARTELLO: Is it really?—please allow me . . .
(*Door. Ping-pong loud. The rally ends with a winning shot—
denoted by the hiatus where one has been led to expect, from the
rhythm, contact with the 'other' bat.*)
SOPHIE: Good shot!
MARTELLO: Gentlemen, I have the honour to present to you
Miss Farthingale.
(*The ping-pong resumes.*)
SOPHIE (*disappointed*): Oh.
MARTELLO: My friends, as you know, are called Mr. Donner
and Mr. Beauchamp. Mr. Beauchamp is to your right, Mr.
Donner to your left.
(*The ball hits the net: familiar sound of small diminishing
bounces on the table.*)
SOPHIE: Bad luck.
MARTELLO: They are not in fact playing ping-pong.
SOPHIE: Oh!
MARTELLO: That is why they are momentarily taken aback.
Turn it off, Beauchamp.
(*Cut ping-pong.*)
SOPHIE: I'm sorry.
DONNER (*hurriedly*): How do you do?

BEAUCHAMP: How do you do?

MARTELLO: There's no point in sticking out your hands like that. Miss Farthingale is blind.

BEAUCHAMP: Really, Martello, you exceed the worst possible taste——

SOPHIE: But I am—blind as a bat, I'm afraid.

BEAUCHAMP: Oh. I'm sorry.

SOPHIE: Please don't mention it.

BEAUCHAMP: I will not, of course.

SOPHIE: Oh, mention it as much as you like. And please don't worry about saying 'you see' all the time. People do, and I don't mind a bit.

MARTELLO: Would you like to sit down, Miss Farthingale . . . Please allow me . . .

SOPHIE: Oh, thank you . . . thank you so much. That is most comfortable. I hope no one will remain standing for me.

MARTELLO: Will you take tea?

SOPHIE: I should love some tea.

DONNER: We were just waiting for the kettle to boil.

MARTELLO: Indian or Singhalese?

SOPHIE: I don't think I'd know the difference.

MARTELLO: Nobody does. That's why we only keep the one.

SOPHIE: And which one is that?

MARTELLO: I haven't the slightest idea.

DONNER: It's best Assam.

(*Kettle whistles.*)

SOPHIE: Is that the gramophone again?

DONNER: Excuse me.

(*Kettle subsides.*)

BEAUCHAMP: I have been making gramophone records of various games and pastimes.

SOPHIE: Is it for the blind?

BEAUCHAMP: Heavens, no. At least . . . the idea is you listen to the sounds with your eyes closed.

SOPHIE: It's very effective. I could have kept the score just by listening.

BEAUCHAMP: Yes!—you see—sorry!—I'm trying to liberate the

visual *image* from the limitations of visual *art*. The idea is to
create images—pictures—which are purely *mental* . . . I
think I'm the first artist to work in this field.

SOPHIE: I should think you are, Mr. Beauchamp.

BEAUCHAMP: The one you heard was my latest—Lloyd George
versus Clara Bow.

SOPHIE: Goodness! However did you persuade them?

BEAUCHAMP: No, you see——

SOPHIE: Oh—of course! Of course I see. What a very good
joke, Mr. Beauchamp.

BEAUCHAMP: Yes . . . Thank you. May I play you another ?—
it's very quiet.

SOPHIE: Please do.

    (DONNER *with tea tray*.)

DONNER: There we are. How would you like your tea, Miss
Farthingale?

MARTELLO: Perhaps *you* will do us the honour, Miss Farthingale?

DONNER: Banjo!

SOPHIE: Yes . . . Yes . . . I think so.

    (*Small sounds of her hands mapping the tea tray*.)
    Now.
    (*Tea in first. One cup. Two. Three. Four*.)
    You will all take milk?
    (*'Yes please' etc. One. Two. Three. Four*.)
    Mr. Donner, how many lumps?

DONNER: Two please, Miss Farthingale . . .

    (*One. Two*.)

DONNER: Thank you.

SOPHIE: Mr. Beauchamp?

BEAUCHAMP: None for me, thank you.

SOPHIE: Mr. Martello?

MARTELLO: And just one for me.

    (*One*.)

SOPHIE: There we are.

    (*The men's tension breaks. They applaud and laugh*.)

DONNER: I say, Miss Farthingale, you're an absolutely ripping
girl.

SOPHIE: How very kind of you, Mr. Donner. Please do not think me 'fast' but I was no less struck by you and your friends. I thought you all very pleasant-looking and good humoured, and there was nothing I wished more than that I should find myself having tea with you all one day.

MARTELLO: I have not in fact explained to my friends . . .

SOPHIE: Oh, forgive me. I must have puzzled you. My late uncle, who was rather progressive in such things, took me to your opening day at the Russell Gallery last year. (*Pause.*)

BEAUCHAMP: Forgive my asking . . . but do you often visit the art galleries?

SOPHIE: Not now, of course, Mr. Beauchamp, but I had not yet lost all of my sight in those days. Oh dear, I'm telling everything back to front.

MARTELLO: Miss Farthingale lives at the Blind School in Prince of Wales Drive. She happened to be sitting on a bench in the public garden next to the School when I walked by. She accosted me in a most shameless manner.

SOPHIE: Absolutely untrue!

MARTELLO: I have been twice to tea at the School since then. She always pours.

SOPHIE: I was in the park with my teacher, but she had left me for a few moments while she went down to the water to feed the ducks. When she looked back she saw a gentleman with a fixed grin and a raised hat staring at me in a most perplexed and embarrassed manner. By the time she returned to rescue me, it was too late.

DONNER: Too late?

SOPHIE: I heard this voice say, 'Forgive me, but haven't we met before? My name is Martello.' Of course he'd never seen me before in his life.

MARTELLO: And she replied, 'Not the artist, by any chance?'

SOPHIE: 'I believe so,' he said, flattered I think.

MARTELLO: 'Frontiers in Art?' she asked. I was astonished. And invited to tea; with great firmness and without preamble. Now there you *were* shameless, admit it.

SOPHIE: Well, I lead such an uneventful life . . . I was naturally excited.

MARTELLO: I thought she was going to *faint* with excitement. The chaperone disapproved, even protested, but Miss Farthingale was possessed!

SOPHIE: Please, Mr. Martello . . .

BEAUCHAMP: Well, of course, the chaperone could see what you look like.

DONNER: You must have been very impressed by the exhibition, Miss Farthingale.

MARTELLO: Not by the exhibition at all! (*A bit of a faux pas, perhaps.*) I mean . . . it was Miss Farthingale's opinion that the pictures were all frivolous and not very difficult to do.

BEAUCHAMP: She was absolutely right.

MARTELLO: As I was quick to explain to her. Why should art be something difficult to do? Why shouldn't it be something very easy?

SOPHIE: But surely it is a fact about art—regardless of the artist's subject or his intentions—that it celebrates a world which includes itself—I mean, part of what there is to celebrate is the capability of the artist.

MARTELLO: How very confusing.

SOPHIE: I think every artist willy-nilly is celebrating the impulse to paint in general, the imagination to paint something in particular, and the ability to make the painting in question.

MARTELLO: Goodness!

SOPHIE: The more difficult it is to make the painting, the more there is to wonder at. It is not the only thing, but it is one of the things. And since I do not hope to impress you by tying up my own shoelace, why should you hope to have impressed me by painting a row of black stripes on a white background? Was that one of yours?

MARTELLO: I don't recall it—you asked me about it when we met.

SOPHIE: So I did. Perhaps one of your friends remembers it— black railings on a field of snow?

MARTELLO: Let me answer for them nonetheless. You seem to forget, or perhaps you do not know, that what may seem very difficult to you may be very easy for the artist. He may paint a perfect apple as easily as you tie your shoelace, and as quickly. Furthermore, anybody could do it—yes, I insist: painting nature, one way or another, is a technique and can be learned, like playing the piano. But how can you teach someone to *think* in a certain way?—to paint an utterly simple shape in order to ambush the mind with something quite unexpected about that shape by hanging it in a frame and forcing you to see it, as it were, for the first time—

DONNER: Banjo . . .

MARTELLO: And what, after all, is the point of excellence in naturalistic art—? How does one account for, and justify, the very notion of emulating nature? The greater the success, the more false the result. It is only when the imagination is dragged away from what the eye sees that a picture becomes interesting.

SOPHIE: I think it is chiefly interesting to the artist, and to those who respond to a sense of the history of art rather than to pictures. I don't think I shall much miss what is to come, from what I know, and I am glad that I saw much of the pre-Raphaelites before my sight went completely. Perhaps you know Ruskin's essay, the one on——

BEAUCHAMP: I say, Miss Farthingale—are you wearing blue stockings?

SOPHIE: I don't know, Mr. Beauchamp. Am I? Whatever happened to the game you were going to play me?

BEAUCHAMP: Oh, it's been on. I'll turn the record over for the continuation.

DONNER: You know . . . I think I *do* remember you.

BEAUCHAMP: Now, now, Mouse.

DONNER: A girl—with spectacles, and a long pig-tail I think.

SOPHIE: Yes!

DONNER: I believe we exchanged a look!

SOPHIE: Perhaps we did. Tell me, Mr. Donner—which one were you?

DONNER: Which one?

SOPHIE: Yes. I have a picture in my mind of the three of you but I never found out, and was too shy at the time to ask, which was Donner, and which Beauchamp, and which Martello. I asked my uncle afterwards, but although he knew which of you was which, I was unable to describe you with enough individuality . . .

DONNER: Shame, Miss Farthingale!

SOPHIE: Well, you were all fair, and well built. None of you had a beard or jug ears—and if you remember you were all wearing your army uniforms, all identical . . .

MARTELLO: Yes, it was a sort of joke. We had not been long back from France.

BEAUCHAMP: Late going, late returning.

SOPHIE: A few months later my blindness descended on me, and the result is that I do not know which of your voices goes with the face that has stayed in my mind—that is, all three faces, of course.

(*Pause.*)

BEAUCHAMP: Is it that you remember one of our faces particularly, Miss Farthingale?

SOPHIE: Well, yes, Mr. Beauchamp.

BEAUCHAMP: Oh.

SOPHIE: I mean, I thought you were all engaging.

BEAUCHAMP: But one of us more engaging than the others.

MARTELLO: Ah. Well, we shall never know!

DONNER: Oh!, but it was my eye you caught.

SOPHIE: As a matter of fact, there is a way of . . . satisfying my curiosity. There was a photographer there, for one of the illustrated magazines . . .

DONNER: The *Tatler*.

SOPHIE: No, there was no photograph in the *Tatler*, I happened to see . . . but this man posed each of you against a picture you had painted.

MARTELLO: I see. And you want to know which of us was the

one who posed against the painting you have described.

SOPHIE: Well, yes. It would satisfy my curiosity. It was a background of snow, I think.

DONNER: Yes, there was a snow scene. Only one.

SOPHIE: A field of snow, occupying the whole canvas——

MARTELLO: Not the whole canvas——

SOPHIE: No—there was a railing——

BEAUCHAMP: Yes, that's it—a border fence in the snow!

SOPHIE: Yes! (*Pause.*) Well, which of you . . . ?

DONNER: It was Beauchamp you had in mind.

SOPHIE: Mr. Beauchamp!

BEAUCHAMP: Yes, Miss Farthingale . . . It seems it was me.
   (*Pause.*)

SOPHIE (*brightly*): Well, is anybody ready for some more tea?

MARTELLO: I will replenish the pot.
   (*Pause.*)
   (GRAMOPHONE: '*Check.*')

SOPHIE: Oh!—is it chess, Mr. Beauchamp?

BEAUCHAMP: It is. Lenin versus Jack Dempsey.

SOPHIE: Oh, that's very good. But do you no longer paint?

BEAUCHAMP: No. Nobody will be painting in fifty years. Except Donner, of course.

SOPHIE: Well, I hope you will paint beauty, Mr. Donner, and the subtlest beauty is in nature.

BEAUCHAMP: Oh, please don't think that I am against beauty, or nature, Miss Farthingale. Indeed, I especially enjoy the garden where you met Martello, a most delightful prospect across the river, isn't it?—I mean——

SOPHIE: You are quite right, Mr. Beauchamp. It is a delightful prospect, for me too. It is only my sight I have lost. I enjoy the view just as much as anyone who sits there with eyes closed in the sun; more, I think, because I can improve on reality, like a painter, but without fear of contradiction. Indeed, if I hear hoofbeats, I can put a unicorn in the garden and no one can open my eyes against it and say it isn't true.

MARTELLO (*returning*): To the Incas, who had never seen a

horse, unicorns had the same reality as horses, which is a
very high degree of reality.—Listen! Miss Farthingale, is
that a hansom or a landau?

(*Carriage in the street below.*)

SOPHIE: Eight hooves, Mr. Martello, but it's not a landau for all
that. Those are shire horses, probably a brewer's dray.

MARTELLO (*at window*): A brewer's dray as I live!—More
games!

BEAUCHAMP: I say—that has suddenly brought to mind—do
you remember——?

MARTELLO: Yes—I was just thinking the same thing——

BEAUCHAMP: Beauchamp's Tenth Horse!

Flashback

(*Clip-clop . . .* BEAUCHAMP'*s Horse. Flies buzzing in the
heat. Feet walking.*)

BEAUCHAMP (*declaiming*): Art consists of constant surprise. Art
should never conform. Art should break its promises. Art is
nothing to do with expertise: doing something well is no
excuse for doing the expected. My God, this is fun. All my
life I have wanted to ride through the French countryside in
summer, with my two best friends, and make indefensible
statements about art. I am most obliged to you, Martello. I
am delighted to know you, Donner. How do you like my
horse?

MARTELLO: Beautiful, your Majesty.

DONNER: Very nice. Why don't you give it a rest?

BEAUCHAMP: Mouse is a bit mousey today. You should have
invested in a horse. It makes an enormous difference. In fact
I have never felt so carefree. When we are old and doddery
and famous and life is given over to retrospection and
retrospectives, this is as far back as I want memory to go——

(*Smack!*)

I've never been so hot . . . and the flies . . .

(*Smack!*)

Are we nearly there?

MARTELLO: Nearly where?

DONNER: How do I know?

BEAUCHAMP: Secondly!—how can the artist justify himself in
the community? What is his role? What is his
reason?—Donner, why are you trying to be an artist?

DONNER: I heard there were opportunities to meet naked
women.

BEAUCHAMP: Donner is feeling cynical.

DONNER: I had never seen a naked woman, and the way things
were going I was never likely to. My family owned land.

BEAUCHAMP: Interesting line of thought; don't pretend to
follow it myself. I repeat—how can the artist justify
himself? The answer is that he cannot, and should stop
boring people with his egocentric need to try. The artist is a
lucky dog. That is all there is to say about him. In any
community of a thousand souls there will be nine hundred
doing the work, ninety doing well, nine doing good, and
one lucky dog painting or writing about the other nine
hundred and ninety-nine. Whoa, boy, whoa . . .

DONNER: Oh, shut up.

BEAUCHAMP: I don't know what to call him.

MARTELLO: I've had the most marvellous idea.

DONNER: So have I.

MARTELLO: A portrait . . . an idealization of female beauty,
based on the Song of Solomon.

BEAUCHAMP: I don't get it.

DONNER: *My* idea is that next year we should go on a motoring
tour, and if we can't afford a car we should stay at home.

MARTELLO: You were dead keen about a walking tour, Mouse.

DONNER: Well, I like some parts more than others. The part I
liked best was the first part when we planned our route,
sitting by the fire at home with a cup of cocoa and a map of
France. If you remember, we decided to make the journey
in easy stages, between one charming village and the next
. . . setting off each morning after a simple breakfast on a
terrace overhung with vines, striking out cross-country
along picturesque footpaths, occasionally fording a laughing

brook, resting at midday in the shade, a picnic, perhaps a
nap, and then another little walk to a convenient inn . . . a
hot bath, a good dinner, a pipe in the tap-room with the
honest locals, and so to bed with a candle and a good book,
to sleep dreamlessly——
(*Smack!*)
take *that* you little devil!

BEAUCHAMP (*hooves skittering*): Whoa—whoa—Try not to
startle my mount, Donner.

DONNER: Oh, shut up, Biscuit. I'm bitten all day by French
flies and at night the mosquitoes take over. I nearly
drowned trying to cross a laughing torrent, the honest locals
have stolen most of our money so that we have had to sleep
rough for three days, I've had nothing to eat today except
for half a coconut, and as for the picturesque footpaths—oh
God, here they bloody come again!
(*Improbably, a convoy of rattletrap lorries roars past.
Between their approach and their decline, nothing else is
audible. At the end of it,* BEAUCHAMP's *horse is skittering
about.*)

BEAUCHAMP: Steady, steady . . . good boy . . .

MARTELLO: Tell you what—give Mouse a go on the horse.

BEAUCHAMP: No. This horse only believes in me. What an
animal!—I've had nine horses at various times counting my
first pony, but none has been remotely like this one . . .
Absolutely no trouble, and he gives me a magical feeling of
confidence. My spirits lift, the road slips by . . . What shall
I call him?

DONNER: Where are we, Banjo? Do you know?

MARTELLO: More or less.

DONNER: Well?

MARTELLO: There's a discrepancy between the map and the last
signpost.

DONNER: There hasn't been a signpost since this morning.
Perhaps they're uprooting them.
(*More lorries.*)

BEAUCHAMP: Steady, steady . . .

DONNER: For God's sake, Beauchamp, will you get rid of that coconut!

BEAUCHAMP: Coconut!—not a bad name. And yet it lacks a certain something. Would Napoleon have called his horse Coconut? . . . Napoleon . . . not a bad name.

DONNER: Apart from anything else, it's becoming increasingly clear that we should have stayed at home because of the international situation.

MARTELLO: What international situation?

DONNER: The war.

MARTELLO: What war? You don't believe any of that rot. Why should there be a war? Those Middle Europeans are always assassinating each other.

DONNER: That's the fourth lot of troop lorries we've met today, and we haven't seen a newspaper all week.

MARTELLO: The French are an excitable people.

DONNER: But they weren't French, they were German.

MARTELLO: Rubbish.

DONNER: Yes they were.

MARTELLO: Where's that bloody map? Biscuit, were those lorries French or German?

BEAUCHAMP: I don't know, Banjo. One lorry is much like another.

MARTELLO: I mean the soldiers. Donner says they were German.

BEAUCHAMP: How does one tell?

MARTELLO: Well, Donner?

DONNER: The uniforms.

MARTELLO: The uniforms. Well, don't worry. They're going in the opposite direction. By the time they get to Paris we'll be in Switzerland.

DONNER: Do you seriously expect me to walk to Switzerland? You're crazy, Martello.

(*Dull distant explosion; field gun.*)

MARTELLO: Quarrying.

BEAUCHAMP: All right, Napoleon, easy, boy . . .

DONNER: Beauchamp's crazy too.

(*Explosion, repeat.*)

BEAUCHAMP: I know!—I'll call him Beauchamp's Tenth
Horse!—He will be the phantom cavalry that turns the
war—now you see him, now you don't—he strikes, and is
gone, his neigh lost on the wind, he leaves no hoofprints;
there is only the sound of his hooves on the empty road—
He's not physical!—He's not metaphysical!—He's
pataphysical!—apocalyptic, clipcloptic, Beauchamp's
Tenth!—Here it comes—! !
(*A squadron of Cavalry gallops in quickly to occupy the
foreground with a thunder of hooves; and recedes, leaving the
men stunned and sobered.*)

MARTELLO: Good Christ.

DONNER: Now do you believe me? They were German cavalry.

BEAUCHAMP: He's right.

MARTELLO: We must have got too far east. Don't worry—good
God, if a man can't go for a walk on the Continent
nowadays, what is the world coming to? Come on; I see
there's a fork in the road—judging by the sun the right fork
is the Swiss one.
(*Explosion.*)
Take no notice.

DONNER: Look, what's that?

MARTELLO: What?—Ah. Men digging a ditch.

BEAUCHAMP: Soldiers.

MARTELLO: It is not unusual for soldiers to do such work in
France. Or Germany. The main thing is to ignore them.

BEAUCHAMP: That's quite a ditch.

MARTELLO: Isn't it? Laying pipes, I shouldn't wonder.

BEAUCHAMP: Would you call that a trench?

MARTELLO: Take no notice.

DONNER: We'll probably be interned. I hope they'll do it with
some kind of transport.

MARTELLO: Beautiful bit of country, this. The road is climbing.
That's a good sign. Come on, Biscuit. What happened to
your Tenth Horse?

BEAUCHAMP: My feet are swelling visibly—Good lord!
(*A shock.*)

MARTELLO (*talking up and out*): Good morning!

BEAUCHAMP (*ditto*): Bonjour!

DONNER: Gut'n tag . . .

(*Pause.*)

BEAUCHAMP (*whisper*): That was a field gun!

MARTELLO: My dear chap, it's nothing to do with us. These Continentals are always squabbling over their frontiers.

DONNER: How are we going to get back?

BEAUCHAMP: By train. I shall telegraph for money.

DONNER: There won't be any *trains*!

BEAUCHAMP: Then I shall wait at the station until there are.

DONNER: They might think we're spies . . . and kill us. That would be ridiculous. I don't want to die *ridiculously*.

BEAUCHAMP: All deaths in war are ridiculous.

MARTELLO: Now look here, you two, you're talking like tenderfeet. I am older than you; I have a little more experience. I have studied the European situation minutely, and I can assure you that there will be no war, at least not this year. You forget I have an Uncle Rupert in the War Office. I said to my uncle, when they shot that absurd Archduke Ferdinand of Ruritania, Uncle!, I said, does this mean war?—must I postpone the walking tour which I and my friends have been looking forward to since the winter?! My boy, he said—go!, go with my personal assurance. There will be no war for the very good reason that His Majesty's Government is not *ready* to go to war, and it will be six months at least before we are strong enough to beat the French.

DONNER: The French?

MARTELLO: Go and walk your socks off, my uncle said, and then take the waters-waters at Baden-Baden, to which my auntie added, perhaps that will cure you of all that artistic nonsense with which you waste your time and an expensive education. You live in a sane and beautiful world, my auntie said, and the least you can do, if you must be a painter, is to paint appropriately sane and beautiful pictures. Which reminds me—I've stopped being auntie

now, by the way—I was going to tell you about my next work, a beautiful woman, as described in the Song of Solomon . . . (*Explosions build.*)
I shall paint her navel as a round goblet which wanteth not liquor, her belly like a field of wheat set about with lilies, yea, her two breasts will be like two young roes that are twins, her neck as a tower of ivory, and her eyes will be like the fishpools in Hebdon by the gate of Bath-rabbim, her nose like the tower of Lebanon which looketh towards Damascus . . . Behold she will be fair! My love will have her hair as a flock of goats that appear from Mount Gilead, her teeth like a flock of sheep that are even shorn . . . I shall paint her lips like a thread of scarlet!, and her temples will be like a piece of pomegranate within her locks . . . ! (*Explosions.*)

End of Flashback

(*The three young men are chanting out directions, sometimes in unison, sometimes just one or two voices.*)

ALL THREE: Left! . . . left . . . right . . . left . . . right . . . right . . . turn . . . right a bit . . . left a bit . . . turn . . . left . . . turn . . . stop!

DONNER: Well?

SOPHIE: I am exactly where I started, standing with my back to my chair.

DONNER: Are you quite sure of that, Miss Farthingale?

SOPHIE (*sits*): There!

(*Gasps; laughs.*)

BEAUCHAMP: You win—but we might have moved the chair.

SOPHIE: I assumed that you would move it back if necessary, or at least catch me in your arms.

BEAUCHAMP: Yes, you may be sure of that.

DONNER: Indeed, yes. In fact, why don't we do it again?

SOPHIE: Not this time, Mr. Donner. I've stayed much longer than I intended, and I don't want them to worry about me at the school.

BEAUCHAMP: Then we'll walk back with you.

SOPHIE: Thank you. But there is really no need to trouble you all.

BEAUCHAMP: I should like to.

SOPHIE: Well, if you would like to, Mr. Beauchamp.

DONNER: We would all like to.

SOPHIE: Goodness, I *will* raise their eyebrows—oh! !
  (*She has knocked over the tea-table.*)

BEAUCHAMP: Martello!—you moved the tea things!

SOPHIE: I'm so sorry—how clumsy—

BEAUCHAMP: It wasn't your fault one bit—please get up—really—There!—oh——

SOPHIE: What is it?

BEAUCHAMP: Only that you *are* wearing blue stockings!
  (SOPHIE *and* BEAUCHAMP *laugh.*)

MARTELLO: You seem to be in very good hands, Miss Farthingale. I'm sure you don't want to be accompanied by a whole gang of people, so permit me to say good-bye, and I hope that you will come again.

SOPHIE: Oh, Mr. Martello—of course. Thank you so much again. And good-bye to you both.

DONNER: Oh . . . Good-bye, Miss Farthingale.

MARTELLO: I hope Mr. Beauchamp will not leave you without inviting you to dinner.

BEAUCHAMP: Wouldn't dream of it.

SOPHIE: I should love to come to dinner. Oh—and there will be no need to dress . . . Come then, Mr. Beauchamp . . . may I hold your hand on the stairs?

BEAUCHAMP: If we are going to hold hands, I think I ought to know your name.

SOPHIE: It's Sophie.

DONNER: Don't fall . . .

BEAUCHAMP: I won't!
  (*Their laughter receding down the stairs.*)

DONNER (*close, quiet*): Don't fall.
  (*Door closes on the laughter.*)

End of Flashback

(Faint accordion as before. Feet descending the stairs, starting outside the closed door of the room, and getting fainter with each succeeding floor. They are still faintly audible at the very bottom, and the last sound, just audible, is the front door slamming. This whole business probably takes half a minute. After the slam, SOPHIE *speaks close up.)*

SOPHIE: I feel blind again. I feel more blind than I did the first day, when I came to tea. I shall blunder about, knocking over the occasional table.

(Cries out.) It's not possible!—What is he thinking of?—What are *you* thinking of, Mouse? . . . We can't live here like brother and sister. I know you won't make demands of me, so how can I make demands of you? Am I to weave you endless tablemats and antimacassars in return for life? . . . And is the servant girl to be kept on? I cannot pay her and I cannot allow you to pay her in return for the privilege of reading to me in the evenings. And yet I will not want to be alone, I cannot live alone, I am afraid of the dark; not *my* dark, the real dark, and I need to know that it's morning when I wake or I will fear the worst and never believe in the dawn breaking—who will do that for me? . . . And who will light the fire; and choose my clothes so the colours don't clash; and find my other shoe; and do up my dress at the back? You haven't thought about it. And if you have then you must think that I will be your lover. But I will not. I cannot. And I cannot live with you knowing that you want me—Do you see that? . . . Mouse? Are you here? Say something. Now, don't do that, Mouse, it's not fair—please, you are here . . . Did you go out? Now please don't . . . How can I do anything if I can't trust you—I beg you, if you're here, tell me. What do you want? Are you just going to watch me?—standing quietly in the room—sitting on the bed—on the edge of the tub—Watch me move about the room, grieving, talking to myself, sleeping, washing, dressing, undressing, crying?—Oh no, there is no way now—I won't—I won't—I won't—no, I won't . . . !

(*Glass panes and wood smash violently. Silence. In the silence, hoofbeats in the street, then her body hitting, a horse neighing.*)

End of Flashback

MARTELLO: She would have killed you, Donner. I mean if she'd fallen a yard to the right. Brained you or broken your back, as you waved us good-bye. I remember I heard the glass go and looked up, but my mind seized and I shouted 'Look out' after she hit. I wouldn't have saved you. Beauchamp said she fell, an accident; otherwise why didn't she open the window, he said. I don't know, though. Why should she have behaved rationally to fulfil an irrational impulse? 'This tragic defenestration,' the coroner said. I remember that. Pompous fool, I thought. But I suppose he looked on it as a rare chance to use the word. It's an odd word to exist, defenestration, isn't it? I mean when you consider the comparatively few people who have jumped or been thrown from windows to account for it. By the way, I'm still missing one of her teeth, can you see it anywhere?—a pearl, it could have rolled under the cupboard . . . Yes, why isn't there a word, in that case, for people being pushed downstairs or stuffed up chimneys . . . ? De-escalate is a word, I believe, but they don't use it for that. And, of course, influence. He was bodily in-fluenced. That's a good idea; let's cheer ourselves up by inventing verbs for various kinds of fatality——

DONNER: Martello, will you please stop it.

(*Pause.*)

MARTELLO: Oh, there it is.

DONNER: Her teeth were broken too, smashed, scattered . . .

MARTELLO: *Donner!* If there is anything to be said it's not that. Fifty years ago we knew a nice girl who was due for a sad life, and she jumped out of a window, which was a great shock and certainly tragic, and here we are, having seen much pain and many deaths, none of them happy, and no doubt due for our own one way or another, and then we will have caught up on Sophie's fall, all much of a

muchness after a brief delay between the fall of one body
and another——

DONNER: No, no, each one is vital and every moment
counts—what other reason is there for trying to work well
and live well and choose well? I think it was a good life
lost—she would have been happy with me.

MARTELLO: Well, Beauchamp thought the same, but they were
only happy for a year or two. How can you tell? A blind
mistress is a difficult proposition.

DONNER: I would have married her without question.

MARTELLO: Well, yes, perhaps one made the wrong choice.

DONNER: There was no choice. She fell in love with him at first
sight. As I did with her, I think. After that, even when life
was at its best there was a small part missing and I knew
that I was going to die without ever feeling that my life was
complete.

MARTELLO: Is it still important, Donner? Would it comfort you
if you thought, even now, that Sophie loved you?

DONNER: I can never think that, but I wish I could be sure that
she had some similar feeling for me.

MARTELLO: Did you ever wonder whether it was you she loved?

DONNER: No, of course not. It was Beauchamp.

MARTELLO: To *us* it was Beauchamp, but which of us did she
see in her mind's eye . . . ?

DONNER: But it *was* Beauchamp—she remembered his
painting, the snow scene.

MARTELLO: Yes. She asked me whether I had painted it within
five minutes of meeting me in the garden that day; she
described it briefly, and I had an image of black vertical
railings, like park railings, right across the canvas, as
though one were looking at a field of snow through the bars
of a cage; not like Beauchamp's snow scene at all.

DONNER: But it was the only snow scene.

MARTELLO: Yes, it was, but—I promise you, Donner, it was a
long time afterwards when this occurred to me, when she
was already living with Beauchamp——

DONNER: What occurred to you, Martello?

MARTELLO: Well, your painting of the white fence——
DONNER: White fence?
MARTELLO: Thick white posts, top to bottom across the whole
    canvas, an inch or two apart, black in the gaps——
DONNER: Yes, I remember it. Oh God.
MARTELLO: Like looking at the dark through the gaps in a
    white fence.
DONNER: Oh my God.
MARTELLO: Well, one might be wrong, but her sight was not
    good even then.
DONNER: Oh my God.
MARTELLO: When one thinks of the brief happiness she enjoyed
    . . . well, we thought she was enjoying it with Beauchamp
    but she was really enjoying it with you. As it were.
DONNER: Oh my God.
MARTELLO: Of course, it was impossible to say so, after she got
    off on the right foot with Beauchamp—I mean, one
    couldn't——
DONNER: Oh my God!
MARTELLO: Now, steady on, Donner, or I'll be sorry I
    mentioned it——
DONNER: *Oh my God* . . .

End of flashback

    (*Smack!*)
BEAUCHAMP: Missed him again! (*Pause.*) All right, don't tell
    me then.
    (BEAUCHAMP's TAPE: *snap crackle pop* . . .)
    Fascinating, isn't it? Layer upon layer of what passes for
    silence, trapped from an empty room—no, trawled—no,
    like—no matter! I know that in this loop of tape there is
    some truth about how we live, Donner. These unheard
    sounds which are our silence stand as a metaphor—a
    correspondence between the limits of hearing and the limits
    of all knowledge: and whose silence is our hubbub?
DONNER: Are you going out, Beauchamp? I'd like to get on.

BEAUCHAMP: I have nothing to go out for.

DONNER: Get some fly-killer.

BEAUCHAMP: All right, if you'll let me record a clean loop while
I'm out. I don't want you whistling and throwing things
about when you can't get the likeness right.

DONNER: I *am* getting it right.

BEAUCHAMP: Yes, she's very good. May I make a small
suggestion?

DONNER: No.

BEAUCHAMP: Her nipples were in fact——

DONNER: Get out!

BEAUCHAMP: Courtesy costs nothing. All right, I'll see if
Martello is in the pub, and I'll be back in an hour or so.
(*Changing tapes.*)
There. Will you press the switch when I'm out of the door?

DONNER: Yes.

BEAUCHAMP: Promise?

DONNER: I promise, Beauchamp.

BEAUCHAMP: Poor Sophie. I think you've got her, Donner.
(BEAUCHAMP's *feet down the stairs. Open and close door. The
fly starts to buzz. It comes close to the microphone and the sound
is distorted slightly into a droning rhythm.*)

End of Flashback

(*The beginning of the* DONNER TAPE. *It is the same sound as
made by the fly.*)

MARTELLO: I don't want to hear it again.
(*Cut* TAPE.)

BEAUCHAMP: Now then. Let's try looking at it backwards.
Coolly. Fact number one: Donner is lying at the bottom of
the stairs, dead, with what looks to my untrained eye like a
broken neck. Inference: he fell down the stairs. Fact
number two: the balustrade up here is broken. Inference:
Donner fell through it, as a result of, er, staggering and
possibly slipping on what is undeniably a slippery floor, as a
result of . . . Well, fact number three: the sounds which

correspond to these inferences were preceded by Donner crying out, preceded by a sort of thump, preceded by two quick footsteps, preceded by Donner remarking, unalarmed—I can't believe it of you, Martello!
(*Pause.*)

MARTELLO: Nor I of you, Beauchamp. (*Pause.*) Well, let's get him upstairs.

BEAUCHAMP: Hang on . . .

(*Fly.*)

That fly has been driving me mad. Where is he?

MARTELLO: Somewhere over there . . .

BEAUCHAMP: Right.

The original loop of TAPE *is hereby reproduced:*

(*a*) *Fly droning.*

(*b*) *Careful footsteps approach. A board creaks.*

(*c*) *The fly settles.*

(*d*) BEAUCHAMP *halts.*

(*e*) BEAUCHAMP: *'Ah! There you are.'*

(*f*) *Two more quick steps and then: Thump!*

BEAUCHAMP: Got him!

(*Laughs shortly.*)

'As flies to wanton boys are we to the Gods: they kill us for their sport.'

Now then.

THE DOG IT WAS THAT DIED

CHARACTERS

RUPERT PURVIS
GILES BLAIR
HOGBIN
SLACK
PAMELA BLAIR
MRS RYAN
COMMODORE ARLON
MATRON
DR SEDDON
VICAR
CHIEF
WREN

SCENE 1

Exterior. City. Night.

PURVIS's *footsteps on the pavement. An occasional vehicle passing, not very close.*

PURVIS *is coming up to retirement age. As he walks he is singing quietly, disjointedly, cheerfully . . . songs of farewell: the one beginning* 'Goodbye–ee . . . ' *. . . and* 'Goodbye, Piccadilly . . . ' *. . . and* 'We Don't Want to Leave You but . . . '

This singing voice is the same time and place as the footsteps and the traffic. Over this is PURVIS's *own voice reading through a letter he has written. The singing voice and the footsteps, together with the occasional road and river traffic, continue intermittently underneath.*

PURVIS: *(Voice over)* Dear Blair. I have decided I have had enough of this game and I'm getting out but before I take the plunge . . . (PURVIS *chuckles briefly but pulls himself together*) . . . before I take the plunge I thought I'd give you a tip which if you handle it right could put you in the top spot in the Department, assuming that that is what you want. I have no fastidious scruples myself about the Chief having an opium den in his house in Eaton Square—perhaps that is something more of us should be doing—but I dare say the Prime Minister would take a different view. That was the tip, by the way. I wish I had something more on him to give you but gone are the days when a man could be brought down by being named in the divorce courts, even for sexual misconduct with the wife of a subordinate, and I only mention it now because your good lady (is she called Pamela?—I only met her once) may have been pulling the wool over your eyes and you have always been more than decent to me. So you will have to do what you can with the opium den, and my only regret is that I won't be here to enjoy the brouhaha . . . .

(*The here-and-now* PURVIS *adds a few ha-has to that one.*) Actually, it's not my *only* regret because I was looking forward to taking a belly dancer to Buckingham Palace—if the invitation was anything to do with you, many thanks for the thought. She's a splendid girl, and would have made a bit of a splash. But now it's left to me to do that. Thanks, anyway. There's something of mine which has been in the family for ages and as I'm the last of the line you may like to have it. It's supposed to have belonged to a one-legged sea captain who inspired the character of Long John Silver and I thought you might find a place for it in your folly. In all honesty, I saw one just like it on a piano in the trophy room at Cork Castle or somewhere, which gives one pause for thought, but I'll send it round anyway.

(PURVIS *is now walking across a bridge over the Thames (Chelsea Bridge) and Big Ben is heard distantly striking the quarter hour.*) Well, I think that's about all. I hope I won't be bobbing up again so there shouldn't be any problem about the remains. I have left enough in the kitty for a plaque on the wall of St Luke's where I am church warden, and I would be grateful if you could make sure this is done. The vicar bears a grudge against me but if he starts making trouble you can take it from me that on the subject of that savoury business the choir is lying its head off man and boy, especially Hoskins, third from the end with the eyelashes. An inquiry would clear my name but I have no wish to see the diocese dragged through the mud. That is a fate I have reserved for—yours ever, Rupert Purvis. (*Now speaking 'live'*) Well, this seems to be about the middle . . . if I can manage the parapet . . . (*He grunts and heaves himself up*) . . . I'm too old for this game . . . nice breeze anyway . . . quiet as the grave and black as your hat— to hell with the lot of them, oh dear me . . . (*He starts to sniffle, all cheerfulness gone*) . . . never mind, it's all over now. Off I . . . go . . .

(*The last word is extended with* PURVIS's *plunge, which ends unexpectedly with the sound of a quite large dog in sudden and short-lived pain.*)

SCENE 2

Exterior.   City park (St James's Park).   Daytime.
Big Ben is striking ten.
BLAIR *is middle-aged and a gentleman.* HOGBIN *is younger and perhaps less of a gentleman.*

BLAIR: Good morning. On the dot.

HOGBIN: I see the tulips are in glorious bloom.

BLAIR: Absolutely. What can I do for you, Hogbin?

HOGBIN: I'm sorry—do we know each other?

BLAIR: I prefer thingummies myself. What's all this about?

HOGBIN: I see the tulips are in glorious bloom.

BLAIR: So you said. I prefer hollyhocks myself. (*Pause.*) Hibiscus?
    (*Pause.*) Come on, Hogbin. I'm Blair. We've met. A couple of
    years ago up in Blackheath, don't you remember?

HOGBIN: I'm afraid not.

BLAIR: Two days and nights in the back of a laundry van watching a
    dead-letter drop for a pigeon who never turned up . . . I'll
    never forget Blackheath.

HOGBIN: (*Carefully*) I was in Blackheath once.

BLAIR: Of course you were. That was you in the white apron,
    brought me chicken in a basket. I mean a laundry basket. So
    stop fooling about. (*Pause.*) Gladioli? (*Pause.*) All right, I'll
    just sit on this bench and enjoy the view. The view north from
    St James's Park is utterly astonishing, I always think. Domes
    and cupolas, strange pinnacles and spires. A distant prospect
    of St Petersburg, one imagines . . . Where does it all go when
    one is in the middle of it, standing in Trafalgar Square with
    Englishness on every side? Monumental Albion, giving credit
    where credit is due to some sketchbook of a Grand Tour, but
    all as English as a 49 bus.

HOGBIN: With or without chips?

BLAIR: As I remember it was a baked potato in silver foil, and a
    KitKat.

HOGBIN: Hydrangeas.

BLAIR: That was it. I prefer Hydrangeas myself.

HOGBIN: I'm sorry, sir, but . . .

BLAIR: Perfectly all right. Keen gardener, are you?

HOGBIN: Do you run a man called Purvis, Mr Blair?

BLAIR: Rupert Purvis?

HOGBIN: Yes. He tried to kill himself last night. He killed a dog instead.

BLAIR: I see.

HOGBIN: Sir?

BLAIR: I said—I see.

HOGBIN: Oh. Well. Well, he jumped off Chelsea Bridge at 3.16 this morning, precisely at high tide. A precise man, Mr Purvis.

BLAIR: Yes.

HOGBIN: Unfortunately he landed on a barge.

BLAIR: You mean fortunately.

HOGBIN: I was looking at it from his point of view.

BLAIR: Of course.

HOGBIN: In fact he landed on a barge dog. The dog broke Purvis's fall. Purvis broke the dog's back. The barge dropped Purvis off downstream at St Thomas's.

BLAIR: And that's where he is now?

HOGBIN: Yes, sir.

BLAIR: Well, I'll pop down and see him. Thank you, Hogbin.

HOGBIN: There is something else, sir.

BLAIR: Yes. What kind of dog was it?

HOGBIN: I don't know, sir.

BLAIR: Well, it wouldn't be anything special. Fifty pounds, more than ample, wouldn't you say?

HOGBIN: I hadn't really thought, sir.

BLAIR: I would say fifty. If your Chief won't wear it, I dare say mine will.

HOGBIN: I didn't want to mention this to your Chief.

BLAIR: Oh, he's all right for fifty, don't worry. You worry too much, Hogbin, if I may say so. I'm grateful to you for taking this trouble but it would have been quite all right for you to come to the office.

HOGBIN: No, sir. I thought it was better to talk outside. It's not about the dog, sir. It's about a letter. Purvis posted a letter a few minutes before he jumped. We retrieved it.

BLAIR: You've been following him, Hogbin.

HOGBIN: We didn't know he was one of our own.

BLAIR: He wasn't yours, he was mine. Still is.

HOGBIN: That's what I meant.

BLAIR: Well, who did you think he was?

HOGBIN: We thought he was one of theirs.

BLAIR: I see.

HOGBIN: He was followed from Highgate Hill to a house in Church Street, Chelsea.

BLAIR: He lives there.

HOGBIN: Yes, so I gather. He left the house again just before three, leaving all the lights on. He knew he wouldn't have to pay any more bills. He walked to the river.

BLAIR: Posting a letter on the way. Whereabouts in Highgate did you follow him from? Highgate Hill Square?

HOGBIN: You obviously know all about it.

BLAIR: Everybody knows their safe house. Red Square we call it.

HOGBIN: We call it Dunkremlin.

BLAIR: Why?

HOGBIN: Sir?

BLAIR: Why did you follow him? Was he acting suspiciously?

HOGBIN: Not exactly suspiciously. He walked out of the front door, slamming it behind him.

BLAIR: Well, I give him a pretty free rein. When did you realize he was Q6?

HOGBIN: It was the letter. Here you are, sir. You understand, sir, that we had to open all the letters in the box in order to ascertain . . .

BLAIR: Yes, of course. Thank you. I'll read it later. Anything else?

HOGBIN: Sir?

BLAIR: I said—anything else?

HOGBIN: Well, the letter's a bit . . . Would you say that Mr Purvis had been overworking lately?

BLAIR: Well, *I* haven't been overworking him. But of course I can't speak for *them*.

SCENE 3

Interior. Hospital.

BLAIR: Well, Purvis, this is all very silly. What on earth did you think you were doing jumping off bridges?

PURVIS: Oh, hello, sir. How good of you to come.

BLAIR: Not at all. Are you quite comfortable?

PURVIS: Yes, thank you. I'm grateful for the private room.

BLAIR: I meant with your feet winched up like that. You put me in mind of a saucy postcard.

PURVIS: I put the nurses in mind of midwifery. But I appreciate your not mincing words. You're the first person who has mentioned the word jump or bridge since I got here. I thought I must have imagined it all. By the way, was there something about a dog?

BLAIR: Yes. You're the first person to jump off a bridge on to a dog. The reverse one often used to see at the Saturday morning cinema, of course.

PURVIS: Men jumping off dogs on to . . . ?

BLAIR: No, dogs jumping off bridges on to . . .

PURVIS: Oh yes. What a relief anyway. I was beginning to think I'd gone cuckoo.

BLAIR: Your relief may be premature. There's nothing cuckoo about imagining things. Cuckoo is jumping off bridges. Are you in any sort of trouble?

PURVIS: Well, one had a bit of a *crise*, you know.

BLAIR: Yes. Do you remember writing me a letter?

PURVIS: Have you received it already?

BLAIR: Special delivery.

PURVIS: I wasn't going to mention it.

BLAIR: I shouldn't have done so.

PURVIS: A bit of a shaker, I expect.

BLAIR: Well, these things happen in all families.

PURVIS: You mean that business about your wife. I'm sorry. It's the last thing one would have expected of a woman who runs a donkey sanctuary—concubine to an opium addict.

BLAIR: (*Huffily*) Now look here, Purvis—

PURVIS: Yes, I'm so sorry—one loses all one's social graces when one expected to be dead.

BLAIR: I didn't mean *my* family. I meant Q6. People having what you call a bit of a *crise*. I suggest we draw the veil, eh? Least said, soonest mended.

PURVIS: You must do as you think fit. Personally I think you'd make an excellent number one, but I can quite see that you might take the view that it's nobody's business what the Chief gets up to in his own time so long as he doesn't bring his pipe to the office. Perhaps you think I'm a bit of a cad for sneaking?

BLAIR: These decisions are never easy. By the way, where did this story come from?

PURVIS: It's all over Highgate.

BLAIR: I see.

PURVIS: I was up there last night actually.

BLAIR: Really?

PURVIS: I went to visit my friend.

BLAIR: Oh yes?

PURVIS: He was none too pleased.

BLAIR: No?

PURVIS: I was after some information.

BLAIR: And did you get it?

PURVIS: No. I said to him, look, I said, can you just remind me— what is the essential thing we're supposed to be in it for?—the ideological nub of the matter? Is it power to the workers; is it the means of production, distribution and exchange; is it each according to his needs; is it the expropriation of the expropriators? Know what he said? Historical inevitability! Historical inevitability! You're joking, I said. Pull the other one, it's got bells on. No, you'll have to do better than that. Something can't be good just because it's *inevitable*. It may be good and it may be inevitable, but that's no *reason*, it may be *rotten* and inevitable. He couldn't see it. So I left. None the wiser. Perhaps you could help me on this one, Blair.

BLAIR: Oh . . . I don't know . . . they did give us a run-down on it years ago . . . one of those know-thy-enemy lectures . . . I didn't take much notice. There was something called the value of labour capital which seemed to be important but I never understood what it was.

PURVIS: No, I mean from your side of the fence.

BLAIR: Mine?

PURVIS: Yes. It's important to me. Can you remind me, what was the gist of it?—the moral and intellectual foundation of Western society in a nutshell.

BLAIR: I'm sorry, my mind's gone blank.

PURVIS: Come on—democracy . . . free elections, free expression, free market forces . . .

BLAIR: Oh yes, that was it.

PURVIS: Yes, but how did we deal with the argument that all this freedom merely benefits the people who already have the edge? I mean, freedom of expression advantages the articulate . . . Do you see?

BLAIR: You're going a bit fast for me, Purvis. I never really got beyond us being British and them being atheists and Communists. There's no arguing with that, is there? Are you quite sure you aren't in any sort of trouble?

PURVIS: Depends what you mean by trouble.

BLAIR: Your letter mentioned some unsavoury business with choirboys.

PURVIS: *Savoury* business, not unsavoury business.

BLAIR: Savoury business?

PURVIS: Yes. You know what a savoury is. Mushrooms on toast . . . sardines . . . or, in this case, Welsh rarebit.

BLAIR: I see. Well, you just have a jolly good rest, Rupert, take the weight off your feet . . .

PURVIS: As you see . . .

BLAIR: Yes, of course. But we'll soon have you back on them. You were lucky.

PURVIS: Luckier than the dog.

BLAIR: Yes. It was the dog that died.

SCENE 4

Exterior.   Garden.

BLAIR: I admit it looks odd. The question is does it look odd enough?

SLACK: It looks odd enough to me, sir.

BLAIR: I'm not convinced, Mr Slack. I *do* like the mullioned window between the Doric columns—that has a quality of coy desperation, like a spinster gatecrashing a costume ball in a flowered frock . . . and the pyramid on the portico is sheer dumb insolence. All well and good. I think it's the Gothic tower that disappoints. It isn't quite *there*. It's Gothic but not Gothick with a 'k'. Should we ruin one of the buttresses?

SLACK: Ruin it, sir?

BLAIR: Mm . . . Make it a bit of a ruin. Or should we wait for the ivy to catch up?

SLACK: I should wait for the ivy, sir. We're going to have our hands full with the obelisk. Is it all right to lower away?

BLAIR: Yes, lower away.

SLACK: (*Calls out*) Lower away!

BLAIR: The crane has to swing it over slightly to the right.

SLACK: No, sir, it's centred on top of the tower.

BLAIR: But it's lop-sided.

SLACK: Only from where we're standing.

BLAIR: But surely, Mr Slack, if it's centred on top of the tower, it should look centred from everywhere.

SLACK: That would be all right with a round Norman tower, sir, but with your octagonal Gothic tower the angles of the parapet throw the middle out.

BLAIR: Throw the middle out—?

SLACK: The obelisk will look centred from the terrace, sir.

BLAIR: But it has to look centred from my study window as well.

SLACK: Can't be done now—you'd have had to have one side of the tower squared up with the window.

BLAIR: Hold everything.

SLACK: (*Shouts*) Hold everything!

BLAIR: This obviously needs the superior intelligence of Mrs B. I'll go and fetch her from the paddock.

SLACK: She's in the drawing room, sir.

BLAIR: I thought she was operating on one of the donkeys.

SLACK: That's right, sir.

SCENE 5

Interior.

Modest donkey noises.

BLAIR: (*Entering*) Pamela . . .

    (*The donkey brays and kicks the floor.*)

PAMELA: Hang on, Mrs Ryan.

BLAIR: I say, do be careful of my clocks.

    (*The room is going tick-tock rather a lot.*)

PAMELA: You've come just at the right moment. Mrs Ryan, you're
    doing very well but I can't do the stitches if there's so much
    movement.

MRS RYAN: Right-ho, dear.

PAMELA: Giles, you hang on to her legs.

BLAIR: I haven't really got time for all this.

PAMELA: Not Mrs Ryan's legs, Giles, Empy's.

BLAIR: Sorry.

PAMELA: There, there, Empy. Soon be over.

BLAIR: Look, Pamela, the donkey sanctuary is supposed to be the
    paddock. The drawing rooom is supposed to be sanctuary *from*
    the donkeys.

PAMELA: This is the only fire lit today and I needed it to sterilize the
    instrument. Hold her neck, Mrs Ryan.

MRS RYAN: Right-ho, dear.

PAMELA: Poor Empy got into a fight with Don Juan. It's only a
    couple of stitches . . . here we go, everybody . . .

    (*Silence, except for the ticking and tocking. Then the donkey brays
    and kicks.*)

BLAIR: For God's sake—she nearly kicked over my American
    Townsend.

PAMELA: Well, hold her *still*.

    (*Tense silence, marked by an orchestra of ticks and tocks.*)

    How long have I got before they all go off?

BLAIR: About a minute.

PAMELA: I don't see why they have to be *going* all the time.

BLAIR: If they weren't going they wouldn't be clocks, they'd be
    bric-à-brac. The long delay in the invention of the clock was
    all to do with the hands going round. If the hands didn't have

to go round, the Greeks could have had miniature Parthenons on their mantelshelves with clock faces stuck into the pediments permanently showing ten past two or eight thirty-five . . .

MRS RYAN: Were you expecting a clock today, sir? A package came for you, special delivery, sender's name Purvis.

BLAIR: Oh yes. Do you remember Purvis, Pamela?

PAMELA: Don't talk to me while I'm stitching. Isn't Empy being brave? Good girl.

BLAIR: I introduced you to him at the Chief's Christmas drinks. You said there was something funny about him. Pretty sharp. He tried to kill himself the other night. He killed a dog instead. He's sent me a family heirloom. I suppose I'll have to send it back now.

PAMELA: That must be what the note from Security was about. They opened your parcel in transit. They thought it was suspicious.

BLAIR: No, no I know all about it. Purvis has sent me an old sea captain's wooden peg-leg.

PAMELA: No he hasn't, he's sent you a stuffed parrot.

BLAIR: That's what I meant. There's one just like it on the piano in the trophy room at Cork Castle. That reminds me, there's a serious problem with the obelisk on the tower. It's going to look lop-sided depending on where one is standing, even though it's in the middle.

PAMELA: That's because of the corners. You should have had a round tower.

BLAIR: Why didn't you tell me?

PAMELA: I didn't think it mattered. The whole thing is fairly loopy anyway.

BLAIR: It's the old story—never change anything that works! I had in mind the obelisk at Plumpton Magna where they have a round tower but I thought I would go octagonal. It's entirely my own fault.

PAMELA: You mean your own folly. Can you reach the forceps?

BLAIR: Where are they?

PAMELA: On the grate.

BLAIR: Right.

(BLAIR *yelps as he drops the forceps. He yelps louder as the donkey kicks him. The donkey brays. All the clocks starts to chime and strike. The donkey gallops across the wooden floor and then out of earshot.*)

She kicked me!

PAMELA: I know just how she felt.

BLAIR: Well, the forceps were red hot.

(*The clocks are still going strong.*)

MRS RYAN: Is it all right if I get on now, dear?

PAMELA: Yes, all right, Mrs Ryan. Good job the french windows were open.

(MRS RYAN *switches on a vacuum cleaner.*

PAMELA *fades out calling for Empy as she leaves the room.*)

MRS RYAN: Can you lift your leg, dear?

BLAIR: No, I can't. The knee is swelling visibly.

MRS RYAN: Don't you worry, dear. I'll vacuum round you.

(*The clocks continue to strike.*)

SCENE 6

Exterior.   City park (St James's).   Day.

Big Ben is striking.

BLAIR: Good morning. I see the tulips are fighting fit.

HOGBIN: There's no need for that, sir.

BLAIR: No, no, just a passing remark. I thought you were keen on the things. Anyway, what's up?

HOGBIN: You remember that letter Purvis wrote you?

BLAIR: Yes?

HOGBIN: It's been on my mind.

BLAIR: You really *do* worry too much.

HOGBIN: Didn't it worry you, Mr Blair?

BLAIR: Well, some of it of course . . . but every family has occasional problems.

HOGBIN: You mean about Mrs Blair?

BLAIR: No, I don't mean anything of the sort. I really don't understand how some people's minds work. I was talking about Q6. We're a small department with, I like to think, a family feeling, and we have occasional problems, that's all.

HOGBIN: I'm sorry. I didn't believe a word of it, of course. The

whole letter was raving mad. I never read anything so
obviously off its trolley. That's what worries me about it, as a
matter of fact. That's why it's on my mind.

BLAIR: What do you mean, Hogbin?

HOGBIN: Well, sir—the opium den in Eaton Square, the belly
dancer at Buckingham Palace, the sea captain's piano leg—

BLAIR: Parrot—it was a stuffed parrot.

HOGBIN: Well, whatever. And some scandal with an entire male-
voice choir.

BLAIR: I asked Purvis about that. He said it involved a Welsh
rarebit.

HOGBIN: You see what I mean.

BLAIR: No.

HOGBIN: I think the letter smells. I think he overdid it. I think he's
shamming, Mr Blair.

BLAIR: Shamming what?

HOGBIN: I think Purvis *wanted* you to think he'd gone off his
trolley.

BLAIR: But Hogbin . . . he did jump off Chelsea Bridge.

HOGBIN: At high tide. The absolute top. To the minute.

BLAIR: Exactly.

HOGBIN: When there was the shortest possible distance to fall.

DLAIR: Everybody goes too fast for me nowadays.

HOGBIN: Think about it, sir. There he is in the Soviet safe house in
Highgate. What he's doing there I leave an open question for
the minute. He makes a conspicuous departure, practically
begging to be followed. He walks all the way home just to
make it easy. He comes out flashing a letter which he posts,
and then off to the bridge and over he goes—just as a handy
barge is there to pick him up.

BLAIR: But he landed *on* the barge.

HOGBIN: It went slightly wrong. Especially for the dog.

BLAIR: You're not serious?

HOGBIN: No, I'm not. It's just not on. Apart from anything else the
bargee and his family have been scudding about the river for
three generations, real Tories, can't abide foreigners,
wouldn't even eat the food. So that one is a non-starter. I'm
just showing that the facts would fit more than one set of

possibilities. There's something wrong with that letter. I
know there is. You wouldn't like to tell me what Purvis was
doing up in Highgate?

BLAIR: He was discussing political theory.

HOGBIN: I suppose you people know what you're doing.

BLAIR: Well, one tries.

HOGBIN: Where is Purvis now?

BLAIR: Convalescing. We maintain a house on the Norfolk coast, as
a rest-home for those of our people who . . . need a rest. Sea
breezes, simple exercise, plain food, TV lounge, own grounds,
wash-basins in every room . . . It's like an hotel, one of those
appalling English hotels. So I'm told—I've never been there.

HOGBIN: A rest-home for people who crack up?

BLAIR: You could put it like that. Or you could say it's a health farm.

HOGBIN: A funny farm?

BLAIR: I think that's about as much as I can help you, Hogbin.

HOGBIN: How is Purvis now?

BLAIR: I'm going to go and see him in a day or two. I'll let you know
how I find him.

HOGBIN: *If* you find him. Is there a gate to this place?

BLAIR: No, as far as I know Purvis could make a dash for it in his
wheelchair any time he chooses.

HOGBIN: I'm sorry if I seem to be obstinate. But there is something
funny about that letter, sir. I don't know what it is.

BLAIR: Well, I'm afraid I must be getting back.

HOGBIN: Thank you for coming out to meet me . . . You seem to
have been in the wars.

BLAIR: Got kicked on the kneecap, nothing serious. Goodbye—
careful with my hand, burned my fingers . . . Oh, how I love
this view!—what a skyline! All the way up Whitehall from
Parliament Square, Trafalgar Square, St James's . . . It's like
one enormous folly.

SCENE 7

*Exterior.   Car arriving on gravel.   Motor mower at work in
background.*
The car draws up and comes to a halt. The car door opens and slams.
ARLON *is an old buffer who is mowing the lawn not far off.*

ARLON: Ahoy there!

BLAIR: Er—good afternoon.

ARLON: (*Approaching*) Spanking day!

BLAIR: Yes, indeed. Where would I find . . . ?

ARLON: Quite a swell.

BLAIR: Thank you.

ARLON: Force three, south-sou'-west, running before the wind all the way down from London, just the ticket.

BLAIR: Where would I find Dr Sed—?

ARLON: Hang on, let me turn this thing off.

(*The engine of the mower is cut to idling speed.*)

That's better. Welcome aboard.

BLAIR: I don't want to interrupt your mowing.

ARLON: Glad of the excuse to heave to, been tacking up and down all morning.

BLAIR: You're doing an excellent job here.

ARLON: Good of you to say so.

BLAIR: Deeply satisfying, I should think.

ARLON: Well, it's not everybody's idea of fun, running a bin for a couple of dozen assorted nervous wrecks and loonies, but I suppose it's better than cleaning spittoons in the fo'c'sle— even when London won't give us the money to pay a proper gardener. Still, there we are—you must be Blair. What happened to your fingers? Ice in the rigging?

BLAIR: How do you do? I'm sorry, I didn't realize . . . You are the warden here?

ARLON: I prefer the term keeper, just as I prefer the term loony. Let's call things by their proper name, eh?

BLAIR: Yes . . . Dr Seddon, isn't it?

ARLON: Commodore.

BLAIR: Commodore Seddon?

ARLON: You've come about Purvis, the scourge of the tidal bestiary, the one-man mission to keep the inland waterways dog-free, correct?

BLAIR: Well, yes.

ARLON: These secret service types, once they crack they can't stop babbling. Are you a member of the Naval and Military Club?

BLAIR: I don't recall.

ARLON: I used to be. But after certain words exchanged between myself and a brother officer in the card room it was not possible for me to remain. I said to the secretary—look chum, I said, the Arlons have been gentlefolk in Middlesex for five generations. We kept our own carriage when Twickenham was a hamlet and the Greenslades were as dust under our wheels, and I will not be called a jumped-up suburban card-sharp by a man whose grandfather bought a baronetcy from the proceeds of an ointment claiming to enlarge the female breast—a spurious claim moreover as an old shipmate of mine, now unhappily gone to her Maker, might have attested. Her Maker having made her the shape of an up-ended punt. Wouldn't you have done the same—?

BLAIR: I . . .

ARLON: I know you would. As far as that nine of hearts was concerned I accept that salting it away behind one's braces for a rainy day does not fall within the rules of Grand National Whist as the game is understood on land, I accept that without reservation, but certain words were uttered and cannot be unuttered, they are utterly and unutterably uttered, Blair, and if you want to do a chap a favour the next time you find yourself in Pall Mall, I'd like you to take out your service revolver and go straight up to Greenslade and—

BLAIR: Absolutely. Consider it done.

ARLON: Thank you, Blair. I shall sleep easier.

BLAIR: Don't mention it. By the way, do you happen to know where I might find Dr Seddon?

MATRON: (*Approaching across the gravel*) Good afternoon!

ARLON: I expect Matron will know. Say nothing about this. Take in a couple of reefs and batten the hatches.

BLAIR: Thank you very much.

MATRON: Mr Blair?

BLAIR: Good afternoon.

MATRON: Thank you, Commodore—please continue with the mowing.

ARLON: I don't take orders from you, you're just a figure-head and I've seen better ones on the sharp end of a dredger.

MATRON: Now, Commodore, do you want your rum ration with your cocoa or don't you?

ARLON: If I mow the lawn it is because it pleases me to do so.

(*The mowing continues.*)

MATRON: Welcome to Clifftops, Mr Blair. I saw you talking to the Commodore from the window. He's one of our more difficult guests. I do hope it wasn't too awkward for you.

BLAIR: It's all right. He caught me on the wrong foot for a moment.

MATRON: You'll be wanting Dr Seddon. Let's go inside.

BLAIR: Thank you.

(*They walk a few yards of gravel and then they are in interior.*)

MATRON: He's probably looking in on the ping-pong players in the library.

BLAIR: Ping-pong in the library? Isn't that rather disturbing?

MATRON: I suppose it is but most of them are already rather disturbed when they get here. See that one over there? He's *dangerous*. Let me take your coat.

BLAIR: I haven't got a coat.

MATRON: Never mind—in here—quick!

(BLAIR *is pushed through a door which then closes.*)

BLAIR: What—?

MATRON: Sssh.

BLAIR: (*Whispering*) Where are we?

MATRON: In the coat cupboard. We haven't got long so don't waste a minute.

BLAIR: Really, Matron . . .

MATRON: Don't Matron me, I blew your cover the moment you showed your limp. I'm match fit and ready to go—parachute, midget submarine, you name it. The last show wasn't my fault, the maps were out of date.

BLAIR: Will you please open the—

(*The door is opened.*)

SEDDON: Who is in there?

BLAIR: Ah, good afternoon— I'm looking for Dr Seddon.

MATRON: (*Sweetly*) And this, of course, is the coat cupboard.

BLAIR: Awfully nice.

SEDDON: Thank you, Bilderbeck. You may leave our visitor to me now.

MATRON: Matron to you, if you don't mind.

SEDDON: Have you had your tablets?

MATRON: (*Receding*) Mind your own business.

SEDDON: That's Bilderbeck. She used to dress up as a matron to oblige a chap she got mixed up with in Washington. When she was confronted with the photographs she insisted that she was giving him first aid and she's been sticking to her story ever since. It's the only uniform we allow here. We found that they tended to set people off. So we're all in civvies. Not even a white coat, as you see. You must be Blair. I'm Dr Seddon.

BLAIR: How do you do. Giles Blair. Look, don't take this amiss but would you have any form of identification?

SEDDON: First sensible remark I've heard today, counting the ones by the staff. Let's go to my office and have a cup of tea.

BLAIR: Thanks very much.

SEDDON: This way. How are things in London?

BLAIR: Relatively sane.

SEDDON: I know what you mean. My time with the firm was excellent preparation for Clifftops.

BLAIR: Oh . . . were you—?

SEDDON: Q10.

BLAIR: Code-breaking?

SEDDON: Code-*making*. You may have heard of consonantal transposition. Scramble your own telephone. That was my contribution to the fun and games.

BLAIR: Really? No, I . . .

SEDDON: We go up these stairs now. Yes, they never took it up. Said it was too difficult, or too simple, one or the other.

BLAIR: How did it work?

SEDDON: Posetransing stantocons, titeg?

BLAIR: Sorry?

SEDDON: Transposing consonants—get it?

BLAIR: (*Faintly*) Ingenious.

SEDDON: The trick was that there were no rules as such. You had to do it like improvising music. It just needed a little tackpris but cos fork the cuffing ditios dookn't tag the feng tif of.

BLAIR: What?

SEDDON: Moo yee sot I wean; tackpris! Well too yot, Blair . . .

BLAIR: Yot?

SEDDON: You see—pick it up in no time! Come up to the belfry, I've got something up there which will interest you.

BLAIR: What?

SEDDON: Bats.

BLAIR: Bats in the belfry?

SEDDON: Had them for years without knowing it. I say, not that way . . .

BLAIR: Excuse me—I've got to find someone.

(BLAIR *starts hurrying back down the stairs.*)

SEDDON: Blair—?

BLAIR: Terribly sorry—I really have to go.

(*He gallops down the stairs. We go with him.*)

SEDDON: (*Distantly*) Blair . . . !

(*At the bottom of the stairs there is a collision.*)

BLAIR: I'm terribly sorry!

PURVIS: Blair!

BLAIR: Purvis! Thank goodness.

PURVIS: I'm very glad to see you.

BLAIR: I'm not sorry to see *you*. I'm damned if I can flush out anyone in authority. Where's the chap who's supposed to be running this show?

PURVIS: You mean Dr Seddon? I'll see if I can raise him for you.

BLAIR: Just as a courtesy . . . It was you I came to see, of course.

PURVIS: Really? That's awfully nice of you. I was about to have my constitutional. Care to accompany me?

BLAIR: Glad to give you a shove. Front door?

PURVIS: Can't do the steps. This way is better.

BLAIR: How do you feel?

PURVIS: Like a mermaid on wheels. Did I hurt your leg?

BLAIR: That wasn't you. Burnt my fingers pulling Pamela's chestnuts out of the fire, nearly knocked my Hilderson lantern clock off the mantel and got kicked by the donkey for my pains.

PURVIS: I'm awfully grateful to you for coming. It's impossible to have a sensible conversation with anyone in this place.

(*They move to the exterior, garden.*)

There's a path through the rhododendrons to a view of the sea.

BLAIR: Tip me off if we run into Seddon.

PURVIS: He's probably up in the bell tower collecting guano for the rose-beds.

BLAIR: Quite a decent clock up there. Reminds me a little of St Giles's in Cambridge. If it's a turret movement, I'd like to have a look at it. Did you say guano?

PURVIS: Yes. Seddon discovered a colony of bats up there the other day.

BLAIR: Bats in the belfry? Oh dear.

PURVIS: What's up?

BLAIR: Perhaps it would be better if I didn't see him. I'll drop him a note.

PURVIS: This is my favourite path. You can follow the top of the cliffs all the way round nearly to Cromer. At least you could if it wasn't for the wheelchair because of the boundary fence. Whoa!

BLAIR: Sorry.

PURVIS: Don't worry, this thing has got brakes. I don't come down this far if I'm on my own.

BLAIR: It *is* rather dangerous.

PURVIS: Not that. It's just a question of getting back up. You need strong wrists. There's a little flat bit to the side here, you could sit on that stump.

BLAIR: Fine. This is very pleasant. Do you mind if I pollute the atmosphere?

(BLAIR *lights his pipe and sucks on it.*)

Which way are we looking?

PURVIS: About north-east. That's the Dogger Bank out there, over the horizon a bit . . . the scene of the last occasion on which the Russian battle fleet engaged the British.

BLAIR: Really? When was that?

PURVIS: Ages ago. The Russian navy fired on some British trawlers.

BLAIR: Why?

PURVIS: It was a mistake. They thought the trawlers were Japanese torpedo boats.

BLAIR: In the North Sea?

PURVIS: As I said it was a mistake. I think it was a bit foggy, too.

BLAIR: It must have been.

PURVIS: It damned nearly led to war.

BLAIR: I should think it did.

PURVIS: The Tsar had to apologize to the King.

BLAIR: Oh . . .

PURVIS: Different Russia, of course.

BLAIR: (*Regretfully*) Yes, indeed.

PURVIS: They're getting there slowly.

BLAIR: Sorry?

PURVIS: Two steps forward, one and a half back. Narrowing the gap between rich and poor. That's what it's all about.

BLAIR: What?

PURVIS: Money, wealth.

BLAIR: I thought it was about freedom.

PURVIS: That's a luxury which has to be paid for. That's why the rich have always had it.

BLAIR: There's nothing in English law about what a man is worth.

PURVIS: There doesn't have to be. People only desire the freedom that is within their imagination. When you limit their horizon economically you limit their imagination. That's why the proletariat need the intellectuals—the failure of the masses to act is a failure of the mass imagination.

BLAIR: Purvis, what are you doing?

PURVIS: Just trying it out. How does it sound?

BLAIR: Like balderdash.

PURVIS: Really?

BLAIR: Doesn't it sound like balderdash to you?

PURVIS: Sometimes it does, sometimes it doesn't. That's my problem.

BLAIR: Well, we knew you had a problem, Purvis. What exactly is it?

PURVIS: Blair . . . you know how it is when you telephone someone and say, shall we meet at the Savoy Grill or Simpson's, and he says, I don't mind, make it Simpson's if you like, or do you prefer the Savoy, and you say no, that's fine, eight thirty suit you?, and he says fine, eight thirty, and you hang up—and *suddenly* you think—did he say Simpson's or the Savoy? It's gone, you know. You've lost it. Well, that's what's happened to me.

BLAIR: The Savoy or Simpson's?

PURVIS: No, it isn't *really* like that, except that when you try to remember back, both ways sound equally right. I'm going back thirty-five years now, when I was still being run by Gell, or Rashnikov. Now Gell is dead and Rashnikov is probably dead too. They set me going between them like one of those canisters in a department store, and they disappeared leaving me to go back and forth, back and forth, a canister between us and you, or us and them.

BLAIR: I didn't quite follow that last bit.

PURVIS: I remember some of it, no problem. I remember striking up a conversation with Rashnikov in one of the stacks in the Westminster Library—political economy. Or perhaps he struck up a conversation with me. I remember having a few dinners with him, meeting some of his friends, arguing long into the night about politics, and I remember finally being asked to look something up for him in our back-numbers room in Whitehall . . . You remember that basement we used to have before we had microfilm? The thing he wanted was perfectly innocuous, but by that time, of course, I knew he was supposedly on the staff of the Soviet Commercial Attaché, so the next time he asked me to look something up, something which wasn't quite so innocuous, I of course reported the whole thing to Gell who was my superior.

BLAIR: Of course.

PURVIS: Sure enough, Gell told me to pretend to swallow the bait and to await instructions.

BLAIR: Straightforward enough.

PURVIS: It wasn't. Rashnikov was playing a subtle game. He had told me to tell Gell.

BLAIR: To tell him what?

PURVIS: To tell Gell that I was being recruited by Rashnikov. So that Gell would be fooled into thinking that I was pretending to be Rashnikov's man while I was really Gell's man.

BLAIR: Looking at it from Rashnikov's point of view.

PURVIS: Yes.

BLAIR: And did you tell Gell that this was going on, that Rashnikov had told you to tell Gell?

PURVIS: Yes. I did. But . . .

BLAIR: But . . . ?

PURVIS: Well, I'm pretty sure that when I told Gell that all this was going on, I was also acting on Rashnikov's instructions.

(Pause.)

BLAIR: But, if that were so, no doubt you told Gell that it was so. No doubt you told Gell that Rashnikov had told you to tell Gell that Rashnikov had told you to tell him that you were being offered the bait.

PURVIS: That's what I can't remember. I've forgotten who is my primary employer and who my secondary. For years I've been feeding stuff in both directions, following my instructions from either side, having been instructed to do so by the other, and since each side wanted the other side to believe that I was working for it, both sides were often giving me genuine stuff to pass on to the other side . . . so the side I was actually working for became . . . well, a matter of opinion really . . . it got lost.

(Pause.)

Blair?

BLAIR: I didn't speak.

PURVIS: Well, I just carried on doing what I was told . . . and one day, not very long ago, I started thinking about my retirement. The sherry party with the Chief. The presentation clock. The London Transport senior citizen's bus pass. The little dacha on the Vistula.

BLAIR: Purvis . . . ?

PURVIS: Exactly. Hang on a sec, I thought—hello!—which—? . . . ? And blow me, I found I had forgotten.

BLAIR: But you worked for Gell. For me.

PURVIS: I worked for Rashnikov too.

BLAIR: Only because we asked you to play along.

PURVIS: He asked me to play along.

BLAIR: Let's not get into that again. You're one of us.

PURVIS: Well, I'd have to be, wouldn't I, to be of any use to him.

BLAIR: You're a church warden.

PURVIS: I thought about that but if one were covering up would one join a left-wing book club instead, for instance? Obviously not. Well, I suppose one might as a double bluff.

Or, then again, one might not, as a triple bluff. I don't think I'm going to get to the bottom of this, to my infinite regress, I mean regret.

BLAIR: This is nonsense.

PURVIS: Rashnikov said to me once, you've got to believe in the lie so strongly that even if you confessed they wouldn't believe you. Or was that Gell? One of the two.

BLAIR: All you've got to do is remember what you believed.

PURVIS: I remember I was very idealistic in those days, a real prig about Western decadence. On the other hand I was very patriotic and really didn't much care for foreigners. Obviously one scruple overcame the other, but as to whether it was the Savoy or Simpson's . . . At some point it must have ceased to matter to me. That's what I find so depressing. Did they tell you I was depressed? It's on my file here: Purvis is extremely depressed.

BLAIR: My dear chap . . .

PURVIS: Well, it *is* extremely depressing to find that one has turned into a canister. A hollow man. Like one of those Russian dolls—how appropriate! Yes, I'm like one of those sets of wooden dolls which fit into one another as they get smaller. Somewhere deep inside is the last doll, the only one which isn't hollow. At least, I suppose there is. There used to be. Perhaps I'm not even a set of dolls any more, perhaps I'm an onion. My idealism and my patriotism, folded on each other, have been peeled away leaving nothing in the middle except the lingering smell of onion.

BLAIR: Please don't cry.

PURVIS: I'm sorry. It's the onion. Oh stuff it, Blair!

BLAIR: That's the spirit. To the taxidermist with the lot of it.
(*Sniffles and pause.*)

PURVIS: Did you get the parrot by the way?

BLAIR: Oh yes. I'll let you have it back, of course.

PURVIS: I'd like you to keep it. Find a place for it in your folly.

BLAIR: Most kind of you. Well, I ought to be getting back.

PURVIS: Thank you for coming.

BLAIR: Let me give you a push up the hill.

PURVIS: No, I'll stay here for a while. I'll manage. I like looking at the sea.

BLAIR: As for that other matter . . . You never told Rashnikov
anything which Gell hadn't told you to tell him, did you?

PURVIS: I never *knew* anything which Gell hadn't told me.

BLAIR: Well, there you are.

PURVIS: And I never knew anything to tell Gell which Rashnikov
hadn't told me.

BLAIR: So the whole thing is rather academic, isn't it?

PURVIS: Thank you for understanding, Blair.

BLAIR: Cheerio, then.

PURVIS: Goodbye, Blair.

SCENE 8

Interior. Funeral service.

A choir. Then BLAIR *and* HOGBIN *conversing under the singing.*

BLAIR: I thought I might find you here, Hogbin. Still worrying?

HOGBIN: Yes, sir.

BLAIR: Too late to worry now.

HOGBIN: Too late for Purvis, you mean.

BLAIR: Yes, poor Purvis. We were all at fault, especially me.

HOGBIN: Why?

BLAIR: Well, one asks oneself . . . with the benefit of hindsight,
was Clifftops the ideal place to put a man who had a tendency
to fling himself from a great height into a watery grave. Of
course, one didn't realize it was a tendency, one thought it
was a one-off, but even so . . .

HOGBIN: You think he jumped?

BLAIR: (*Sighs.*) What now?

HOGBIN: Just asking.

BLAIR: He wheeled. He rolled.

HOGBIN: Has anyone thought of checking the brakes on that
wheelchair, sir?

BLAIR: The wheelchair has not surfaced, Hogbin. Can you think of
anyone who required Purvis's death, or even stood to gain by it?

HOGBIN: He had friends in High . . .

(*The organ drowns him momentarily.*)

BLAIR: High places?

HOGBIN: Highgate. But then one would need to know more about
that than I'm allowed to know. I don't know anything. I don't
know what I'm doing here.

BLAIR: You're checking out the mourners. That's what you're
doing here, Hogbin. You smell a mystery. You're looking for
a lead. And as is often the case after sudden death, a good place
to start looking is the funeral. Any interesting mourners?
Anybody unusual? Unexpected? Anybody who looks wrong?
Too aloof? Too engaged? Too glamorous?

HOGBIN: I spotted her. Any idea who she is?

BLAIR: None. Have you spotted Hoskins?

HOGBIN: Hoskins?

BLAIR: Third from the end with the eyelashes.

SCENE 9

Exterior. Churchyard.

The VICAR *is saying goodbye to the mourners.*

VICAR: Goodbye . . . goodbye . . . sad occasion . . . would have
been so pleased . . . goodbye . . . goodbye . . .

HOGBIN: Thank you, reverend. A beautiful service. The choristers
in glorious voice . . .

VICAR: Thank you . . . Mr . . . ?

HOGBIN: Hogbin.

VICAR: I noticed you at the back of the church, with the other
gentleman. Were you colleagues of Mr Purvis's?

HOGBIN: Mr Blair is representing the firm. I was following in
Purvis's footsteps. Perhaps I could walk along with you for a
moment?

VICAR: I'm only going to the vicarage. We can take the side gate.
We weren't quite sure what exactly Mr Purvis was doing.

HOGBIN: Quite. Incidentally, that lady in the red dress with the
fingernails . . .

VICAR: She lodged with Mr Purvis in Church Street. Quite
innocently, of course. One has to make the point nowadays,
on the rare occasions when one is able to make it. I only met
her once, a Turkish lady. She's a ballet dancer.

HOGBIN: Did you say ballet dancer or belly dancer?

VICAR: Ballet dancer. At least, I assumed she said ballet dancer.
But now I come to think of it she does seem rather the wrong
shape, and when I asked her where she danced she said
Rotherhithe. Do you think she might possibly be a belly dancer?

HOGBIN: I'd put money on it. Let me hold the gate for you.

VICAR: Would you care for a spot of cheese?

HOGBIN: Thank you very much.

SCENE 10

Interior.

VICAR: Try this one, Mr Hogbin. This is a Caerphilly.

HOGBIN: (*With mouth full*) Welsh? I was going to ask you—

VICAR: Hardly any Caerphilly made in Wales any more—mostly in Somerset. A hundred years ago every farmhouse in that part of South Wales made its own cheese. A hundred and fifty years ago—what do you think?

HOGBIN: I don't know.

VICAR: It wasn't made at all! It's a newcomer, invented for the miners, makes an ideal meal underground, doesn't dry up, very digestible, and you can make it in two or three hours using hardly more than its own weight in milk. A Cheddar needs ten times its own weight in milk.

HOGBIN: I like toasted cheese. Welsh rarebit. Incidentally, Purvis mentioned—

VICAR: Now your cheese for Welsh rarebit is red Leicester. It'll never be so fine as a Cheshire because it doesn't go on maturing the same way, it's ready at three months, good for nine, finished at a year. But it's the best English cheese for melting. The orange colour is a tint, of course—carrot juice originally, but since the eighteenth century tinted with annatto, an extract from the *Bixa orellana* tree from the West Indies. You need one dram to every two and a half gallons of milk.

HOGBIN: Amazing.

VICAR: I'm always glad to meet a man who appreciates cheese.

HOGBIN: Did Purvis appreciate cheese . . . on toast perhaps?

VICAR: One doesn't like to speak ill of the dead, but I tell you now that Purvis may have liked the odd piece of cheese but he knew nothing about it, nothing at all. Purvis was a man who would melt an Epoisses on a slice of Mother's Pride as soon as look at you.

HOGBIN: An Epoisses?

VICAR: Purvis blamed the choir, but I'm not convinced. You would have really liked my Epoisses. I brought it back from Dijon. I chose one which had been renneted with fennel. The curd is milled, salted and then refined on rye straw. As soon as the mould starts forming the cheese is soaked in Marc de Bourgogne, an eau-de-vie distilled from local grape pulp. A beautiful thing, brick red on the outside, of course.

HOGBIN: Of course.

VICAR: I put it in the vestry because it can't abide central heating. That was a Wednesday.

HOGBIN: Don't tell me Purvis . . . ?

VICAR: Cut a great wedge out of it. The electric grill was still warm. I held up Matins for ten minutes while I searched the vestry for evidence.

HOGBIN: Did you find any?

VICAR: A half-eaten rarebit in Purvis's hymn book.

HOGBIN: An unsavoury business.

SCENE 11

Interior.

BLAIR'*s chiming and striking clocks signal one o'clock. They require a spread of several seconds between them.*

PAMELA: Come and sit down, Giles. Soup's getting cold.

(BLAIR *grunts.*)

Are you going back to the office after lunch?

BLAIR: I suppose so.

PAMELA: Your funeral seems to have got you down.

BLAIR: It wasn't exactly *my* funeral.

PAMELA: Well, don't stand there brooding and looking out at the rain. What's worrying you?

BLAIR: Just thinking . . . I could have had a rustic pagoda.

(*A late clock strikes the hour.*)

The Graham bracket isn't itself, it's sickening for something. I'm pretty sure I know what it is. I'll have a look at it at the weekend. I think I've run out of copper sheeting . . . if I write down what I need could you pick some up for me from that place in Pimlico?

PAMELA: Must I?

BLAIR: It would be quite convenient for you, if you are in the
vicinity, it's practically next door to Eaton Square.

PAMELA: Proximity and convenience aren't necessarily the same
thing. Well, I'll try to fit it in.
(*Doorbell.*)
Are you expecting someone?

BLAIR: Half expecting. I'll go and see.
(*He goes through a door.*)
Don't worry Mrs Ryan, I'll get it!
(*He opens the front door.*)
Come in, Hogbin.

HOGBIN: I'm sorry to . . .

BLAIR: It's all right, I was half expecting you.

HOGBIN: Only half?

BLAIR: I was half expecting you to come here and half expecting
you to telephone me to meet you in the park.
(*He closes the door.*)
Come in.

HOGBIN: Thank you, sir.
(BLAIR *closes a second door.*)

BLAIR: An interesting little funeral.

HOGBIN: Yes. I hardly know where to begin.

BLAIR: You talked to the vicar, of course.

HOGBIN: Yes.

BLAIR: A parochial scandal, as scandals go. I don't think for a
moment that Purvis was guilty.

HOGBIN: Of what, exactly, Mr Blair?

BLAIR: Purvis wasn't your left-wing book-club type who would do
down his vicar.

HOGBIN: What type was Purvis?

BLAIR: I would say he was loyal.

HOGBIN: Did you know he had an invitation to Buckingham
Palace? To a garden party?

BLAIR: Yes. As a matter of fact I rather put it his way. The
Department was due for one and, speaking for myself, I
don't get much of a thrill any more from queueing up for a
cup of tea and a fancy cake.

HOGBIN: He was going to take his lodger. She was most

disappointed that the invitation was not transferable.

BLAIR: The belly dancer?

HOGBIN: Exactly. I said there was something funny about Purvis's letter. And that's what it was—it's all true.

BLAIR: Well, of course.

(*Door opens.*)

PAMELA: Giles—

BLAIR: Darling, this is Mr Hogbin, a policeman. My wife, Pamela . . .

HOGBIN: (*Overcome with embarrassment*) Oh . . . how do you do . . . Mrs Blair . . .

PAMELA: How do you do, Mr Hogbin—please sit down.

HOGBIN: Thank you—oh! Sorry! I'm *terribly* sorry! I sat on your parrot.

PAMELA: It's not as bad as it looks, he was already dead. Giles, do remove him. I've given up on lunch. I'm off to see Don Juan—he hasn't been getting his oats. See you later perhaps, Mr Hogbin.

(*She leaves, closing the door.*)

BLAIR: You were saying.

HOGBIN: Yes. I'm awfully sorry.

BLAIR: What about? Oh, I see, yes. Would you like to give me the parrot? Thank you.

HOGBIN: Look, sir, if everything in Purvis's letter is true . . .

BLAIR: Oh, it's true all right.

HOGBIN: It's a situation. A bit of a bombshell.

BLAIR: Oh, come now. What sort of fool do you take me for?

HOGBIN: You mean you knew it was true?

BLAIR: Of course. One mustn't get over-dramatic about these things. One must try to be civilized about them. Keep them in the family.

HOGBIN: But surely, sir . . . the head of Q6 . . . an opium den in his own house . . .

BLAIR: Oh, *that*. That's a different matter. On that subject I would be inclined to say . . . that one mustn't get over-dramatic about these things.

HOGBIN: Over-dramatic? I don't see how one can be over-dramatic. You asked me a few days ago who might want

Purvis out of the way. It looks as if the answer is your Chief.

BLAIR: Why? I don't follow.

HOGBIN: An opium den in Eaton Square?!

BLAIR: Hogbin, you're in danger of making yourself look foolish. Too many tuppenny dreadfuls in your childhood reading. You and Purvis. A shiver of delicious horror runs right through your Farnham Royal morality. Opium den! The quintessence of moral depravity combined with dubious foreign habits. The Chief stoned to the eyeballs in a brocade dressing-gown, beating a gong when he is ready for the other half. Look, I've been in his den. TV, hi-fi, books, writing desk, dead animals poking their heads out of the wall, Axminster on the floor. It's not an opium den, it's a *den*. And to him, enjoying an occasional pipe would be simply a souvenir of a Far Eastern posting. Something brought home in the baggage like a carved ivory elephant. It isn't some ghastly secret for which you drive all the way to Cromer in order to tamper with the brakes of a wheelchair. You really are absurd, Hogbin.

HOGBIN: Are you trying to tell me to forget all about it?

BLAIR: Certainly not. You must make your report and give it to your Chief.

HOGBIN: That's what I intend to do. Mr Wren may have a different attitude.

BLAIR: I doubt it. In any case, if I were you I wouldn't bother Mr Wren with your murder theory.

HOGBIN: Why?

BLAIR: Because I had another farewell letter from Purvis.

SCENE 12

Purvis letter.

PURVIS: Dear Blair. Well, goodbye again, assuming that I don't fall into a fishing boat. Please don't feel badly. Suicide is no more than a trick played on the calendar. You may like to know that whether or not I left the fold all those years ago when my intellect aspired to rule my actions, I found at the end that my remaining affinity was with the English character, a curious bloom which at Clifftops merely appears in its overblown form. Looking around at the people I've rubbed up against, I see that with the significant exception of my friend in Highgate they all inhabit a sort of Clifftops catchment area; if we lowered our entry qualifications we would be inundated. I find this reassuring. I realize I am where I belong, at last, even though, in common with all the other inmates, I have the impression that I am here by mistake while understanding perfectly why everybody else should be here. In this respect Clifftops has an effect precisely opposite to being in a Marxist discussion group. I'm grateful to you for our chat. It led me to think about Gell and the way he used to wear hunting pink to the office in the season, and the way he used to complain about not being able to eat asparagus without dripping the butter after the first time he broke his neck, and I thought I *couldn't* have lied to Gell, not to Gell, not for a mere conviction. The man was so much himself that one would have been betraying him instead of the system. I hope I'm right, though I would settle for *knowing* that I'm wrong. Oddly enough, my friend from Highgate came to visit me, or rather to meet me at the boundary of the fence, and he tells me that the reason Rashnikov disappeared was that he had been recalled under suspicion of having been duped by Gell and me. Rashnikov said there was a logical reason why this should have been the impression given, but unfortunately he died of a brainstorm while trying to work it out. You might say that the same happened to me. My regards to your good lady. Yours sincerely, Rupert Purvis.

SCENE 13

Interior.
A cosy atmosphere. All three men, the CHIEF, WREN *and* BLAIR *are smoking pipes.*

BLAIR: There is something else, sir.

CHIEF: Yes. This dog. Now let's be reasonable about this, Wren.
   Quite unexpectedly the bargee has sent in a bill for three
   hundred pounds, claiming that his wretched dog was a

member of the Kennel Club and runner up in his class in the South of England Show. Is that correct, Blair?

BLAIR: Quite correct, sir, but . . .

WREN: I don't dispute any of that. I'm only saying that the dog was killed, in effect, by Q6, not by Q9.

CHIEF: We killed him but your man Hogbin filed the report confirming the dog's death as an incident during *his own case*. All the paper work is Q9, and, crucially, the bill for the dog was sent to Q9.

WREN: Look, I'm good for fifty if it helps. I'll put it in under dog-handling. I suppose Hogbin must have handled the dog.

CHIEF: Let's go halves. One-fifty each.

BLAIR: Excuse me, sir. Why can't we use Purvis's money? After all, he killed the dog.

CHIEF: Purvis's money?

BLAIR: Highgate kept giving him odd sums for film and bus fares, which we made him accept to preserve his credibility, and which Highgate made him declare for the same reason. There must be several hundred pounds by now, lying in some account somewhere.

CHIEF: Excellent. Well thought, Blair. Would you care for a pipe?

BLAIR: No thank you, sir. I'll stick to the old briar.

CHIEF: How is your pipe, Wren? Ready for another?

WREN: No thanks, it's bubbling along very nicely.

CHIEF: Jolly good. Well, that's that.

BLAIR: Actually it wasn't about the dog. It was about the opium. And your . . . your private life generally. Purvis said it was all over Highgate. I'd like to know how it got there.

CHIEF: Purvis took it up there. I put it into his Highgate package a couple of months ago. He was coming up for retirement and I thought that if they thought they had something on me I might get a tickle as his replacement . . . Nothing doing so far. Perhaps it's just as well. These double and triple bluffs can get to be a bit of a headache. It got to be a bit of a headache for Purvis.

WREN: How did it work?

(*The* CHIEF *speaks, slowly, deliberately, reflectively. The pauses filled with the gentle bubbling of his pipe.*)

CHIEF: Well, in the beginning the idea was that if they thought
that we knew that they thought Purvis was their
man . . . they would assume that the information we gave
Purvis to give to them . . . would be information designed to
mislead . . . so they would take that into account . . . and,
thus, if we told Purvis to tell them that we were going to do
something . . . they would draw the conclusion that we were
not going to do it . . . but as we were on to that, we naturally
were giving Purvis genuine information to give to them,
knowing that they would be drawing the wrong conclusions
from it . . . This is where it gets tricky . . . because if they
kept drawing these wrong conclusions while the other thing
kept happening . . . they would realize that we had got to
Purvis first after all . . . So to keep Purvis in the game we
would have to *not* do some of the things which Purvis told
them we *would* be doing, even though our first reason for
telling Purvis was that we did intend to do them . . . In
other words . . . in order to keep fooling the Russians, we
had to keep doing the opposite of what we really wanted to
do . . . Now this is where it gets *extremely* tricky . . .
Obviously we couldn't keep doing the opposite of what we
wished to do simply to keep Purvis in the game . . . so we
frequently had to give Purvis the wrong information from
which the Russians would draw the right conclusion, which
enabled us to do what we wished to do, although the
Russians, thanks to Purvis, knew we were going to do
it . . . In other words, Purvis was acting, in effect, as a
genuine Russian spy in order to maintain his usefulness as a
bogus Russian spy . . . The only reason why this wasn't
entirely disastrous for us was that, of course, during the
whole of this time, the Russians, believing us to believe that
Purvis was in their confidence, had been giving Purvis
information designed to mislead *us* . . . and in order to
maintain Purvis's credibility they have been forced to do
some of the things which they told Purvis they *would* do,
although their first reason for telling him was that they didn't
wish to do them.
(*Pause.*)
In other words, if Purvis's mother had got kicked by a horse

things would be more or less exactly as they are now.
(*Pause.*)
If I were Purvis I'd drown myself.

PURVIS: PS—Incidentally, Dr Seddon thinks that you ought to be in here yourself, but I'll leave you to field that one.

IN THE NATIVE STATE

FLORA CREWE, aged thirty-five
NIRAD DAS, aged thirty-three
MRS SWAN, aged eighty-three
ANISH DAS, aged forty
DAVID DURANCE, about thirty, officer class
NAZRUL, young or middle-aged, a Muslim, speaks no
English
PIKE, age not crucial (thirty-five to fifty-five), educated
American, Southern accent
COOMARASWAMI, middle-aged, fat, cheerful; Indian accent
RESIDENT, aged forty-plus, Winchester and Cambridge
RAJAH, aged late fifties, educated at Harrow
NELL (Mrs Swan), aged twenty-three; middle-class
bluestocking
FRANCIS, say thirty-three, Indian Civil Service
EMILY EDEN (a real person), was forty-two in 1839

In addition
Indian QUESTIONER
Club SERVANT
English MAN and WOMAN at the Club

In the Native State was first transmitted on BBC Radio 3 on 21 April 1991. The cast was as follows:

FLORA CREWE	Felicity Kendal
NIRAD DAS	Sam Dastor
MRS SWAN	Peggy Ashcroft
ANISH DAS	Lyndam Gregory
NELL	Emma Gregory
DAVID DURANCE	Simon Treves
NAZRUL	Amerjit Deu
PIKE	William Hootkins
COOMARASWAMI	Renu Setnar
RESIDENT	Brett Usher
RAJAH	Saeed Jaffrey
FRANCIS/Englishman	Mark Straker
EMILY EDEN/Englishwoman	Auriol Smith
Directed by John Tydeman	

The play is set in two places and periods: India in 1930, and England in the present day.

We come to learn that Nirad Das was educated initially at a 'vernacular school', unlike Anish Das, who went to a 'convent school'. The significance of this is that Nirad speaks English with a stronger Indian accent than Anish.

The verandah of a guesthouse. Jummapur would be a considerable
town, but the guesthouse is conceived as being set somewhat on its
own; the ambient sound would not be urban. There are references to
monkeys, parrots, dogs, chickens. The surround would be sandy, not
metalled.

FLORA: (*Interior voice*)

    'Yes, I am in heat like a bride in a bath,
    without secrets, soaked in heated air
    that liquifies to the touch and floods,
    shortening the breath, yes,
    I am discovered, heat has found me out,
    a stain that stops at nothing,
    not the squeezed gates or soft gutters,
    it brims as I shift,
    it webs my fingers round my pen,
    yes, think of a woman in a blue dress
    sat on a straight-backed chair at a plain table
    on the verandah of a guesthouse,
    writing about the weather.
    Or think, if you prefer, of bitches,
    cats, goats, monkeys at it like knives
    in the jacaranda – '

NIRAD DAS: Do you want me to stop, Miss Crewe?

FLORA: What?

DAS: Would you like to rest?

FLORA: No, I don't want to rest. Do you?

DAS: Not at all, but you crossed your legs, and I thought
    perhaps –

FLORA: Oh! I'm so sorry! So I did. There. Is that how I was?

DAS: You are patient with me. I think your nature is very kind.

FLORA: Do you think so, Mr Das?

DAS: I am sure of it. May I ask you a personal question?

FLORA: That *is* a personal question.

DAS: Oh, my goodness, is it?

FLORA: I always think so. It always feels like one. *Carte blanche* is what you're asking, Mr Das. Am I to lay myself bare before you?

DAS: (*Panicking slightly*) My question was only about your poem!

FLORA: At least you knew it was personal.

DAS: I will not ask it now, of course.

FLORA: On that understanding I will answer it. My poem is about heat.

DAS: Oh. Thank you.

FLORA: I resume my pose. Pen to paper. Legs uncrossed. You know, you are the first man to paint my toenails.

DAS: Actually, I am occupied in the folds of your skirt.

FLORA: Ah. In that you are not the first.

DAS: You have been painted before? But of course you have! Many times, I expect!

FLORA: You know, Mr Das, your nature is much kinder than mine.

SCENE TWO: ENGLAND

Interior. We come to learn that Mrs Swan is serving tea (on a brass table-top) in a bungalow in Shepperton, a garden's length from the (quiet) road.

MRS SWAN: Do you think you take after your father?

ANISH: I don't know. I would like to think so. But my father was a man who suffered for his beliefs, and I have never had to do that, so . . .

MRS SWAN: I meant being a painter. You are a painter like your father.

ANISH: Oh . . . yes. Yes, I am a painter like my father. Though not at all like my father, of course.

MRS SWAN: Your father was an Indian painter, you mean?

ANISH: An Indian painter? Well, I'm as Indian as he was. But yes. I suppose I am not a particularly *Indian* painter . . . not an Indian painter *particularly*, or rather . . .

MRS SWAN: Not particularly an Indian painter.

ANISH: Yes. But then, nor was he. Apart from being Indian.

MRS SWAN: As you are.

ANISH: Yes.

MRS SWAN: (*Pouring tea*) Though you are not at all like him.

ANISH: No. Yes. Perhaps if you had seen my work . . . (*Accepting the teacup.*) Oh, thank you.

MRS SWAN: Of course, *you* are a successful painter.

ANISH: I didn't mean that, Mrs Swan . . . only that my father was a quite different kind of artist, a portrait painter, as you know . . .

MRS SWAN: I can't say I do, Mr Das. Until I received your letter your father was unknown to me. In fact, the attribution 'unknown Indian artist' summed up the situation exactly, if indeed it was your father who made the portrait of my sister.

ANISH: Oh, the portrait is certainly my father's work, Mrs Swan! And I have brought the evidence to show you! I have been in such a state! I have done no work for a week!

You simply cannot imagine my feelings when I saw the book in the shop window – my excitement! You see, I carry my copy everywhere.

MRS SWAN: Well, I hope there'll be lots like *you*, Mr Das.

ANISH: There will be no one like me, Mrs Swan! It was not the book, of course, but the painting on the jacket and the same on the frontispiece inside! My father was not 'unknown' in Jummapur. Surely the publishers or somebody . . .

MRS SWAN: They made inquiries by letter, but it was all sixty years ago.

ANISH: Yes. If only my father could have known that one day his portrait of Flora Crewe would . . .

MRS SWAN: By the way, what *were* your father's beliefs?

ANISH: (*Surprised*) Why . . . we are Hindu . . .

MRS SWAN: You said he had suffered for his beliefs.

ANISH: Oh. I meant his opinions. For which he suffered imprisonment.

MRS SWAN: Who put him in prison?

ANISH: You did.

MRS SWAN: I did?

ANISH: I mean, the British.

MRS SWAN: Oh, I see. *We* did. But how did we know what his opinions were?

ANISH: Well . . . (*Uncertainly.*) I suppose he took part in various actions . . .

MRS SWAN: Then he was imprisoned for his actions not his opinions, Mr Das, and obviously deserved what he got. Will you have a slice of cake?

ANISH: Thank you.

MRS SWAN: Victoria sponge or Battenberg?

ANISH: Oh . . .

MRS SWAN: The sponge is my own, the raspberry jam too.

ANISH: I would love some.

(*A clock chimes in the room.*)

MRS SWAN: Ignore it. The clock has decided to be merely decorative. It chimes at random. There we are, then . . .

ANISH: Thank you.

MRS SWAN: But all that must have been before you were born
. . . Independence . . .

ANISH: Oh, yes, long before. I was the child of my father's
second marriage. I was born in '49, and these events took
place in Jummapur in 1930.

MRS SWAN: 1930! But that was when Flora was in Jummapur!

ANISH: Yes, I know. That is why I am here.

SCENE THREE: INDIA

On the verandah.

FLORA: Mr Das, I am considering whether to ask you a delicate question, as between friends and artists.

DAS: Oh, Miss Crewe, I am transported beyond my most fantastical hopes of our fellowship! This is a red-letter day without dispute!

FLORA: If you are going to be so Indian I shan't ask it.

DAS: But I cannot be less Indian than I am.

FLORA: You could if you tried. I'm not sure I'm going to ask you now.

DAS: Then you need not, dear Miss Crewe! You considered. The unasked, the almost asked question, united us for a moment in its intimacy, we came together in your mind like a spark in a vacuum glass, and the redness of the day's letter will not be denied.

FLORA: You are still doing it, Mr Das.

DAS: You wish me to be less Indian?

FLORA: I did say that but I think what I meant was for you to be *more* Indian, or at any rate *Indian*, not Englished-up and all over me like a labrador and knocking things off tables with your tail – so *waggish* of you, Mr Das, to compare my mind to a vacuum. You only do it with us. I don't believe that left to yourself you can't have an ordinary conversation without jumping backwards through hoops of delight, *with* whoops of delight, I think I mean; actually, I do know what I mean, I want you to be with me as you would be if *I* were Indian.

DAS: An Indian Miss Crewe! Oh dear, that is a mental construction which has no counterpart in the material world.

FLORA: A *unicorn* is a mental construction which has no counterpart in the material world but you can imagine it.

DAS: You can imagine it but you cannot mount it.

FLORA: Imagining it was all I was asking in my case.

DAS: (*Terribly discomfited*) Oh! Oh, my gracious! I had no
intention – I assure you –

FLORA: (*Amused*) No, no, you cannot unwag your very best
wag. You cleared the table, the bric-à-brac is on the
parquet – the specimen vase, the snuff box, the souvenir of
Broadstairs – (*But she has misjudged.*)

DAS: (*Anguished*) You are cruel to me, Miss Crewe!

FLORA: (*Instantly repentant*) Oh! I'm so sorry. I didn't want to
be. It's my nature. Please come out from behind your easel
– look at me.

DAS: May we fall silent, please. I prefer to work in silence.

FLORA: I've spoiled everything. I'm very sorry.

DAS: The shadow has moved. I must correct it.

FLORA: Yes, it has moved. It cannot be corrected. We must wait
for tomorrow. I'm so sorry.

SCENE FOUR: ENGLAND

ANISH: When my father met Flora Crewe he had been a
  widower for several years, although he was still quite a
  young man, a year or two younger than her, yes . . . the
  beginning of the Hot Weather in 1930: he would have been
  not yet thirty-four. He had lost his wife to cholera and he
  was childless. I knew nothing of my father's life before
  Swaraj. The British Empire was prehistory to me. By the
  time I was old enough to be curious, my father was over
  sixty, an old gentleman who spoke very little except when
  he sometimes read aloud to me. I say read to me but really
  he read to himself, with me in attendance. He liked to read
  in English. Robert Browning, Tennyson, Macaulay's *Lays
  of Ancient Rome*, and Dickens, of course . . .

MRS SWAN: How surprising.

ANISH: Oh, yes. (*Meaning 'no'.*) He went from a vernacular
  school to Elphinstone College in Bombay, and you only
  have to look at Elphinstone College to know it was built to
  give us a proper British education.

MRS SWAN: I really meant, how surprising in view of his
  'opinions'. But I spoke without thinking. Your father
  resented the British and loved English literature, which was
  prefectly consistent of him, and I have interrupted you.
  You haven't mentioned your mother.

ANISH: My mother speaks no English. She is from a village,
  peasant farmers, no, plot-holders. She was born in the year
  Flora Crewe came to Jummapur, and she married when she
  was sixteen. It was not from her that I learned . . .
  that . . .

MRS SWAN: That . . . ?

ANISH: That my father was a thorn in the flesh of the British;
  and was still remembered for it – I might say, is honoured
  for it.

MRS SWAN: By whom?

ANISH: By his son.

MRS SWAN: It does you credit.

ANISH: In Bengal and the United Provinces, all over British India, of course, there were thousands of people who did as much and more, and went to gaol, but in Jummapur we were 'loyal', as you would say, we had been loyal to the British right through the First War of Independence.

MRS SWAN: The . . . ? What war was that?

ANISH: The Rising of 1857.

MRS SWAN: Oh, you mean the Mutiny. *What* did you call it?

ANISH: Dear Mrs Swan, imperial history is only the view from . . . no, no – please let us not argue. I promise you I didn't come to give you a history lesson.

MRS SWAN: You seem ill-equipped to do so. We were your Romans, you know. We might have been your Normans.

ANISH: And did you expect us to be grateful?

MRS SWAN: That's neither here nor there. I don't suppose I'd have been grateful if a lot of Romans turned up and started laying down the law and the language and telling us we were all one country now, so Wessex had to stop fighting Mercia, and so forth. 'What a cheek,' is probably what I would have thought. 'Go away, and take your roads and your baths with you.' It doesn't matter what I would have thought. It's what I think now that matters. You speak English better than most young people I meet. Did you go to school here?

ANISH: No, I went to a convent school in . . . You are spreading a net for me, Mrs Swan.

MRS SWAN: What net would that be? Have some more cake.

ANISH: Mrs Swan, you are a very wicked woman. You advance a preposterous argument and try to fill my mouth with cake so I cannot answer you. I will resist you and your cake. *We* were the Romans! We were up to date when you were a backward nation. The foreigners who invaded *you* found a third-world country! Even when you discovered India in the age of Shakespeare, we already had our Shakespeares. And our science, architecture, our literature and art, we had a culture older and more splendid, we were rich! After all, that's why you came. (*But he has misjudged.*)

MRS SWAN: (*Angrily*) We made you a proper country! And when
we left you fell straight to pieces like Humpty Dumpty!
Look at the map! You should feel nothing but shame!

ANISH: Oh, yes . . . I am ashamed. I am a guest in your house
and I have been . . .

MRS SWAN: . . . no, only provocative. We will change the
subject.

ANISH: I'm sorry.

(*The clock chimes.*)

MRS SWAN: That clock has gone quite mad. It has gained
twenty minutes since this morning . . . There seems no
point in putting it back.

ANISH: No, we cannot put it back. I'm so sorry.

SCENE FIVE: INDIA

FLORA: While having tiffin on the verandah of my bungalow I
spilled kedgeree on my dungarees and had to go to the
gymkhana in my pyjamas looking like a coolie.

DAS: I was buying chutney in the bazaar when a thug who had
escaped from the choky ran amuck and killed a box-wallah
for his loot, creating a hullabaloo and landing himself in the
mulligatawny.

FLORA: I went doolally at the durbar and was sent back to
Blighty in a dooley feeling rather dikki with a cup of char
and a chit for a chotapeg.

DAS: Yes, and the burra sahib who looked so pukka in his topi
sent a coolie to the memsahib –

FLORA: No, no. You can't have memsahib *and* sahib, that's
cheating – and anyway, I've already said coolie.

DAS: I concede, Miss Crewe. You are the Hobson-Jobson
champion!

FLORA: You are chivalrous, Mr Das. So I'll confess I had help. I
found a whole list of Anglo-Indian words in my bedside
drawer, for the benefit of travellers.

DAS: But I know both languages, so you still win on handicap.

FLORA: Where did you learn everything, Mr Das?

DAS: From books. I like Dickens and Browning and
Shakespeare of course – but my favourite is Agatha
Christie! *The Mysterious Affair at Styles*! Oh, the woman is a
genius! But I would like to write like Macaulay.

FLORA: Oh dear.

DAS: I have to thank Lord Macaulay for English, you know. It
was his idea when he was in the government of India that
English should be taught to us all. He wanted to supply the
East India Company with clerks, but he was sowing
dragon's teeth. Instead of babus he produced lawyers,
journalists, civil servants – he produced Gandhi! We have
so many, many languages, you know, that English is the

only language the nationalists can communicate in! That is a very good joke on Macaulay, don't you think?

FLORA: Are *you* a nationalist, Mr Das?

DAS: Ah, that is a very interesting question! But we shouldn't have stopped. It's getting late for you. I must work more quickly.

FLORA: It's only half-past ten.

DAS: No, it's already April, and that is becoming late.

FLORA: Yes, it seems hotter than ever. Would you like some more lemonade?

DAS: No, thank you, no lemonade. Miss Crewe, you haven't looked at my painting yet.

FLORA: No. Not yet. I never look. Do you mind?

DAS: No.

FLORA: You do really. But I once asked a painter, 'Can I look?' and he said, 'Why? When I paint a table I don't have to show it to the table.'

DAS: I said you had been painted before.

FLORA: Only once.

DAS: A portrait?

FLORA: Not in the way you mean. It was a nude.

DAS: Oh.

FLORA: Unusually. He painted his friends clothed. For nudes he used models. I believe I was his friend. But perhaps not. Perhaps a used model only. It hardly matters. He was dead so soon afterwards. He was not so kind to me as you are. I had to lie with my shoulders flat but my hips twisted towards the canvas; I could hardly move afterwards.

DAS: Do you have the painting?

FLORA: No.

DAS: Where is it?

FLORA: Nowhere. A man I thought I might marry destroyed it. So after that, I didn't want to be painted again.

DAS: Oh . . .

FLORA: But luckily I forgot that, when you asked me. I must have got over it without realizing. My goodness, what a red-letter day you are having. There's a man on a horse.

DURANCE: (*Off*) Good morning! Miss Crewe, I think!

FLORA: Yes, good morning! (*Aside to* DAS.) Do you know him?
  (*To* DURANCE.) How do you do!
DAS: He is the Assistant.
DURANCE: (*Off*) May I get down a moment?
FLORA: Of course. What a beautiful animal! (*Aside to* DAS.)
  Assistant what?
DAS: Captain Durance!
DURANCE: Thank you!
FLORA: Come on up, do join us.
  (*We have heard the horse walking forward, perhaps snorting,
  and* DURANCE *dismounting, and now coming up the three or
  four wooden steps on to the verandah.*)
DURANCE: (*Arriving*) Oh, it's Mr Das, isn't it?
DAS: Good morning, sir. But we have never met.
DURANCE: Oh, but I know you. And Miss Crewe, your fame
  precedes you.
FLORA: Thank you . . . but . . .
DURANCE: I'm from the Residency. David Durance.
FLORA: How do you do?
DURANCE: Oh, but look here – I'm interrupting the artist.
FLORA: We had stopped.
DURANCE: May one look? Oh, I say! Coming along jolly well!
  Don't you think so, Miss Crewe?
DAS: I must be going. I have overstayed my time today.
FLORA: But we'll continue tomorrow?
DAS: Yes. Perhaps a little earlier if it suits you. I will leave
  everything just inside the door, if that is all right . . . and
  the easel . . . (DAS *is moving the objects, bumping them down
  in the interior.*)
FLORA: Yes, of course. Why don't you leave the canvas too? It
  will be quite safe.
DAS: I . . . yes . . . I have a drape for it. Thank you. There.
FLORA: Like shutting up the parrot for the night.
DAS: There we are. Thank you for the lemonade, Miss Crewe.
  An absolute treat. I promise you! Goodbye, sir – and –
  yes – and until tomorrow . . . (*He goes down the steps to the
  outside and mounts a bicycle and pedals away.*)
FLORA: Yes . . . goodbye! (*To* DURANCE.) I'll put my shoes on.

Sorry about my toes, but I like to wriggle them when I'm working.

DURANCE: I'll only stay a moment. My chief asked me to look in. Just to make sure there's nothing we can do for you.

FLORA: There's a servant who seems to come with the guesthouse, though he has a way of disappearing, but would you like some tea?

DURANCE: No, nothing for me. Really. We might have found you more comfortable quarters, you know, not quite so in-the-town.

FLORA: How did you know I was here?

DURANCE: Now there's a point. Usually we know of arrivals because the first thing they do is drop in a card, but in your case . . . rumours in the bazaar, so to speak. Are you an old hand here, Miss Crewe?

FLORA: No, I've never been to India before. I came up from Bombay just a few days ago.

DURANCE: But you have friends here, perhaps?

FLORA: No. I got on a boat and I came, knowing no one. I have friends in England who have friends here. Actually, one friend.

DURANCE: In Jummapur, this friend?

FLORA: No – the *friend* – my friend – is in London, of course; *his* friends are in different places in Rajputana, and I will also be going to Delhi and then up to the Punjab, I hope.

DURANCE: Now I see. And your friend in London has friends in Jummapur?

FLORA: Yes.

DURANCE: Like Mr Das?

FLORA: No. Are you a policeman of some kind, Mr Durance?

DURANCE: Me? No. I'm sorry if I sound like one.

FLORA: Well, you do a bit. I'm travelling with letters of introduction from Mr Joshua Chamberlain to a number of social clubs and literary societies. I speak on the subject of 'Literary Life in London', in return for board and lodging . . . So you see I couldn't have taken advantage of your kindness without giving offence to my hosts.

DURANCE: The game is different here. By putting up at the Residency you would have gained respect, not lost it.

FLORA: Thank you, but what about *self* respect?

DURANCE: Well . . . as long as all is well. So you are following in Chamberlain's footsteps. All is explained.

FLORA: I don't think *I* explained it. But yes, I am. He spoke in Jummapur three years ago, on the subject of Empire.

DURANCE: Yes. Is he a good friend?

FLORA: Yes.

DURANCE: Did you know he was some sort of Communist?

FLORA: I thought he might be. He stood twice for Parliament as the Communist candidate.

DURANCE: (*Unoffended, pleasant as before*) I amuse you. That's all right, amusing our distinguished visitors is among my duties.

FLORA: Well, don't be so stuffy. And call again if you like.

DURANCE: Thank you. How long will you be with us?

FLORA: I'm expected in Jaipur but they don't mind when I come.

DURANCE: I'm sure you'll have a marvellous time. There are wonderful things to see. Meanwhile, please consider yourself an honorary member of the Club – mention my name, but I'll put you in the book.

FLORA: Thank you.

DURANCE: Well . . .

FLORA: I wish I had a lump of sugar for your horse. Next time.

DURANCE: He's my main indulgence. I wish I'd been here when a good horse went with the job.

FLORA: Yes . . . what *is* your job? You mentioned your chief.

DURANCE: The Resident. He represents the government here.

FLORA: The British government?

DURANCE: Delhi. The Viceroy, in fact. Jummapur is not British India . . . you understand that?

FLORA: Yes . . . but it's all the Empire, isn't it?

DURANCE: Oh, yes. Absolutely. But there's about five hundred rajahs and maharajahs and nabobs and so on who run bits of it, well, nearly half of it actually, by treaty. And we're here to make sure they don't get up to mischief.

FLORA: I knew you were a kind of policeman.

DURANCE: (*Laughs*) Miss Crewe, would you have dinner with us while you are here?

FLORA: With you and your wife, do you mean?

DURANCE: No . . . at the Club. Us. With me. I don't run to a wife, I'm afraid. But do come. We're a reasonably civilized lot, and there's usually dancing on Saturdays; only a gramophone but lots of fun.

FLORA: I'd love to. On Saturday, then.

DURANCE: Oh . . . splendid! I'll come by. (*He mounts his horse.*)

FLORA: I haven't got a horse, you know.

DURANCE: We have a Daimler at the Residency. I'll see if I can wangle it. Pick you up about eight?

FLORA: Yes.

DURANCE: We don't dress, normally, except on dress nights. (*Laughs at himself.*) Obviously.

FLORA: I'll be ready.

DURANCE: Jolly good.

FLORA: Goodbye.

DURANCE: Goodbye.

FLORA: (*Calling out*) Wangle the Daimler!

SCENE SIX: ENGLAND

ANISH: I apologize if I was rude. *You* didn't put my father in gaol, after all.

MRS SWAN: Not in any sense. Jummapur was a native state, so your father was put in gaol by his own people.

ANISH: (*Cautiously*) Well . . .

MRS SWAN: (*Firmly*) Whatever your father may have done, the Resident would have had no authority to imprison an Indian. The Rajah of Jummapur had his own justice.

ANISH: Even so, you – (*corrects himself*) the British . . .

MRS SWAN: Oh, I'm not saying we wouldn't have boxed his ears and sent him packing if he forgot which side his bread was buttered, but facts are facts. The Rajah put your father in the choky. How long for, by the way?

ANISH: Six months, actually.

MRS SWAN: There you are. In Bengal or the UP he would have got a year at least. After the war it may have been different. With Independence round the corner, people were queuing up to go to prison; it was their ticket to the show. They'd do their bit of civil disobedience and hop into the paddy-wagon thoroughly pleased with themselves. Francis – that's my husband – would let them off with a small fine if he thought they were Johnny-come-latelies, and they'd be furious. That was when Francis had his District. We were right up near Nepal . . .

ANISH: Yes, I noticed your . . .

MRS SWAN: Of course you did. In India we had pictures of coaching inns and fox hunting, and chintz covers from Liberty's and all sorts of knick-knackery from home . . . and now I've landed up in Shepperton I've got elephants and prayer-wheels cluttering up the window ledges, and the tea table is Nepalese brass. One could make a comment about human nature, but have a slice of Battenberg instead.

ANISH: Thank you.

MRS SWAN: I got it specially, an artistic sort of cake, I always think. What kind of paintings are they, these paintings that are not like your father's? Describe your latest. Like the cake?

ANISH: (*Eating*) Delicious. Thank you.

MRS SWAN: No, are they like the cake?

ANISH: Oh. No. They are all . . . like each other really. I can't *describe* them.

MRS SWAN: Indescribable, then. But modern, I suppose?

ANISH: (*Becoming slightly impatient*) It's not *my* paintings I have come about.

MRS SWAN: No, of course. You recognized your father's work in the window of a bookshop. Still, he might have been more pleased to be in one art gallery than in a hundred bookshops.

ANISH: Perhaps not. I'm sure my father never had a single one of his paintings reproduced, and that is an extraordinary pleasure for an artist. I know! The painting under one's hand is everything, of course . . . unique. But replication! *That* is popularity! If we are allowed a little worldly pride, put us on thousands and thousands of book jackets – on calendars – biscuit tins!

MRS SWAN: Well, it's only *three* thousand of the *Selected Letters*, but America is still to come. Mr Pike thinks Flora's letters will do very well in America, and he should know, being an American himself.

ANISH: Mr Pike?

MRS SWAN: The editor. He put the book together. A serious man, Mr Pike, with a surprising *Gone with the Wind* sort of accent.

ANISH: Editor? Oh, yes. So he is. 'Edited with an introduction by Eldon Cooper Pike.' What does it mean – edited – exactly? Are there more letters that are not in the book?

MRS SWAN: Naturally. *Selected Letters of Flora Crewe*, that is what it means. And then there's the footnotes. Mr Pike did those too.

ANISH: Oh yes . . . the footnotes.

MRS SWAN: Far too much of a good thing, the footnotes, in my opinion; to be constantly interrupted in a Southern drawl

by someone telling you things you already know or don't
need to know at that moment. I hear Mr Pike's voice every
time I go to the bits at the bottom of the page. He teaches
Flora Crewe at a university in Maryland. It makes her
sound like a subject, doesn't it? Like biology, or in her
case, botany. Flora is widely taught in America. I have
been written to, even visited, and on one occasion
telephoned, by young women doing Flora Crewe.

ANISH: Always young women?

MRS SWAN: Almost always, yes. She has become quite a
heroine. Which she always was to me. I was only five when
Mother died, so it was Flora who . . . oh dear, I'm going to
need a hanky.

ANISH: Oh, I say! I'm sorry if I –

MRS SWAN: (*Snuffling*) Found it. (*She blows her nose.*) It makes
me so cross that she missed it all, the *Collected Poems*, and
now the *Letters*, with her name all over the place and
students and professors so *interested* and so sweet about her
poetry. Nobody gave tuppence about her while she was
alive except to get her knickers off. Never mind, how is
your tea?

ANISH: Erm . . . sorry. Very nice, very nice tea.

MRS SWAN: I'll have to go and repair myself. Yes, I like it well
enough but I can't get the tea here to taste as it should. I
expect it's the water. A reservoir near Staines won't have
the makings of a good cup of tea compared to the water we
got in the Hills. It came straight off the Himalayas. (*With
the help of a stick she has walked to the door and closed it
behind her.*)

SCENE SEVEN: INDIA

FLORA: (*Interior voice*)
    'Yes, I am in heat like a corpse in a ditch,
    my skin stained and porous as a photograph
    under a magnifying lens that shows each hair
    a lily stem straggling out of a poisoned swamp.
    Heat has had its way with me,
    yes, I know this ditch, I have been left for dead before,
    my lips gone slack and the wild iris
    flickers in the drooling cavity, insects
    crawl like tears from behind my eyes – '
    Oh, fiddlesticks! May we stop for a moment. (*She gets up.*)
    I'm sticking to myself.

DAS: Of course! Forgive me!

FLORA: You musn't take responsibility for the climate too, Mr
    Das.

DAS: No, I . . .

FLORA: No, I'm sorry. I'm bad-tempered. Should we have some
    tea? I wouldn't mind something to eat too. (*Calls out.*)
    Nazrul! Am I saying his name right? There's a jar of duck
    pâté in the refrigerator . . .
    (NAZRUL *is a male servant. He speaks Urdu.*)
    Oh, Nazrul . . . char and . . .

NAZRUL: (*In Urdu*) Yes, madam, I will bring tea
    immediately . . .

FLORA: . . . bread . . . and in the fridge, no, don't go, listen to
    me –

DAS: Would you allow me, please?
    (DAS *and* NAZRUL *speak in Urdu.* DAS *orders bread and butter
    and the duck pâté from the fridge. But* NAZRUL *has dramatic
    and tragic disclosures to make. Thieves have stolen the pâté.*
    DAS *berates him.*)

FLORA: (*Over the conversation*) . . . a jar with a picture of a
    duck . . .

(NAZRUL *is promising to fetch bread and butter and cake, and he leaves.*)

What was all that?

DAS: He will bring tea, and bread and butter and cake. The pâté has been taken by robbers.

FLORA: What?

DAS: (*Gravely*) Just so, I'm afraid.

FLORA: But the fridge is padlocked. Mr Coomaraswami pointed it out to me particularly.

DAS: Where do you keep the key?

FLORA: Nazrul keeps it, of course.

DAS: Ah well . . . the whole thing is a great mystery.

(FLORA *splutters into laughter and* DAS *joins in.*)

FLORA: But surely, isn't it against his religion?

DAS: Oh, certainly. I should say so. Not that I'm saying Nazrul stole the pâté, but stealing would be against his religion, undoubtedly.

FLORA: I don't mean stealing, I mean the pork.

DAS: But I thought you said it was duck.

FLORA: One must read the small print, Mr Das. 'Duck pâté' in large letters, 'with pork' in small letters. It's normal commercial practice.

DAS: Yes, I see.

FLORA: We must hope he only got the duck part . . .

DAS: That is your true nature speaking, Miss Crewe!

FLORA: . . . though of course, if they use one pig for every duck, Nazrul will have been lucky to get any duck at all.

DAS: The truth will never be known, only to God, who is merciful.

FLORA: Yes. Which God do you mean?

DAS: Yours if you wish, by all means.

FLORA: Now, Mr Das, there is such a thing as being too polite. Yours was here first.

DAS: Oh, but we Hindus can afford to be generous; we have gods to spare, one for every occasion. And Krishna said, 'Whichever god a man worships, it is I who answer the prayer.'

FLORA: I wasn't sure whether Krishna was a god or a person.

DAS: Oh, he was most certainly a god, one of the ten
　　incarnations of Vishnu, and a favourite subject of the old
　　Rajasthani painters. He had a great love affair, you see,
　　with a married lady, Radha, who was the most beautiful of
　　the herdswomen. Radha fell passionately in love with
　　Krishna and she would often escape from her husband to
　　meet him in secret.

FLORA: I think that's what confused me. Come and sit down,
　　Mr Das. Take the cane chair. I'll keep mine for posture.

DAS: (*Sitting*) Thank you.

FLORA: I've been looking at temples with Mr Coomaraswami.

DAS: Yes. Do you find them interesting?

FLORA: I like some of the sculptures. The women have such
　　serene faces. I mean, the goddesses.

DAS: Yes, they are beautiful.

FLORA: Breasts like melons, and baby-bearing hips. You must
　　think me ill-favoured.

DAS: No. My wife was slightly built.

FLORA: Oh . . .
　　(NAZRUL *arrives with a noisy tray.*)
　　Thank you, Nazrul. Two kinds of cake!
　　(NAZRUL *leaves, saying in Urdu that he will return with bread
　　and butter.*)

DAS: He will return with bread and butter.

FLORA: (*Arranging teacups*) How is your painting today?

DAS: Altered. Your face . . . I think your work was
　　troublesome.

FLORA: Yes.

DAS: Is it the rhyming that is difficult?

FLORA: No.

DAS: The metre?

FLORA: No. The . . . emotion won't harmonize. I'm afraid I'm
　　not much good at talking about it.

DAS: I'm sorry.

FLORA: That's why I don't keep nipping round to your side of
　　the easel. If I don't look there's nothing to say. I think that
　　that's better.

DAS: Yes. It is better to wait. My painting has no *rasa* today.

FLORA: What is *rasa*?

DAS: *Rasa* is juice. Its taste. Its essence. A painting must have its *rasa* . . . which is not *in* the painting exactly. *Rasa* is what you must feel when you see a painting, or hear music; it is the emotion which the artist must arouse in you.

FLORA: And poetry? Does a poem have *rasa*?

DAS: Oh yes! Without *rasa* it is not a poem, only words. That is a famous dictum of Vishvanata, a great teacher of poetry, six hundred years ago.

FLORA: *Rasa* . . . yes. My poem has no *rasa*.

DAS: Or perhaps it has two *rasas* which are in conflict.

FLORA: Oh . . .

DAS: There are nine *rasas*, each one a different colour. I should say mood. But each mood has its colour – white for laughter and fun, red for anger, grey for sorrow . . . each one has its own name, and its own god, too.

FLORA: And some don't get on. Is that it?

DAS: Yes. That is it. Some do and some don't. If you arouse emotions which are in opposition to each other the *rasas* will not . . . harmonize, you said.

FLORA: Yes.

DAS: Your poem is about heat.

FLORA: Yes.

DAS: But its *rasa* is perhaps . . . anger?

FLORA: Sex.

DAS: (*Unhesitatingly*) The *rasa* of erotic love is called Shringara. Its god is Vishnu, and its colour is *shyama*, which is blue-black. Vishvanata in his book on poetics tells us: Shringara requires, naturally, a lover and his loved one, who may be a courtesan if she is sincerely enamoured, and it is aroused by, for example, the moon, the scent of sandalwood, or being in an empty house. Shringara goes harmoniously with all other *rasas* and their complementary emotions, with the exception of cruelty, disgust and sloth.

FLORA: I see. Thank you. Empty house is very good. Mr Das, you sounded just like somebody else. Yourself, I expect. I knew you could. The other one reminded me of Dr Aziz in

Forster's novel. Have you read it yet? I kept wanting to kick him.

DAS: (*Offended*) Oh . . .

FLORA: For not knowing his worth.

DAS: Then perhaps you didn't finish it.

FLORA: Yes, perhaps. Does he improve?

DAS: He alters.

FLORA: What is your opinion of *A Passage to India*?

DAS: Was that the delicate question you considered to ask me?

FLORA: (*Laughs happily*) Oh, Mr Das!

SCENE EIGHT: ENGLAND

MRS SWAN *re-enters the room.*

MRS SWAN: There . . . that's better . . .

ANISH: I was looking at your photographs. I hope you don't mind.

MRS SWAN: I took that one myself, in Venice, the summer before Flora went to India. I had a Kodak which let down in front in pleats. It took very good snaps; I wonder what happened to it? That was the day Diaghilev died. But we didn't know that till afterwards. We crossed to the Lido to have dinner with him at the hotel and he was dead.

ANISH: Is this one your husband?

MRS SWAN: Yes. That's Francis in Rawalpindi before we were married. Have you been up there?

ANISH: No. We have always lived in Rajasthan.

MRS SWAN: But you do not live there now?

ANISH: No. I live here now.

MRS SWAN: You wrote from St John's Wood.

ANISH: Yes. London is my home now. I have spent half my life here. I married here.

MRS SWAN: An English girl?

ANISH: Yes. Australian.

MRS SWAN: What an odd reply.

ANISH: Yes. I suppose so. Mrs Swan, it says in the book that your sister's portrait is reproduced by your permission. Does that mean you have it?

MRS SWAN: Yes.

ANISH: Here? In the house?

MRS SWAN: Oh, yes. Would you like to see it?

ANISH: Very much! I half expected to see it the moment I entered.

MRS SWAN: Pride of place, you thought. That's because you're a painter. Flora would not have cared to be on show. The portrait has always fended for itself rather . . .

ANISH: I understand. Where do you keep it?

MRS SWAN: Nowhere particularly. We always took it around
with us from house to house and sometimes it ended up on
top of a wardrobe. Oh dear, that must seem rather rude.

ANISH: It's all right.

MRS SWAN: Come along. It's in the bedroom, wrapped up.
You're lucky. It only just came back from being
photographed for the book. You can unwrap it for me.
Where's my stick? Has it fallen down?

ANISH: Here . . . let me . . .

MRS SWAN: Thank you.

ANISH: Do you need me to help you?

MRS SWAN: I hope not. Otherwise what would I do when you'd
gone? But you may open the door. You can see why I got a
bungalow.
(*They are moving now, she with her stick. They enter another
room.*)
I wonder what we called bungalows before India, and
verandahs and so on. It must have made certain
conversations quite awkward. 'I'm looking for a house with
no upstairs and an outside-inside bit stuck on the
front . . .'
Well, there you are! Rather well wrapped up. Will you
need the kitchen scissors, do you think?

ANISH: We'll see. What is in the boxes?

MRS SWAN: Flora's letters. Mr Pike had them photographed
too. Try to save the brown paper – it looks a good size to
be useful.

ANISH: Yes, I will . . .

MRS SWAN: Oh, it's quite easy . . . that's it . . .
(*The painting is unwrapped.*)
Well, there she is.

ANISH: Oh . . .

MRS SWAN: Yes, a bit much, isn't it?

ANISH: Oh . . . it's . . . so vibrant . . .

MRS SWAN: Vibrant. Yes . . . Oh . . . I say, *you're* not going to
blub too, are you?

ANISH: (*Weeping*) I'm sorry.

MRS SWAN: Don't worry. Borrow my hanky . . . It just goes to show, you need an eye. And your father, after all, was, like you, an Indian painter.

SCENE NINE: INDIA

FLORA: 'Jummapur. April 5th. Darling Nell, I'm having my
     portrait painted by an artist I met here, and I'm not using
     the historical present, I mean he's at it as I write, so if you
     see a painting of me in my cornflower dress sitting writing
     on a verandah you'll know I was writing *this* – some of the
     time anyway. He thinks I'm writing a poem. Posing as a
     poet, you see, just as the Enemy once said of me in his
     rotten rag.'
     (PIKE'*s voice, which does sound rather like Clark Gable in*
     Gone with the Wind, *comes in immediately, intimate and*
     slightly hushed, rather in the manner of the continuity voice
     which introduces live concerts on the radio.)
PIKE: 'The Enemy' was J.C. Squire (1884–1958), poet, critic,
     literary editor of the *New Statesman*, and editor of the
     London *Mercury*. FC is evidently referring to an
     anonymous editorial in the London *Mercury* (April 1920)
     complaining about, 'an outbreak of versifying flappers who
     should stop posing as poets and confine themselves to
     posing as railway stations'. The magazine was sued by the
     poets Elizabeth Paddington (1901–88) and Lavinia
     Clapham (1899–1929), both cases being settled out of
     court. FC poured a pint of beer over Squire's head in the
     Fitzroy Tavern in January 1921.
FLORA: 'I am installed in a little house with a verandah and
     three good-sized rooms under a tin roof. The verandah is at
     the front and you go into the main room which has an
     electric ceiling-fan and electric light, and an oil lamp which
     I prefer even when the electricity hasn't failed. There's a
     nice big window at the back, looking out at a rather
     hopeless garden, and then there is a nice plain bedroom
     with a big bed and a desk and one wooden chair and a
     wash-stand, and through another door a little bathroom
     with a Victorian bath and also a shower which is, alas,
     contemporary makeshift. Over on the other side is a

kitchen bit with a fridge, but my cook and bottle-washer disregards the electric stove and makes his own arrangements on a little verandah of his own. And all this is under a big green tree with monkeys and parrots in the branches and it's called a duck bungalow – '

PIKE: Dak bungalow, literally post-house.

FLORA: ' – although there is not a duck to be seen, only some scrawny chickens and a peahen. This is my first proper stop since I got off the boat and posted my Bombay letter. Yours overtook me and was waiting for me – why didn't I think of posting myself overland? – and thank you for it, but, darling, you mustn't expect me to be Intelligence from Abroad, as the *Times* used to say – you obviously know much more than I do about the Salt March – '

PIKE: Gandhi's 'March to the Sea' to protest the salt tax began at Ahmedabad on March 12th. He reached the sea on the day this letter was written.

FLORA: ' – nobody has mentioned it to me – and you'd better explain to Josh that the earthshaking sensations of Lord Beaverbrook's new Empire Party, etc. – '

PIKE: See Appendix G.

FLORA: ' – cause little stir in Jummapur. Sorry to disappoint.'
(*The appropriate sound effects creep in to illustrate Flora's letter, so here we begin to hear a slow steam train, followed in due course by the hubbub of the station, the clip-clop of the horse pulling the buggy as mentioned and the bicycle bells etc. which accompany the ride into town. Further down the letter, it is intended that Flora's questioner at her lecture will be heard in the appropriate physical ambience. In general, Flora's letter becomes an immediate presence – we can hear her pen scratching now and then, and insects, distant life, etc. – but when her letter takes us into an event, the sound-plot turns into the appropriate accompaniment.*)
'I arrived here on a huffing and puffing local with as many people riding on the roof as inside, and the entire committee of the Jummapur Theosophical Society was on the platform, bunch of flowers at the ready, not quite a red carpet and brass band but almost, and I thought there must

be someone important on the train and it turned out to be me – '

COOMARASWAMI: Miss Crewe! Welcome to Jummapur!

FLORA: Thank you! How nice!

' – which was very agreeable.'

Are you Mr Coomaraswami?

COOMARASWAMI: That is me! Is this suitcase your only luggage?

FLORA: 'And in no time at all they put me in a buggy and the President of the Theosophical sat beside me holding a yellow parasol while the committee bicycled alongside, sometimes two to a bike, and here I came in triumph like Britannia in a carnival float representing Empire, or, depending on how you look at it, the Oppression of the Indian People, which is how you *will* look at it and no doubt you're right but I never saw anyone less oppressed than Mr Coomaraswami, whose entire twenty stone shakes with laughter all the time. The Hot Weather, they tell me, is about to start, but I can't imagine anything hotter than this, and it will be followed by the Wet Season, though I already feel as though I am sitting in a puddle. Everything which requires movement must be accomplished between sunrise and breakfast, by which time inside is too hot to move and outside is too hot to think. My bedroom, apart from the ceiling fan, also has a punkah, which is like a line of washing worked by a punkah-wallah who sits outside and flaps the thing by a system of ropes and pulleys – or would if he were ever here, which he isn't. At sundown, gentle movement may be contemplated, and on Monday I was brought forth to deliver my lecture to a packed house, Mr C's house, in fact, and a much more sensible house than mine – built round a square courtyard, with a flat roof all around so I had an audience in the gods like gods in the audience, and though I say it myself I did a good one, encouraged by the sight of several copies of *Venus* and *Nymph*, in the front rows, and it all went terribly well except for a nasty moment when questions were invited and the very first one went – '

QUESTIONER: Miss Crewe, it is said you are an intimate friend
of Mr H. G. Wells –

FLORA: ' – and I thought, God, how unfair! – to have come all
this way to be gossiped about as if one were still in the
Queen's Elm – '

PIKE: A public house in the Fulham area of Chelsea.

FLORA: ' – but it turned out nothing was meant by it except – '

QUESTIONER: Does Mr Wells write his famous books with a
typewriter or with pen and ink?

FLORA: (*Firmly*) With pen and ink, a Waterman fountain pen, a
present from his wife.
'Not that I had the least idea – Herbert did damn little
writing when I was around, and made sure I did even less.'

PIKE: FC's liaison with Wells began no earlier than November
1929 and was therefore short, possibly the weekend of
December 7th and 8th.

FLORA: 'After which there was a reception with lemonade and
whisky and delicious snacks and conversation – darling, it's
so moving, they read the *New Statesman* and *Time and
Tide* and the *TLS* as if they were the Bible in parts (well, I
don't mean the *Bible* but you know what I mean) and they
know who wrote what about whom; it's like children with
their faces jammed to the railings of an unattainable park.
They say to me – '

QUESTIONER: What is your opinion of Gertrude Stein, Miss
Crewe?

FLORA: ' – and I can't bring myself to say she's a poisonous old
baggage who's travelling on a platform ticket – '

PIKE: FC's animosity towards Gertrude Stein should not lend
credence to Hemingway's fanciful assertion (in a letter to
Marlene Dietrich) that Stein threatened to scratch FC's or
(the possessive pronoun is ambiguous) Alice Toklas's eyes
out. If FC over-praised the chocolate cake, it would have
been only out of politeness. (See 'Bunfight at 27 Rue de
Fleurus' by E.C. Pike, Maryland Monographs, UMP,
1983).

FLORA: ' – but anyway that's when I met my artist.'

DAS: Miss Crewe, may I congratulate you on your lecture. I found it most interesting!

FLORA: Thank you . . . !

DAS: I was surprised you did not mention Virginia Woolf.

FLORA: I seldom do.

DAS: Have you met George Bernard Shaw?

FLORA: Yes. I was nearly in one of his plays once.

DAS: But are you not an actress . . . ?

FLORA: No, that was the trouble.

DAS: What do you think of Jummapur?

FLORA: Well, I only arrived on Saturday but –

DAS: Of course. How absurd of me!

FLORA: Not at all. I was going to say that my first impressions –

DAS: Jummapur is not in any case to be compared with London. Do you live in Bloomsbury?

FLORA: No, I live in Chelsea.

DAS: Chelsea – of course! My favourite part of London!

FLORA: Oh! you . . . ?

DAS: I hope to visit London one of these days. The Chelsea of Turner and the Pre-Raphaelite Brotherhood! Rossetti lived in Cheen Walk! Holman Hunt lived in Old Church Street! 'The Hireling Shepherd' was *painted* in Old Church Street! What an inspiration it would be to me to visit Chelsea!

FLORA: You are a painter!

DAS: Yes! Nirad Das.

FLORA: How do you do?

DAS: I am top hole. Thank you. May I give you a present?

FLORA: Oh . . .

DAS: Please do not judge it too harshly, Miss Crewe . . .

FLORA: But it's wonderful. Thank you.

' – and he gave me a pencil sketch of myself holding forth on the literary life, and the next thing I knew I'd agreed to sit for him. He is charming and eager and looks like a rosewood Charlie Chaplin, not the jumpy one in the films, the real one who was at Iris's tennis party.'

PIKE: Iris Tree was the daughter of Sir Herbert Beerbohm Tree, who, soon after the Crewe family arrived in London, gave FC her first employment, fleetingly as a cockney bystander in the original production of *Pygmalion*, and, after objections from Mrs Patrick Campbell, more permanently 'in the office'. It was this connection which brought FC into the orbit of Iris and her friend Nancy Cunard, and thence to the Sitwells, and arguably to the writing of poetry. FC's first poems, written in 1914–15, now lost, were submitted to the Sitwell magazine *Wheels*, and although they were not accepted (how they could have been worse than Miss Tree's contributions to *Wheels* is difficult to imagine), FC remained to become a loyal footsoldier in the Sitwells' war against 'the Enemy'.

FLORA: 'He is rather virile in a compact sort of way, with curly hair and hot brown eyes; he smiles a lot, he's got the teeth for it, white as his pyjamas.'

(DAS, *painting, is heard grunting in exasperation.*)

'Not that he's smiling at the moment. When I glance up I can see him frowning at me and then at the canvas as if one of us had misbehaved. By the way, I don't mean I've seen him in his pyjamas, darling, it's what he goes about in. At the Theosophical there was everything from loincloths like Gandhi to collars and ties. Which reminds me, I had a visit from a clean young Englishman who has asked me to dinner tonight at the Brits' Club. It was a bit of an afterthought really. I think I made a gaffe by not announcing myself to the Resident, the Senior Brit, and the young man, he was on a horse, was sent to look me over. I think he ticked me off but he was so nice it was hard to tell.'

(DAS *is heard sighing.*)

'I've a feeling I'm going to have to stop in a minute. My poem, the one I'm not writing, is about sitting still and being hot. It got defeated by its subject matter. Ask Dr Guppy – '

PIKE: Dr Alfred Guppy had been the Crewe family doctor since the move from Ashbourne to London in 1913. His notes on FC's illness, with references to pulmonary congestion, are first dated 1926.

FLORA: ' – if this is what he meant by a warm climate.'

DAS: Oh, fiddlesticks!

FLORA: I'm sorry. Is it my fault?

DAS: No, how can it be?

FLORA: Is that so silly?

DAS: No . . . forgive me! Oh dear, Miss Crewe! Yesterday I felt
. . . a communion and today –

FLORA: Oh! It *is* my fault! Yesterday I was writing a poem, and
today I have been writing a letter. That's what it is.

DAS: A letter?

FLORA: I am not the same sitter. How thoughtless of me. How
could I expect to be the same writing to my sister as for
writing my poem.

DAS: Yes. Yes.

FLORA: Are you angry?

DAS: I don't know. Can we stop now? I would like a cigarette.
Would you care for a cigarette? They are Goldflake.

FLORA: No. But I'd like you to smoke.

DAS: Thank you. You were writing to your sister? She is in
England, of course.

FLORA: Yes. Her name is Eleanor. She is much younger than
me; only twenty-three.

DAS: Then she cannot be so much younger.

FLORA: Routine gallantry is disappointing in a man.

DAS: I'm sorry.

FLORA: I am thirty-five and I look well enough on it.

DAS: I guessed your age to be thirty-two, if it is all right to say
so.

FLORA: Yes, it is all right to say so.

DAS: Where does your sister live?

FLORA: That's almost the first thing you asked *me*. Would it
mean anything to you?

(DAS *is loosening up again, regaining his normal good nature.*)

DAS: Oh, I have the whole of London spread out in my
imagination. Challenge me, you will see!

FLORA: All right, she lives in Holborn.

DAS: (*Pause*) Oh. Which part of London is that?

FLORA: Well, it's – oh dear – between the Gray's Inn Road
and –

DAS: Holl-born!

FLORA: Yes. Holborn.

DAS: But of course I know Holl-born! Charles Dickens lived in Doughty Street.

FLORA: Yes. Eleanor lives in Doughty Street.

DAS: But, Miss Crewe, *Oliver Twist* was written in that very street!

FLORA: Well, that's where Eleanor lives, near her work. She is the secretary to the editor of a weekly, the *Flag*.

DAS: The *Flag*!

FLORA: You surely have never read that too?

DAS: No, but I have met the editor of the *Flag* –

FLORA: (*Realizing*) Yes, of course you have! That is how I came to be here. Mr Chamberlain gave me letters of introduction.

DAS: His lecture in Jummapur caused the Theosophical Society to be suspended for one year.

FLORA: I'm sorry. But it's not for me to apologize for the Raj.

DAS: Oh, it was not the Raj but the Rajah! His Highness is our only capitalist! Do you agree with Mr Chamberlain's theory of Empire? I was not persuaded. Of course I am not an economist.

FLORA: That wouldn't deter Mr Chamberlain.

DAS: It is not my impression that England's imperial adventure is simply to buy time against revolution at home.

FLORA: I try to keep an open mind. Political theories are often, and perhaps entirely, a function of temperament. Eleanor and Mr Chamberlain are well suited.

DAS: Your sister shares Mr Chamberlain's opinions?

FLORA: Naturally. For reasons I have implied.

DAS: Yes. Being his secretary, you mean.

FLORA: Being his mistress.

DAS: Oh.

FLORA: You should have been a barrister, Mr Das.

DAS: I am justly rebuked!

FLORA: It was not a rebuke. An unintended slight, perhaps.

DAS: I am very sorry about your sister. It must be a great sadness for you.

FLORA: I am very happy for her.

DAS: But she will never be married now! Unless Mr Chamberlain marries her.

FLORA: He is already married, otherwise he might.

DAS: Oh my goodness. How different things are. Here, you see, your sister would have been cast out – for bringing shame on her father's house.

(FLORA *chuckles and he becomes angry.*)

Yes, perhaps we are not so enlightened as you.

FLORA: I'm sorry. I was only laughing because the difference is not the one you think. My father cast Eleanor out but the shame for him was Mr Chamberlain's politics. Poor father. A poet and a Communist . . . he must have felt like King Lear. Well, you have had your cigarette. Are we going to continue?

DAS: No, not today.

FLORA: I'll go back to my poem.

DAS: I have an appointment I had forgotten.

FLORA: Oh.

DAS: Actually you mustn't feel obliged . . . (DAS *is heard gathering together his paraphernalia, apparently in a hurry now.*)

FLORA: What have I done?

DAS: Done? What should you have done?

FLORA: Stop it. Please. Stop being Indian. (*Pause.*) Oh, I understand. (*Pause.*) Yes, yes. I did look.

DAS: Yes.

FLORA: I had a peep. Why not? You wanted me to.

DAS: Yes, why not? You looked at the painting and you decided to spend the time writing letters. Why not?

FLORA: I'm sorry.

DAS: You still have said nothing about the painting.

FLORA: I know.

DAS: I cannot continue today.

FLORA: I understand. Will we try again tomorrow?

DAS: Tomorrow is Sunday.

FLORA: The next day.

DAS: Perhaps I cannot continue at all.

FLORA: Oh. And all because I said nothing. Are you at the mercy of every breeze that blows? Or fails to blow? Are you an artist at all?

DAS: Perhaps not! A mere sketcher – a hack painter who should be working in the bazaar!

FLORA: Stop it.

DAS: Or in chalks on the ghat.

FLORA: Stop! I'm ashamed of you. And don't cry.

DAS: I will if I wish. Excuse me. I cannot manage the easel on my bicycle. I will send for it.

(It becomes a physical tussle, a struggle. She begins to gasp as she speaks.)

FLORA: You will not! And you will not take your box either. Give it to me – put it back –

DAS: I do not want to continue, Miss Crewe. Please let go!

FLORA: I *won't* let you give in –

DAS: Let go, damn you, someone will see us!

(FLORA falls over, gasping for breath.)

Oh . . . oh, Miss Crewe – oh, my God – let me help you. I'm sorry. Please. Here, sit down –

(She has had an attack of breathlessness. He is helping her to a chair. FLORA speaks with difficulty.)

FLORA: *(Her voice coming back)* Really, I'm all right. *(Pause.)* There.

DAS: What happened?

FLORA: I'm not allowed to wrestle with people. It's a considerable loss. My lungs are bad, you see.

DAS: Let me move the cushion.

FLORA: It's all right. I'm back now. Panic over. I'm here for my health, you see. Well, not *here* . . . I'll stay longer in the Hills.

DAS: Yes, that will be better. You must go high.

FLORA: Yes. In a day or two.

DAS: What is the matter with you?

FLORA: Oh, sloshing about inside. Can't breathe under water. I'm sorry if I frightened you.

DAS: You did frighten me. Would you allow me to remain a little while?

FLORA: Yes. I would like you to. I'm soaking.

DAS: You must change your clothes.

FLORA: Yes. I'll go in now. I've got a shiver. Pull me up. Thank you. Ugh. I need to be rubbed down like a horse.

DAS: Perhaps some tea . . . I'll go to the kitchen and tell –

FLORA: Yes. Would you? I'll have a shower and get into my Wendy House.

DAS: Your . . . ?

FLORA: My mosquito net. I love my mosquito net. My big towel is on the kitchen verandah – would you ask Nazrul to put it in the bedroom?

(DAS *is shouting for* NAZRUL *in the inner part of the house. The action stays with* FLORA *as she goes into the interior, undressing, and through a door. She turns a squeaky tap. There is no sound of water, only a thumping in the pipes.*)

Oh, damn, come on, damn you.

DAS: (*Off*) Miss Crewe! I'm sorry, there's –

FLORA: Yes, no water.

DAS: (*Off*) It's the electricity for the pump.

FLORA: Yes. (*She turns the tap again. The thumping in the pipes ceases.*) I have to lie down. (*She moves.*) There's water in the pitcher, on the washstand.

DAS: Nazrul is not – oh! Oh, I'm so sorry! –

FLORA: I'm sorry, Mr Das, but really I feel too peculiar to mind at the moment.

DAS: Please take the towel.

FLORA: Thank you. No, please, get the water jug and my face cloth from the wash-stand.

(*He moves; he lifts the jug.*)

Is there any water?

DAS: Yes, it's full . . . Here –

FLORA: Thank you. Hold the towel. (*She pours a little water over herself.*) Oh, heaven. Would you pour it – over my back, not too much at a time. Oh, thank you. I'm terribly sorry about this. And my head. Oh, that's good. I feel as weak as a kitten. (*The water splashes down over her and on to the floor.*)

DAS: I'm afraid that's all.

FLORA: Thank you.

DAS: Here . . . should I dry you?

FLORA: My back please. Rub hard. Thank you. (*Her voice comes out shivery.*) Thank you. Stop a minute.
(*She takes the towel. She uses it and gives it back to* DAS.)
There. Thank you. And my legs. Thank you.

DAS: There was no one in the kitchen. And no water for tea.

FLORA: Never mind. I'll get into bed now. (*She does so. She has to draw the net aside.*)

DAS: Do you have soda water?

FLORA: I think so.

DAS: I will fetch it.

FLORA: Yes please. In the fridge.

DAS: Yes. Oh, but is it locked?

FLORA: Oh . . . perhaps. Now I'm hot again, and no electricity for the fan. The sheet's too hot. It's too late for modesty. Anyway, I'm your model.

DAS: I will fetch soda water.

FLORA: That was the thing I was going to ask you.

DAS: When?

FLORA: The delicate question . . . whether you would prefer to paint me nude.

DAS: Oh.

FLORA: I preferred it. I had more what-do-you-call-it.

DAS: *Rasa.*

FLORA: (*Laughs quietly*) Yes, *rasa.*

SCENE TEN: ENGLAND

MRS SWAN: I remember the frock. It was not quite such a royal blue. Her cornflower dress, she called it.

ANISH: And her? Is it a good likeness?

MRS SWAN: Well, it's certainly Flora. She always sat upright and square to the table; she hated slouchers. She would have made a good schoolmistress, except for the feet. She always slipped her shoes off to work, and placed them neatly to one side like that. Yes, it's a very faithful portrait.

ANISH: But unfinished.

MRS SWAN: Is it? Why do you say that?

ANISH: It wasn't clear from the book, the way they cropped the painting. See here, my father has only indicated the tree – and the monkey – especially the doorway beyond . . .

MRS SWAN: Oh, but it's a portrait of *her*.

ANISH: Yes but he wasn't satisfied with her. He would have gone back to complete the background only when he considered the figure finished. Believe me. My father abandoned this portrait. I wondered why he hadn't signed it. Now I know. Thank you for showing it to me.

MRS SWAN: Mr Das, you said you had come to show *me* something. *Evidence* you said –

ANISH: Yes! I did. Come into the hall, Mrs Swan. Can you guess what it is?

MRS SWAN: A photograph of your father looking like Charlie Chaplin.

ANISH: (*Off*) No, better evidence than that. You may be shocked.

MRS SWAN: (*Approaching*) Oh dear, then you had better prepare me.

ANISH: It's a painting of course . . . wrapped up in this paper for sixty years.

(*He unwraps the paper.*) We need a flat surface, in the light –

MRS SWAN: The table in the bay . . .

ANISH: Yes, please come to the window –
    (*They are moving, she with her stick.*)
    May I use the elephants? To hold it flat.
MRS SWAN: Very suitable.
ANISH: And there you are, then.
MRS SWAN: (*Taken aback*) Oh, good heavens.
ANISH: A second portrait of Flora Crewe.
MRS SWAN: Oh . . . How like Flora.
ANISH: More than a good likeness, Mrs Swan.
MRS SWAN: No . . . I mean *how like Flora*!

SCENE ELEVEN: INDIA

DAS: (*Approaching*) Nazrul has returned, most fortunately. I was able to unlock the refrigerator. I have the soda water.

FLORA: Thank you. You must have some too.

DAS: I will put it on the table.

FLORA: Yes. No – no, the table by me. It's quite safe, I've covered myself.

DAS: May I move this book?

FLORA: Thank you. Do you know it? I found it here.

DAS: *Up the Country* . . . No. It looks old.

FLORA: A hundred years before my time, but it's just my book.

DAS: Oh – let me – let me pour the water for you.

FLORA: Thank you.

DAS: (*While pouring water from the bottle into a glass*) Nazrul was delayed at the shops by a riot, he says. The police charged the mob with lathis, he could have easily been killed, but by heroism and inspired by his loyalty to the memsahib he managed to return only an hour late with all the food you gave him money for except two chickens which were torn from his grasp.

FLORA: Oh dear . . . you thanked him, I hope.

DAS: I struck him, of course. You should fine him for the chickens.

FLORA: (*Drinking*) Oh, that's nice. It's still cold. Perhaps there really was a riot.

DAS: Oh, yes. Very probably. I have sent Nazrul to fetch the dhobi – you must have fresh linen for the bed. Nazrul will bring water but you must not drink it.

FLORA: Thank you.

(*The noise of the punkah begins quietly.*)

DAS: I'm sure the electricity will return soon and the fan will be working.

FLORA: What's that? Oh, the punkah!

DAS: I have found a boy to be punkah-wallah.

FLORA: Yes, it makes a draught. Thank you. A *little* boy?

DAS: Don't worry about him. I've told him the memsahib is sick.

FLORA: The memsahib. Oh dear.

DAS: Yes, you are memsahib. Are you all right now, Miss Crewe?

FLORA: Oh yes. I'm only shamming now.

DAS: May I return later to make certain?

FLORA: Are you leaving now? Yes, I've made you late.

DAS: No, not at all. There is no one waiting for me. But the servants will return and . . . we Indians are frightful gossips, you see.

FLORA: Oh.

DAS: It is for yourself, not me.

FLORA: I don't believe you, Mr Das, not entirely.

DAS: To tell you the truth, this is the first time I have been alone in a room with an Englishwoman.

FLORA: Oh. Well, you certainly started at the deep end.

DAS: We need not refer to it again. It was an accident.

FLORA: I didn't think you blushed.

DAS: (*Coldly*) Oh, yes. I assure you our physiology is exactly the same as yours.

FLORA: Well said, but I didn't mean that. I was being personal. I didn't expect an artist to blush.

DAS: Then perhaps I am not an artist, as you said.

FLORA: I did not. All I did was hold my tongue and you wanted to cut and run. What would you have done in the ordinary rough and tumble of literary life in London – on which, as you know, I am an expert. I give lectures on it. I expect you would have hanged yourself by now. When *Nymph In Her Orisons* came out one of the reviewers called it *Nymph In Her Mania*, and made some play with 'free verse' and 'free love', as if my poems, which I had found so hard to write, were a kind of dalliance, no more than that. *I* cried a bit too. *I* wanted to cut and run. Oh, the dreadful authority of print. It's bogus. If free verse and free love have anything in common it's a distrust of promiscuity. Quite apart from it not applying to me . . .

DAS: Of course not!

FLORA: Bogus and ignorant. My poems are not free verse.

DAS: Oh . . .

FLORA: I met my critic somewhere a few months later and poured his drink over his head and went home and wrote a poem. So that was all right. But he'd taken weeks away from me and I mind that now.

DAS: Oh! You're not dying are you?

FLORA: I expect so, but I intend to take years and years about it. You'll be dead too, one day, so let it be a lesson to you. Ignore everything, including silence. I was silent about your painting, if you want to know, because I thought you'd be an *Indian* artist.

DAS: An Indian artist?

FLORA: Yes. You *are* an Indian artist, aren't you? Stick up for yourself. Why do you like everything English?

DAS: I do not like everything English.

FLORA: Yes, you do. You're enthralled. Chelsea, Bloomsbury, *Oliver Twist*, Goldflake cigarettes . . . even painting in oils, that's not Indian. You're trying to paint me from my point of view instead of yours – what you *think* is my point of view. You *deserve* the bloody Empire!

DAS: (*Sharply*) May I sit down, please?

FLORA: Yes, do. Flora is herself again.

DAS: I will move the chair near the door.

FLORA: You can move the chair on to the verandah if you like, so the servants won't –

DAS: I would like to smoke, that is what I meant.

FLORA: Oh. I'm sorry. Thank you. In that case, can you see me through the net from over there?

DAS: Barely.

FLORA: Is that no or yes? Oof! That's better! That's what I love about my little house – you can see out but you can't see in.

DAS: (*Passionately*) But you are looking out at such a house! The bloody Empire finished off Indian painting! (*Pause.*) Excuse me.

FLORA: No, I prefer your bark.

DAS: Perhaps your sister is right. And Mr Chamberlain. Perhaps we have been robbed. Yes; when the books are balanced.

The women here wear saris made in Lancashire. The
cotton is Indian but we cannot compete in the weaving. Mr
Chamberlain explained it all to us in simple Marxist
language. Actually, he caused some offence.

FLORA: Yes, you mean the Rajah . . .

DAS: No, no – he didn't realize we had Marxists of our own,
many of them in the Jummapur Theosophical Society. For
some, Marx is the god whose wisdom the Society honours
in its title!

FLORA: Mr Coomaraswami . . . ?

DAS: No, not Mr Coomaraswami. *His* criticism is that you
haven't exploited India *enough*. 'Where are the cotton mills?
The steel mills? No investment, no planning. The Empire
has failed us!' That is Mr Coomaraswami. Well, the
Empire will one day be gone, like the Mughal Empire
before it, and only their monuments remain – the visions of
Shah Jahan! – of Sir Edwin Lutyens!

FLORA: 'Look on my works, ye mighty, and despair!'

DAS: (*Delighted*) Oh, yes! Finally like the empire of
Ozymandias! Entirely forgotten except in a poem by an
English poet. You see how privileged we are, Miss Crewe.
Only in art can empires cheat oblivion, because only the
artist can say, 'Look on my works, ye mighty, and despair!'

FLORA: Well, it helps if he happens to be Shelley.

DAS: There are Mughal paintings in the museum in London.

FLORA: Yes. Rajput miniatures in the Victoria and Albert.

DAS: You have seen them?

FLORA: Yes.

DAS: And you like them, of course.

FLORA: Yes. Very much.

DAS: Eighteenth and early nineteenth century, or earlier,
nothing much good later.

FLORA: I didn't mean I expected you to paint like that. I just
didn't like you thinking English was better because it was
English. If that is what you were thinking.
Did you consider my question?

DAS: What question?

FLORA: Can't you paint me without thinking of Rossetti or

Millais? Especially without thinking of Holman Hunt. Would your nudes be Pre-Raphaelite too?

DAS: The Pre-Raphaelites did not paint nudes. Their models were clothed.

FLORA: Oh, yes, weren't they though! The Brotherhood painted life as if it were a costume drama put on by Beerbohm Tree. I knew him, you know. He gave me my first job. And my second. All right, Alma-Tadema, then. I bet you like Alma-Tadema.

DAS: Yes, very much. When you stood . . . with the pitcher of water, you were an Alma-Tadema.

FLORA: Well, I don't want to be painted like that either – that's C. B. Cochran, if only he dared.

DAS: I don't understand why you are angry with me.

FLORA: You were painting me as a gift, to please me.

DAS: Yes. Yes, it was a gift for you.

FLORA: If you don't start learning to *take* you'll never be shot of us. Who whom? Nothing else counts. Mr Chamberlain is bosh. Mr Coomaraswami is bosh. It's your country, and we've got it. Everything else is bosh. When I was Modi's model I might as well have *been* a table. 'Lie down – thrust your hips.' When he was satisfied, he got rid of me. There was no question who whom. You'd never change his colour on a map. But please light your Goldflake.

(*Pause.* DAS *lights his cigarette with a match.*)

DAS: I like the Pre-Raphaelites because they tell stories. That is my tradition too. I am Rajasthani. Our art is narrative art, stories from the legends and romances. The English painters had the Bible and Shakespeare, King Arthur . . . We had the Bhagavata Purana, and the Rasikpriya, which was written exactly when Shakespeare had his first play. And long before Chaucer we had the Chaurapanchasika, from Kashmir, which is poems of love written by the poet of the court on his way to his execution for falling in love with the king's daugher, and the king liked the poems so very much he pardoned the poet and allowed the lovers to marry.

FLORA: Oh . . .

DAS: But the favourite book of the Rajput painters was the Gita Govinda, which tells the story of Krishna and Radha, the most beautiful of the herdswomen.

(*The ceiling-fan starts working.*)

FLORA: The fan has started. The electricity is on.

DAS: You will be a little cooler now.

FLORA: Yes. I might have a sleep.

DAS: That would be good.

FLORA: Mr Durance has invited me to dinner at the Club.

DAS: Will you be well enough?

FLORA: I am well now.

DAS: That is good. Goodbye, then.

FLORA: Were Krishna and Radha punished in the story?

DAS: What for?

FLORA: I should have come here years ago. The punkah boy can stop now. Will you give him a rupee? I'll return it tomorrow.

DAS: I will give him an anna. A rupee would upset the market.

SCENE TWELVE: ENGLAND

ANISH: I was in England when my father died. It was Christmas day, 1967. My first Christmas in London, in a house of student bedsits in Ladbroke Grove. An unhappy day.

MRS SWAN: Yes, of course.

ANISH: I mean it was already unhappy. The house was cold and empty. All the other students had gone home to their families, naturally. I was the only one left. No one had invited me.

MRS SWAN: Well, having a Hindu for Christmas can be tricky. Francis would invite his Assistant for Christmas lunch, and I always felt I should be apologizing for rubbing something in which left him out, if you follow me. It quite spoiled the business of the paper hats too. There's nothing like having an Indian at table for making one feel like a complete ass handing round the vegetables in a pink paper fez. That was after I-zation, of course.

ANISH: I heard the telephone . . .

MRS SWAN: Did you? Well, it's stopped now. The mistletoe was another problem.

ANISH: . . . no, there was a coin box in the hall. I could hear it ringing all day. It would stop and then start again. I ignored it. The phone was never for me. But finally I went up and answered it, and it was my uncle calling from Jummapur to say my father was dead.

MRS SWAN: Oh, how sad. Did you go home?

ANISH: Yes. There was great sadness in our house.

MRS SWAN: Of course . . .

ANISH: I'm ashamed of it but I found the rituals of death and grief distasteful. I wanted to return to England. And I did, as soon as permitted. There were legal matters which I was grateful to leave to my father's elder brother. So I was in England again when I learned that I had a legacy from my father. He had left me his tin trunk which had always stood at the foot of his bed.

MRS SWAN: Ah, yes . . .

ANISH: It arrived finally and it was locked. There had been no mention of a key. So I broke the hasp. There was nothing of value in the trunk that I could see.

MRS SWAN: You were disappointed?

ANISH: Well, yes. It was mainly letters and old bills, my report cards from school, and so on. But at the bottom of everything was a painting rolled up in paper. An extraordinary painting, a nude, a portrait of a woman. Even more amazing, a European woman, apparently painted many years before. I couldn't imagine who she was or what it meant.

MRS SWAN: Did you ask anyone? Your uncle?

ANISH: No. It was clear that this was something my father was sharing with me alone. A secret he was passing on. So I rolled the picture up again and put it away. I never hung it, of course. I never showed it to anyone, until years later I showed it to my wife.

MRS SWAN: Until now.

ANISH: Yes, until a week ago. The book in the shop window. It was like seeing a ghost. Not her ghost; his. It was my father's hand – his work – I had grown up watching him work, his portrait-work, in oils – local bigwigs, daughters of well-to-do businessmen. I had seen a hundred original Nirad Dases, and here was his work, not once but repeated twenty times over. It filled the window of the bookshop, a special display . . . *The Selected Letters of Flora Crewe*, and in the next instant I saw it was the same woman.

MRS SWAN: Yes. Oh, yes, it's Flora. It's as particular as an English miniature. A watercolour, isn't it?

ANISH: Watercolour and gouache, on paper.

MRS SWAN: It's fascinating. It looks Indian but he hasn't made *her* Indian.

ANISH: Well, she was *not* Indian.

MRS SWAN: Yes, I know. I'm not gaga, I'm only old. I mean he hasn't painted her flat. But everything else looks Indian, like enamel . . . the moon and stars done with a pastry cutter. And the birds singing in the border. Or is that the ceiling of the room, that line?

ANISH: I'm not sure.

MRS SWAN: And the foliage in bloom, so bright. Is it day or night? I know what's odd. The different parts are on different scales. The tree is far too small, or it's the right size too close. You can't tell if the painter is in the house or outside looking in.

ANISH: She is in a house within a house . . . look.

MRS SWAN: This edge must be the floor. Flora wrote about animals scratching about under the bungalow. There's a snake, look. Oh, but there couldn't have been gazelles under the house, could there? Perhaps it's a border after all . . . or a touch of fancy.

ANISH: Symbolism, yes.

MRS SWAN: I like the book on the pillow. That's Flora.

ANISH: And a pitcher on the table next to her, and bread on the plate . . . Do you see the lettering on the book?

MRS SWAN: Too small. I could find a magnifying glass . . .

ANISH: It says 'Eden'.

MRS SWAN: Eden? . . . (*Understanding.*) Oh!

ANISH: A book of verses underneath the bough, a jug of wine, a loaf of bread and thou beside me singing in the wilderness!

MRS SWAN: That's not Indian.

ANISH: No. The Mughals brought miniature painting from Persia when they made their Indian empire. But Muslim and Hindu art are different. The Muslim artists were realists. To a Hindu every object has an inner meaning, everything is to be interpreted in a language of symbols –

MRS SWAN: Which you understand, Mr Das?

ANISH: Not in detail. I'd have to look it up.

MRS SWAN: (*Amused*) Look it up! (*Apologizing.*) Oh, I'm sorry.

ANISH: But this flowering vine that winds itself around the dark trunk of the tree . . .

MRS SWAN: Oh . . .

ANISH: The vine is shedding its leaves and petals, look where they're falling to the ground. I think my father knew your sister was dying.

MRS SWAN: It upsets me, to see her nakedness.

ANISH: Yes . . . it's unguarded; she is not posing but resting –

MRS SWAN: No, I did not mean that. I don't make
    presumptions.

ANISH: Oh . . . but . . .

MRS SWAN: I was not there to nurse her . . . bathe her . . . I
    never saw her body at the end.

ANISH: Yes. Let me put it away now.

MRS SWAN: No, leave it, please. I want to look at it more. Yes.
    Such a pretty painting.

ANISH: It was done with great love.

MRS SWAN: He was certainly taken with her. Whether she posed
    for him, or whether it's a work of the imagination . . .

ANISH: Oh . . . but the symbolism clearly –

MRS SWAN: Codswallop. Your 'house within a house', as anyone
    can see, is a mosquito net. I had one which was gathered at
    the top in exactly that way. And a drink and a sandwich
    don't add up to the *Rubáiyát of Omar Khayyám* by a long
    chalk. Eden, indeed! Why would a Hindu call it Eden?

ANISH: *Her* paradise, not his –

MRS SWAN: Don't be a fool. The book is a volume of Indian
    travels. It was Flora's bedside reading. She mentions it in
    one of her letters – you should read the footnotes.

SCENE THIRTEEN: INDIA

FLORA: 'Jummapur. Sunday. April 6th. Darling Nell, I posted a
    letter only hours ago – at least I put it in the box at the
    Club last night and no doubt it's still there – but I'll make
    this the next page of my journal and probably post it when
    I leave Jummapur. We had an excitement in town
    yesterday morning, a riot, and half a street of shops burned
    to the ground, with the police out in force – the Rajah's
    police. The Rajah of Jummapur is Hindu (otherwise it
    would more likely be Jumma*bad* – not – *pur*) but the
    Muslims got the best of it according to my cook, who was
    in the heat of the battle. The Brits here shake their heads
    and ask where will it all end when we've gone, because
    going we are. That's official. Tell Josh. I got it from the
    Resident, whose view is that (a) it is our moral duty to
    remain and (b) we will shirk it. So now it's Sunday after
    breakfast, and I've been horse riding! – in a long skirt like
    the Viceroy's daughters twenty years ago, the first women
    to ride astride in India. Do you remember Llandudno? No,
    you surely can't. I think that was the last time I was ever
    on anything resembling a horse.'

PIKE: The Crewe family spent August at the seaside resort in
    North Wales from 1904 until 1911, the year of Mrs Crewe's
    elopement. FC's allusion is evidently to donkey rides on
    the sands, and her comment is of some interest, since, if
    she is right, a recently published photograph described as
    showing FC and Maynard Keynes on horseback at
    Garsington in 1924 (*Ottoline Morrell and Her Circle in Hell*,
    by Toshiro Kurasaki, 1988) misidentifies her; if not him.

FLORA: 'If I start coming over a bit dated it's because in my
    bungalow, which is not duck but dak, i.e. for travellers (as
    Josh has probably told you by now), I have discovered
    among a box of dilapidated railway novels a book of letters
    written from India a hundred years ago by an English

spinster – hand on my heart – to her sister Eleanor in
London, and this is now my only reading.'

PIKE: The spinster was Emily Eden and the book was *Up the
Country*, 1866. The Hon. Miss Eden was accompanying her
brother, the Governor-General Lord Auckland, on an
official progress up country. The tour, supported by a
caravan of ten thousand people, including Auckland's
French chef, and almost as many animals, lasted thirty
months, from October 1837, and Emily wrote hundreds of
letters to sisters and friends at home, happily unaware that
the expedition's diplomatic and strategic accomplishment
was to set the stage for the greatest military disaster ever to
befall the British under arms, the destruction of the army
in Afghanistan.

FLORA: 'I shall steal the book when I leave here in a day or two
and pick up Emily's trail in Delhi and Simla and up into
the Punjab, where the literary societies are holding their
breath. Speaking of which, I am doing pretty well with
mine, well enough to go dancing last night. My suitor (I
suppose I must call him that, though I swear I did nothing
to encourage him) came to fetch me in an enormous open
Daimler which drew a crowd.'

(*Sound of the Daimler and the crowd.*)

(*Calling out from off*) You wangled it!

(*Sounds of* DURANCE *opening the driver's door and closing it
again.* FLORA *has opened the passenger door, got into the car
and slammed the door. The ambience is the hubbub of Indian
voices, children, dogs, chickens . . . general excitement.*)

Can I drive?

DURANCE: Next time. Is that a bargain?

FLORA: It's a bargain.

DURANCE: Done. By the way, I hope you'll call me David. First
names are generally the drill with us.

FLORA: David.

(*Sounds of* DURANCE *shouting, in Urdu, to clear a path. The
car honks its horn and moves.*)

'And off we went, pushing through the mob of curiosity
seekers, scattering children and dogs and chickens right

and left, rather like leaving Bow Street in a police van. My God, how strange; that was ten years ago almost to the day.'

PIKE: In fact, nine. See 'The Woman Who Wrote What She Knew', by E. C. Pike (Maryland Monographs, UMP, 1981).

FLORA: 'I fully expected the Club to be like a commercial hotel in the hotter part of Guildford, but not at all – it's huge and white and pillared, just like the house of your first memory, perhaps – poor mama's nearly-house, which was ours for six months and then no more. I've never been back to Maybrook, perhaps we should make a pilgrimage one day.'

PIKE: The Crewe family met Sir George Dewe-Lovett of Maybrook Hall, Lancashire, on the promenade at Llandudno in August 1911. Catherine Crewe never returned to the house at Ashbourne. She eloped with Dewe-Lovett, a director of the White Star Shipping Line, and took her daughters, who were aged four and sixteen, to live at Maybrook. Percival Crewe proved to be unacrimonious and divorce proceedings were under way when the girls returned to Ashbourne to stay with their father for the Easter holidays of 1912, while their mother joined Dewe-Lovett at Southampton. The *Titanic* sailed on April 10th and FC never saw her mother or Maybrook again.

FLORA: 'And everyone at the Club was very friendly, going out of their way to explain that although they didn't go in much for poetry, they had nothing against it, so that was all right, and dinner was soup, boiled fish, lamb cutlets, sherry trifle and sardines on toast – eight of us at the Resident's table – '

WOMAN: Are you writing a poem about India, Flora?

FLORA: Trying to.

MAN: Kipling – there's a poet! 'And the dawn comes up like thunder on the road to Mandalay!'

WOMAN: I thought that was a *song*.

FLORA: 'The Resident was a different matter – '

RESIDENT: The only poet I *know* is Alfred Housman. I expect
    you've come across him.

FLORA: Of course!

RESIDENT: How is he nowadays?

FLORA: Oh – come *across* him –

RESIDENT: He hauled me through *Ars Amatoria* when I was up
    at Trinity –

FLORA: *The Art of Love?*

RESIDENT: When it comes to love, he said, you're either an
    Ovid man or a Virgil man. *Omnia vincit amor* – that's Virgil
    – 'Love wins every time, and we give way to love' – *et nos
    cedamus amori.* Housman was an Ovid man – *et mihi cedet
    amor* – 'Love gives way to me'.

FLORA: I'm a Virgil man.

RESIDENT: Are you? Well, you meet more people that way.

FLORA: ' – and his sources of information were impressive.'

RESIDENT: I believe you're here on doctor's orders.

FLORA: Why . . . yes . . . how . . . ?

RESIDENT: If there's anything you need or want, you tell David
    – right, David?

DURANCE: Yes, sir.

FLORA: Thank you. He's already promised me a go in the
    Daimler.

DURANCE: (*Embarrassed*) Oh . . .

RESIDENT: If you like cars, the Rajah has got about eighty-six of
    them – Rollses, the lot. With about ten miles on the clock.
    Collects them like stamps. Well, don't let me stop you
    enjoying yourselves.

DURANCE: Would you like to dance, Flora?

FLORA: 'And it turned out to be an easy evening to get through,
    which only goes to show, when in Rome, etc., and I wish
    I'd remembered that when I *was* in Rome.'

PIKE: FC was in Rome twice, in 1920 and 1926, en route to
    Capri in each case. It is unclear what she means here.

FLORA: 'Interrupted!'

    (*The gramophone dance music, which has been in the
    background, becomes the dominant sound as* DURANCE *and*
    FLORA *begin to dance.*)

DURANCE: Do you mean you've come to India for your health?

FLORA: Is that amusing?

DURANCE: Well, it is rather. Have you seen the English cemetery?

FLORA: No.

DURANCE: I must take you there.

FLORA: Oh.

DURANCE: People here drop like flies – cholera, typhoid, malaria – men, women and children, here one day, gone the next. Are you sure the doctor said India? Perhaps he said Switzerland and you weren't paying attention.

FLORA: He didn't say India. He said a sea voyage and somewhere warm – but I wanted to come to India.

DURANCE: Then good for you. Live dangerously, why not?

FLORA: Oh – you're too energetic for me – slow down!

DURANCE: Well, I suppose this is somewhere warm. In a month you can't imagine it – but you'll be gone to the hills, so you'll be all right.

FLORA: Yes. Let's sit down.

DURANCE: Slow one coming up . . . ?

FLORA: No, I'm out of puff.

(*They stop dancing.*)

DURANCE: Yes, of course. You're not really bad, are you, Flora?

FLORA: No, but I'd rather sit down. Do you think there might be more air outside?

DURANCE: On the verandah? Any air that's going. Should we take a peg with us?

(*He calls to a* SERVANT.)

Koi-hai! Thank you – two burra pegs.

SERVANT: Yes, sir.

FLORA: Lots of soda with mine, please.

(*They move further away from the music, which has continued, and come to the exterior, which makes its own noise, crickets, insects, leaves . . .*)

DURANCE: There we are. Long-sleever? Good for putting the feet up.

FLORA: Yes – long-sleever. Thank you. How pretty the
lanterns . . .

DURANCE: I hope you don't mind the moths.

FLORA: No, I like moths.

DURANCE: If they make a whining noise, kill them.

FLORA: It's a nice Club.

DURANCE: Yes, it's decent enough. There are not so many
British here so we tend to mix more.

FLORA: With the Indians?

DURANCE: No. In India proper, I mean *our* India, there'd be
two or three Clubs. The box-wallahs would have their own
and the government people would stick together, you know
how it is – and the Army . . .

FLORA: Mr Das called you Captain.

DURANCE: Yes, I'm Army. Seconded, of course. There are two
of us Juniors – political agents we call ourselves when we're
on tour round the states. Jummapur is not one of your
twenty-one-gun salute states, you see – my Chief is in
charge of half-a-dozen native states.

FLORA: In charge?

DURANCE: Oh yes.

FLORA: Is he Army? No – how silly –

DURANCE: He's ICS. The heaven-born. A Brahmin.

FLORA: Not seriously?

DURANCE: Yes, seriously. Oh no, not a Brahmin seriously. But
it might come to that with I-zation.

(FLORA *is puzzled by the word.*)

Indianization. It's all over, you know. We have Indian
officers in the Regiment now. My fellow Junior here is
Indian, too, terribly nice chap – he's ICS, passed the exam,
did his year at Cambridge, learned polo and knives-and-
forks, and here he is, a pukka sahib in the Indian Civil
Service.

FLORA: But he's not here.

DURANCE: At the Club? No, he can't come into the Club.

(*The* SERVANT *arrives.*)

Ah, here we are. Thank you . . .

(*The* SERVANT *leaves.*)

Cheers. Your health, Flora. I drink to your health for which you came. I wish you were staying longer. I mean, only for my sake, Flora.

FLORA: Yes, but I'm not. So that's that. Don't look hangdog. You might like me less and less as you got to know me.

DURANCE: Will you come riding in the morning?

FLORA: Seriously.

DURANCE: Yes, seriously. Will you?

FLORA: In the Daimler?

DURANCE: No. Say you will. We'll have to go inside in a minute if no one comes out.

FLORA: Why?

DURANCE: There's nothing to do here except gossip, you see. Everyone is agog about you. One of the wives claims . . . Were you in the papers at home? Some scandal about one of your books, something like that?

FLORA: I can see why you're nervous, being trapped out here with me – let's go in –

DURANCE: No – I'm sorry. Flora . . . ? Pax? Please.

FLORA: All right. Pax.

(*He kisses her, uninvited, tentatively.*)

DURANCE: Sealed with a kiss.

FLORA: No more. I mean it, David. Think of your career.

DURANCE: Are you really a scandalous woman?

FLORA: I was for a while. I was up in court, you know. Bow Street.

DURANCE: (*Alarmed*) Oh, not really?

FLORA: Almost really. I was a witness. The publisher was in the dock, but it was my poems – *Venus In Her Season*, my first book.

DURANCE: Oh, I say.

FLORA: The case was dismissed on a technicality, and the policemen were awfully sweet; they got me away through the crowd in a van. It was all most enjoyable actually, and it gave me an entrée to several writers I admired, most of whom, it turned out, were hoping it worked the other way round. My sister was asked to leave school. But that was mostly my own fault – the magistrate asked me why all the poems seemed to be about sex, and I said, 'Write what you know' – just showing off, I was practically a virgin, but it got me so thoroughly into the newspapers my name rings a bell even with the wife of a bloody jute planter or something in the middle of Rajputana, damn, damn, damn. No, let's go inside.

DURANCE: Sit down, that's an order. How's your whisky?

FLORA: Excellent. All the better for being forbidden. My God, where did that moon come from?

DURANCE: Better. I love this country, don't you?

FLORA: Yes, I think I do. What's going to happen to it? The riot in town this morning . . . does that happen often?

DURANCE: Not here, no. The gaols are filling up in British India.

FLORA: Well, then.

DURANCE: It wasn't against us, it was Hindu and Muslim. Gandhi's salt march reached the sea today, did you hear? Our Congress Hindus closed their shops in sympathy, and the Muslims wouldn't join in, that's all it was about. The Indian National Congress is all very well, but to the Muslims, Congress means Gandhi . . . a Hindu party in all but name.

FLORA: Will Gandhi be arrested?

DURANCE: No, no. The salt tax is a lot of nonsense actually.

FLORA: Yes, it does seem hard in a country like this.

DURANCE: Not that sort of nonsense. It works out at about four annas a year. Most Indians didn't even know there *was* a salt tax.

FLORA: Well, they do now.

DURANCE: Yes. They do now. Would you like one more turn round the floor before they play the King?

FLORA: No, I'm tiring. (*She gets up.*) Will you finish my whisky? I'd like to go back to my little house.

DURANCE: Yes, of course. Would you mind saying goodnight to my Chief? It would go down well.

FLORA: I'd like to. The Brahmin.

DURANCE: Yes. The highest caste of Hindu, you see, and the ICS are the highest caste of Anglo-India. There's about twelve hundred ICS and they run the continent. That's three for every million Indians.

FLORA: Why do the Indians let them?

DURANCE: Why not? They're better at it.

FLORA: Are they?

DURANCE: Ask them.

FLORA: Who?

DURANCE: The natives. Ask them. We've pulled this country together. It's taken a hundred years with a hiccup or two but the place now works.

FLORA: That's what you love, then? What you created?

DURANCE: Oh no, it's India I love. I'll show you.

(*A sudden combination of animal noises is heard – buffalo snorting, horses whinnying, Flora crying out.* FLORA *and* DURANCE *on horseback.*)

DURANCE: Did he frighten you? He's big but harmless.

FLORA: Oh my!

DURANCE: We surprised him in his bath.

FLORA: He's immense! Thank you!

DURANCE: Me?

FLORA: He was *my* surprise really.

DURANCE: Oh yes. Just for you.

FLORA: I've never been given a buffalo before.

DURANCE: Look – sand grouse! (*He makes a noise to represent the firing of a shotgun, both barrels.*) A nice left and right!

FLORA: Don't shoot them, they're mine! (*Her interior voice comes in, 'inside' the scene itself.*)

'Where life began at the lake's edge,
water and mud convulsed,
reared itself and became shaped
into buffalo.
The beast stood dismayed,
smeared with birth, streaming
from his muzzle like an infant, celebrated
with lily flowers about his horns.
So he walked away to meet his death
among peacocks, parrots, antelopes.
We watched him go, taller than he,
mounted astride, superior beasts.'

DURANCE: Time to trot – sun's up.

FLORA: Oops – David – I'll have to tell you – stop! It's my first time on a horse, you see.

DURANCE: Yes, I could tell.

FLORA: (*Miffed*) Could you? Even walking? I felt so proud when we were walking.

DURANCE: No, no good, I'm afraid.

FLORA: Oh, damn you. I'm going to get off.

DURANCE: No, no, just sit. He's a chair. Breathe in. India smells wonderful, doesn't it?

FLORA: Out here it does.

DURANCE: You should smell chapattis cooking on a camel-dung fire out in the Thar Desert. Perfume!

FLORA: What were you doing out there?

DURANCE: Cooking chapattis on a camel-dung fire. (*Laughs.*) I'll tell you where it all went wrong with us and India. It was the Suez Canal. It let the women in.

FLORA: Oh!

DURANCE: Absolutely. When you had to sail round the Cape this was a man's country and we mucked in with the natives. The memsahibs put a stop to that. The memsahib won't muck in, won't even be alone in a room with an Indian.

FLORA: Oh . . .

DURANCE: Don't point your toes out. May I ask you a personal question?

FLORA: No.

DURANCE: All right.

FLORA: I wanted to ask *you* something. How did the Resident know I came to India for my health?

DURANCE: It's his business to know. Shoulders back. Reins too slack.

FLORA: But I didn't tell anybody.

DURANCE: Obviously you did.

FLORA: Only Mr Das.

DURANCE: Oh, well, say no more. Jolly friendly of you, of course, sharing a confidence, lemonade, all that, but they can't help themselves bragging about it, telling all they know.

FLORA: (*Furious*) Rubbish!

DURANCE: Well . . . I stand corrected.

FLORA: I'm sorry. I don't believe you, though.

DURANCE: Righto.

FLORA: I'm sorry. Pax.

DURANCE: Flora.

FLORA: No.

DURANCE: Would you marry me?

FLORA: No.

DURANCE: Would you think about it?

FLORA: No. Thank you.

DURANCE: Love at first sight, you see. Forgive me.

FLORA: Oh, David.

DURANCE: Knees together.

FLORA: 'Fraid so.

> (*She laughs without malice but unrestrainedly. He punishes her without malice by breaking his horse into a trot. Her horse follows, trotting.* FLORA *squealing with fright and laughing.*)

SCENE FOURTEEN: INDIA

Inside the bungalow.

FLORA: 'Next day. Oh dear, guess what? You won't approve. Quite right. So I think it's time to go. Love 'em and leave 'em.'

PIKE: What, if anything, came of this is not known. The man was most probably the Junior Political Agent at the Residency, Captain David Arthur Durance, who took FC dancing and horse riding. He was killed in Malaya in 1942 during the Japanese advance on Singapore.

FLORA: 'I feel tons better, though. The juices are starting to flow again, as you can see from the enclosed.'

PIKE: 'Buffalo' and 'Pearl', included in *Indian Ink*, 1932.

FLORA: 'I'll keep sending you fair copies of anything I finish in case I get carried away by monsoons or tigers, and if I do, look after the comma after "astride", please, it's just the sort of thing they leave out – printers have taken more years off my life than pulmonary congestion, I can tell you. Send "Buffalo" to *Blackwood's* and "Pearl" to *Transition*, and if you get a pound for them put it in the Sacha Fund.'

PIKE: The reference is obscure.

FLORA: 'I'm writing this at my table on the verandah, looking longingly to the hills I can't see. The dak menagerie is subdued by the heat, except for a pi-dog barking under the house – and I'd better start with what interrupted me yesterday after my early morning ride – which was a Rolls Royce *circa* 1912 but brand new, as it were, driven by a Sikh in a turban called Singh – '

PIKE: A tautology: all Sikhs are named Singh (however, not all people named Singh are Sikhs).

FLORA: Oh, shut up! (*She is shouting at the dog, which is responding. She manages to get rid of the dog – clapping her hands and generally making a dog-dismissing row. The dog departs, whining and yelping.*)
'He was a chauffeur with a note from His Highness the

Rajah of Jummapur, inquiring after my health and assuring me that the spiritual beauty of Jummapur had been increased a thousandfold by my presence, and asking my indulgence towards his undistinguished collection of motor cars, which nevertheless might be worthy of my interest during an idle hour since he understood I was a connoisseur of the automobile . . . Well, what is a poor girl to do? Hop into the back of the Rolls, that's what.'

(*Sound of* FLORA *getting into the Rolls.*)

Thank you!

(*The car moves, etc.*)

'The Rajah's palace didn't exactly have a garage, more of a cavalry barracks with the Motor Show thrown in, and he himself was there to greet me.'

RAJAH: Miss Crewe! How delightful that you were able to come!

FLORA: Oh, how sweet of you to ask me . . . your Highness . . . oh – sorry!

RAJAH: Please!

FLORA: 'And I made a mess of that, sticking my hand out at his bow, bowing at his hand – '

What a wonderful sight!

' – but he was very sporting about it, and there were all these cars gleaming in the courtyard – with a dozen grooms standing by, one couldn't think of them as mechanics.'

RAJAH: Let me show you one or two.

FLORA: Thank you! Oh – a Hispano-Suiza!

'He's a large soft-looking man with beautiful eyes like a seal and wearing a long buttoned-up brocade coat over white leggings, no jewellery except a yellow diamond ring not much bigger than my engagement ring from Gus, only real, I suppose – '

PIKE: Augustus de Boucheron enjoyed brief celebrity as a millionaire philanthropist and patron of the arts. FC met him, and received his proposal of marriage, on October 11th 1918, at a party given for the Russian Ballet by the Sitwells at Swan Walk (it was at the same party that Maynard Keynes met the ballerina Lopokova). FC had returned from France only hours earlier and was wearing her auxiliary nurse's uniform. Her fortunes were at their lowest ebb, for she was supporting her sister, still at school, and also her father, who, since being invalided out of the Army, had given up the Bar and enjoyed few periods of lucidity. The engagement to de Boucheron was announced on January 1st 1919 and ended on August 1st in a furniture store (see note on page 334).

FLORA: ' – and he knew very little about cars, he just liked the look of them, which was endearing, and I know how badly this must be going down in Doughty Street but we soon got on to politics – he was at school with Winston Churchill.'

RAJAH: But I'm afraid I can't remember him at all. Look at this one! I couldn't resist the headlamps! So enormous, like the eggs of a mythical bird!

FLORA: Yes – a Brancusi!

RAJAH: Is it? I don't know their names. All the same, I read Churchill's speeches with great interest. He is right in what he says, don't you agree, Miss Crewe? The loss of India would reduce Britain to a minor power.

FLORA: That may be, but one must consider India's interests too.

RAJAH: But what about Jummapur's interests?

FLORA: Yes, of course, but aren't they same thing?

RAJAH: No, no. Independence would be the beginning of the end for the Native States. Though in a sense you are right too – Independence may be the beginning of the end for Indian nationalism too. Only yesterday, you may have heard about the hullabaloo in town.

FLORA: Yes.

RAJAH: The Princes stood firm with the British during the First Uprising in my grandfather's day –

FLORA: The . . . ?

RAJAH: In '57 the danger was from fundamentalists –

FLORA: The Mutiny . . .

RAJAH: – today it is the progressives. Marxism. Civil disobedience. But I told the Viceroy, you have to fight them the same way, you won't win by playing cricket. (*He*

presses a bulb-horn, which honks.) My father drove this one.
It's a Bentley.

FLORA: Yes.

RAJAH: He won it at Monte Carlo. He spent much of his time in
the south of France, for his health. (*He laughs.*) But *you*
have come to India for *your* health!

FLORA: (*Not pleased*) Well . . . yes, your Highness. Everybody
seems to know everything about me.

RAJAH: Should we have some refreshment? (*He opens the door of
a car.*)

FLORA: (*Puzzled*) Oh . . . thank you.

RAJAH: After you.

FLORA: You mean in the car?

RAJAH: Do you like this one?

FLORA: I . . . yes, of course. It's a Packard.

RAJAH: It's quite a step to my apartments. Why walk in the sun
when we have so many motorcars?

FLORA: Oh I see. Thank you. (*She gets into the car.*)

RAJAH: I keep them all ready. Would you care to drive?

FLORA: Yes, I'd love to. I'll slip over.
(*She moves over to the steering wheel. The* RAJAH *gets into the
car and closes the door.*)

RAJAH: Jolly good, we'll have some tiffin. When do you leave
Jummapur?

FLORA: ' – and we drove all of two hundred yards past saluting
sentries, into the palace proper, which had a fountain
inside, and we walked through a series of little gardens into
his reception room, where we had sherbet – you can
imagine the rest, can't you? – me sat on silk cushions being
peeped at by giggling ladies of the harem through the
latticework of carved marble – well, no such thing. We had
tea and cold cuts and little iced cakes, and the furniture
was from Heals, three-piece suite and all, and I know it was
Heals because the sofa was absolutely the one I broke my
engagement on when I took Gus to the French Pictures –
my God, I thought, that's the Modigliani sofa!'

PIKE: The exhibition of Modern French Art at Heal and Sons in
the Tottenham Court Road enlivened the hot early-August

days of 1919. Modigliani was one of several newer artists shown with the better-known Matisse, Picasso and Derain, and it was his nudes, including the 'Peasant Girl', now in the Tate Gallery, which provoked such comments in the press as that the show was glorying in prostitution. FC had met Modigliani in Paris at his first show, on December 3rd 1917 (the date is fixed by the fact that the show was closed by the police on the opening day) and she sat, or rather reclined, for the artist soon afterwards. Concurrently with the French pictures, Messrs Heals were showing a model flat. FC arrived at Heals with de Boucheron, expecting to see her portrait, only to discover that her fiancé had bought the painting from the artist and, as he triumphantly confessed, burned it. The ensuing row moved from the gallery to the model flat, and it was on the sofa of the model sitting-room that FC returned de Boucheron's engagement ring (though not the lease on the Flood Street house, which was to be the Crewes' London home from then on). De Boucheron, under his real name, Perkins Butcher, went to prison in 1925 for issuing a false prospectus. His end is unknown.

FLORA: 'I started to tell his Highness about Heals but when I said French pictures he got hold of the wrong end of the stick entirely – '

RAJAH: French pictures?

FLORA: Yes. There was a tremendous fuss – the pictures were wallowing in prostitution, that sort of thing. And of course those of us who defended them were simply admitting our depravity!

RAJAH: My dear Miss Crewe, you are quite the emancipated woman!

FLORA: Not at all. What has being a woman got to do with it?

RAJAH: Oh, I agree with you! I was guilty of male prejudice!

FLORA: In fact they are probably more to my taste than yours – surely it's more a matter of culture than gender?

RAJAH: Ah, but we have 'French pictures' of our own. Of course, you have never seen them.

FLORA: I'm not sure that I understand.

RAJAH: In *our* culture, you see, erotic art has a long history and
a most serious purpose. (*Walking away*.) These drawings,
for example – if I may be so bold – are the depictions not of
depravity . . . (*walking back*) but of precepts towards a
proper fulfilment of that side of life which . . .

FLORA: 'And he produced an album of exquisite water colours –
medieval, I think – which we admired solemnly together,
he determined to acknowledge me as an enlightened
woman, I determined to be one. Really what a muddle, and
not entirely honest, of course – he insisted I chose one as a
gift – '
No, really, I couldn't –

RAJAH: Yes, yes – which one would you like?

FLORA: ' – like pondering a big box of chocolates – should one
go for the Turkish Delight or plump for the nut cluster?'
Well, this one is rather sweet . . .

RAJAH: Ah, yes . . .

FLORA: How very kind.
' – and he invited me to move into the palace for the
remainder of my visit but I got away finally in a yellow
Studebaker and was brought home at lamp-lighting
time . . .'
(*Sounds of the Studebaker arriving, Flora getting out and
closing the car door; the car leaving.* FLORA *calls out.*)
Thank you very much, Mr Singh! (*She comes up the wooden
steps to the verandah.*) Oh, Mr Das!

DAS: Good evening, Miss Crewe! I'm sorry if we frightened you.

FLORA: And Mr Coomaraswami!

COOMARASWAMI: Yes, it is me, Miss Crewe.

FLORA: Good evening. What a surprise.

COOMARASWAMI: I assure you – I beg you – we have not come
to presume on your hospitality –

FLORA: I wish I had some whisky to offer you, but will you
come inside.

COOMARASWAMI: It will be cooler for you to remain on the
verandah.

FLORA: Let me find Nazrul.

COOMARASWAMI: He is not here, evidently. But perhaps now

that the mistress has returned it is permitted to light the lamp?

FLORA: Yes, of course.

COOMARASWAMI: So much more pleasant than sitting in the electric light. (*He lights the oil lamp.*) There we are. And the moon will clear the house tops in a few minutes . . . but where is it? Perhaps on the wrong side of the house. Never mind.

FLORA: Please sit down.

COOMARASWAMI: May I take this chair?

FLORA: No, that's Mr Das's chair. And this is mine. So that leaves you with the sofa.

COOMARASWAMI: Ah, never, never has my fatness received more charming, more delicate acknowledgement! (*He sits down.*) Oh yes, very comfortable. Thank you, Miss Crewe. Mr Das told me that I was exceeding our rights of acquaintance with you in coming to see you without proper arrangement, and even more so to lie in wait for you like *mulaquatis*. If it is so, he is blameless. Please direct your displeasure to me.

DAS: Miss Crewe does not understand *mulaquatis*.

COOMARASWAMI: Petitioners!

FLORA: In my house you are always friends.

COOMARASWAMI: Mr Das, what did I tell you!

FLORA: But what can I do for you?

DAS: Nothing at all! We require nothing!

FLORA: Oh . . .

COOMARASWAMI: Have you had a pleasant day, Miss Crewe?

FLORA: Extremely interesting. I have been visiting his Highness the Rajah.

COOMARASWAMI: My goodness!

FLORA: I believe you knew that, Mr Coomaraswami.

COOMARASWAMI: Oh, you have found me out!

FLORA: He showed me his cars . . . and we had an interesting conversation, about art . . .

COOMARASWAMI: And poetry, of course.

FLORA: And politics.

COOMARASWAMI: Politics, yes. I hope, we both hope – that

your association with, that our association with, in fact – if
we caused you embarrassment, if you thought for a
moment that I personally would have knowingly brought
upon you, compromised you, by association with –

FLORA: Stop, stop. Mr Das, I am going to ask *you*. What is the
matter?

DAS: The matter?

FLORA: I shall be absolutely furious in a moment.

DAS: Yes, yes, quite so. My friend Coomaraswami, speaking as
President of the Theosophical Society, wishes to say that if
his Highness reproached you or engaged you in any
unwelcome conversation regarding your connection with
the Society, he feels responsible, and yet at the same time
wishes you to know that –

FLORA: His Highness never mentioned the Theosophical
Society.

DAS: Ah.

COOMARASWAMI: Not at all, Miss Crewe?

FLORA: Not at all.

COOMARASWAMI: Oh . . . well, jolly good!

FLORA: What has happened?

COOMARASWAMI: Ah well, it is really of no interest. I am very
sorry to have mentioned it. And we must leave you, it was
not right to trouble you after all. Will you come, Mr Das?

FLORA: I hope it is nothing to do with my lecture?

COOMARASWAMI: (*Getting up*) Oh no! Certainly not!

DAS: Nothing!

COOMARASWAMI: Mr Das said we should not mention the thing,
and how truly he spoke. I am sorry. Goodnight, Miss
Crewe. (*He shouts towards somebody distant, in Urdu, and the
explanation is an approaching jingle of harness, horse and
buggy. He goes down the steps to meet it and climbs aboard.*)

DAS: I am coming, Mr Coomaraswami. Please wait for me a
moment.

FLORA: If you expect to be my friends, you must behave like
friends and not like whatever-you-called it. Tell me what
has happened.

COOMARASWAMI: (*Off*) Mr Das!

DAS: (*Shouts*) Please wait!

FLORA: Well?

DAS: The Theosophical Society has been banned, you see. The order came to Mr Coomaraswami's house last night.

FLORA: But why?

DAS: Because of the disturbances in the town.

FLORA: The riot?

DAS: Yes, the riot.

FLORA: I know about it. The Hindus wanted the Muslims to close their shops. What has that to do with the Theosophical Society?

COOMARASWAMI: (*Off*) I am going, Mr Das!

DAS: (*Shouts*) I come now!

Mr Coomaraswami is a man with many hats! And his Highness the Rajah is not a nationalist. I must leave you, Miss Crewe. But may I step inside to fetch my painting away?

FLORA: If you like.

DAS: I do not have my bicycle this evening, so I can manage the easel also.

FLORA: Mr Das, did you tell people I was ill?

DAS: What do you mean?

FLORA: That I came to India for my health?

COOMARASWAMI: (*Off*) I cannot wait, Mr Das!

DAS: (*Shouts*) A moment!

Why do you ask me that?

FLORA: He is leaving you behind.

(*The horse and buggy are heard departing.*)

DAS: I will walk, then.

FLORA: It seems that everyone from the Rajah to the Resident knows all about me. I told no one except you. If I want people to know things, I tell them myself, you see. I'm sorry to mention it but if there's something wrong between two friends I always think it is better to say what it is.

DAS: Oh . . . my dear Miss Crewe . . . it was known long before you arrived in Jummapur. Mr Chamberlain's letter said exactly why you were coming. Mr Coomaraswami told me himself when I began to paint your portrait. But, you see, I already knew from talking with others. This is how it is with us, I'm afraid. The information was not considered to be private, only something to be treated with tact.

FLORA: Oh . . .

DAS: As for the Rajah and the Resident, I am sure they knew before anybody. A letter from England to Mr Coomaraswami would certainly be opened.

FLORA: Oh . . . (*She is merely making sounds, close to tears.*)

DAS: You must not blame yourself. Please.

FLORA: Oh, Mr Das . . . I'm so glad . . . and so sorry. Oh dear, have you got a hanky?

DAS: Yes . . . certainly . . .

FLORA: Thank you. How stupid I am.

(DAS *opens the door to the interior.*)

DAS: I will fetch the canvas.

(*We go with him. He moves the easel, folds it, etc.*)

FLORA: (*Off*) Don't take it.

(*Approaching.*) If it is still a gift, I would like to keep it, just as it is.

DAS: Unfinished?

FLORA: Yes. All portraits should be unfinished. Otherwise it's like looking at a stopped clock. Your handkerchief smells faintly of . . . something nice. Is it cinnamon?

DAS: Possibly not. The portrait is yours, if you would like it. Of course. I must take it off the frame for you, or it will not travel easily in your luggage. Perhaps I can find a knife in the kitchen, to take out the little nails.

FLORA: There are scissors on the table.

DAS: Ah – yes. Thank you. No – I think I would damage them. May I call Nazrul?

FLORA: I thought –

DAS: Yes – Mr Coomaraswami sent him away, he is suspicious of everyone. I'm sorry.

FLORA: It doesn't matter.

DAS: No. There is no hurry.

FLORA: No. But I am leaving tomorrow.

DAS: Tomorrow?

FLORA: I think I must. Every day seems hotter than the day before. Even at dawn.

DAS: Yes, you are right of course.

FLORA: But I will see you again, because I'll come back this way to Bombay, by July 10th at the latest. My boat sails on the 12th.

DAS: You may take a later boat.

FLORA: No, I cannot. My sister . . . oh, you'll be horrified, but never mind; my sister is having a baby in October.

DAS: That is joyful news.

FLORA: Oh, good.

DAS: I can keep the painting for you until you come back if you like.

FLORA: No, I'd like to have it with me.

DAS: Miss Crewe . . . actually I have brought something to show you. I decided I must not show it to you after all, but if we are friends again . . . I would like you to see it.

FLORA: What is it?

DAS: I left it in my briefcase outside.

FLORA: I would like to see it.

DAS: (*Hesitates*) Well . . . I will bring it.

FLORA: All right.

(DAS *walks the few steps back to the verandah, and returns, speaking.*)

DAS: I have wrapped it, although it is itself only a sheet of paper.

FLORA: Oh . . . shall I open it?

DAS: You must look at it in the light. Let me –

FLORA: No – not the electric light. I seldom cry, but never in the electric light. Do you mind? There is enough light in the other window; Mr Coomaraswami was quite right about the moon. (*She moves. She unwraps the paper.*) It's going to be a drawing, isn't it? Oh!

DAS: (*Nervous, bright*) Yes! A good joke, is it not? A Rajput miniature, by Nirad Das!

FLORA: (*Not heeding him*) Oh . . . it's the most beautiful thing . . .

DAS: (*Brightly*) I'm so pleased you like it! A quite witty pastiche –

FLORA: (*Heeding him now*) Are you going to be Indian? Please don't.

DAS: (*Heeding her*) I . . . I am Indian.

FLORA: An Indian artist.

DAS: Yes.

FLORA: Yes. This one is for yourself.

DAS: You are not offended?

FLORA: No, I'm pleased. It has *rasa*.

DAS: I think so. Yes. I hope so.

FLORA: I forget its name.

DAS: (*Pause*) Shringara.

FLORA: Yes. Shringara. The *rasa* of erotic love. Whose god is Vishnu.

DAS: Yes.

FLORA: Whose colour is blue-black.

DAS: Shyama. Yes.

FLORA: It seemed a strange colour for love.

DAS: Krishna was often painted shyama.

FLORA: Yes. I can see that now. It's the colour he looked in the moonlight.

SCENE FIFTEEN: ENGLAND

MRS SWAN: 'Which only goes to show, when in Rome, etc., and
I wish I'd remembered that when I *was* in Rome.
Interrupted! Next day. Oh dear, guess what? You won't
approve. Quite right. So I think it's time to go. Love 'em
and leave 'em . . .'

ANISH: May I see?

MRS SWAN: It's no different from what you can read in the
book. Though it's a relief not to have Clark Gable butting
in all the time. I decided not to tell Mr Pike about Rome,
even though it was several Popes ago and Norman Douglas
wouldn't have given a hoot. Let sleeping dogs lie, that's
what I say.

ANISH: 'You won't approve . . . Oh dear, guess what? You
won't approve . . .'

MRS SWAN: I wish I'd kept the envelopes, they'd be worth
something now to a collector, a philatelist, I mean.

ANISH: Mr Pike's footnote talks about the political agent,
Captain Durance.

MRS SWAN: Gratuitously.

ANISH: Yes! Why wouldn't you approve of Captain Durance?
Surely it's more likely she meant . . .

MRS SWAN: Meant what, Mr Das?

ANISH: I don't mean any offence.

MRS SWAN: Then you must take care not to give it.

ANISH: Would you have disapproved of a British Army officer –
Mrs Swan? – more than an Indian painter?

MRS SWAN: Certainly. Mr Pike is spot-on there. In 1930 I was
working for a Communist newspaper. Which goes to show
that people are surprising. But you know that from your
father, don't you?

ANISH: Why?

MRS SWAN: He must have surprised you too. The thorn in the
lion's paw.

ANISH: Yes. Yes, I was surprised.

MRS SWAN: In any case, if you read Flora's words simply for what they say, you would see that when she said I wouldn't *approve*, she did not mean this man or that man. Flora was ill. As it turned out she was dying. Cigarettes, whisky and men, and for that matter the hundred-yard dash, were not on the menu. She didn't need Dr Guppy to tell her that. No, I would not have approved. But Flora's weakness was always romance. To call it that.

ANISH: She had a romance with my father, then.

MRS SWAN: Quite possibly. Or with Captain Durance. Or his Highness the Rajah of Jummapur. Or someone else entirely. It hardly matters, looking back. Men were not really important to Flora. If they had been, they would have been fewer. She used them like batteries. When things went flat, she'd put in a new one.

SCENE SIXTEEN: INDIA

FLORA: 'Sweat collects and holds as a pearl at my throat,
  lets go and slides like a tongue-tip
  down a Modigliani,
  spills into the delta, now in the salt-lick,
  lost in the mangroves and the airless moisture,
  a seed-pearl returning to the oyster –
  et nos cedamus amori –
  (*She is on the verandah, at dawn. The Daimler car is
  approaching.*)
  (*Hearing the car*) Oh . . .
  (*The Daimler arrives. The engine is cut, the car door opens.*)
  David . . . ?

DURANCE: You're up!

FLORA: Up with the dawn. What on earth are *you* doing?

DURANCE: (*Approaching*) I'm afraid I came to wake you. Don't
  you sleep?

FLORA: Yes, I slept early and woke early.

DURANCE: The grapevine says you're leaving today.

FLORA: Yes.

DURANCE: I promised you a turn with the Daimler –
  remember?

FLORA: Yes.

DURANCE: I wanted to show you the sunrise. There's a pretty
  place for it only ten minutes down the road. Will you
  come?

FLORA: Can I go in my dressing-gown?

DURANCE: Well . . . better not.

FLORA: Righto. I'll get dressed.

DURANCE: Good.

FLORA: Come up.
  (DURANCE *comes up the verandah steps.*)

DURANCE: Writing a poem?

FLORA: Writing *out* a poem, to send to my sister.
  (*Going.*) I'll be quick.

DURANCE: The damnedest thing happened to me just now.

FLORA: (*Inside*) Can't hear you! Come in, it's quite safe.

(DURANCE *also enters the interior. He is now in the living-room.* FLORA *is further within the bungalow.*)

DURANCE: That fellow Das was on the road. I'm sure it was him.

FLORA: (*Off*) Well . . . why not?

DURANCE: He cut me.

FLORA: (*Off*) What?

DURANCE: I gave him a wave and he turned his back. I thought – 'Well, that's a first!'

FLORA: (*Further off*) Oh! There's hope for him yet.

DURANCE: They'll be throwing stones next.
What did you say?

FLORA: (*Off*) Wait – I'm going into the shower!

DURANCE: Oh. Do you want any help?

FLORA: (*Further off*) No, thank you, not today. (*After a few moments the shower is turned off.*)
(*In the bathroom*) Oh – yes, I do – my towel is in there – will you bung it on the bed?
(DURANCE *does this. He enters the bedroom.* FLORA's *voice is still beyond a closed door.*)

DURANCE: It's very damp.

FLORA: Yes. Second shower today. Out you go.

DURANCE: Oh . . . !

FLORA: What?

DURANCE: You're reading Emily Eden. I read it years ago.

FLORA: We'll miss the sunrise.

DURANCE: (*With the book*) There's a bit somewhere . . . she reminds me of you. 'Off with their heads!'

FLORA: (*Off*) Whose heads? Are you out?

(DURANCE *leaves the bedroom and enters the living-room.*)

DURANCE: Yes, I'm out. I'll see if I can find it.

(*Now* FLORA *is in the bedroom.*)

FLORA: (*Off*) I'll be two shakes.

DURANCE: Here it is – listen! – 'Simla, Saturday, May 25th, 1839. The Queen's Ball "came off" yesterday with great success . . .' Oh!

FLORA: (*Off*) What!

DURANCE: Nothing. I found your bookmark.

FLORA: (*Off*) Oh . . . (*Now she enters the living-room.*) I'm sort of decent – wet hair will have to do. It's not my bookmark – I put it in the book for safekeeping.

DURANCE: Where did you get such a thing?

FLORA: His Highness gave it to me.

DURANCE: Why?

FLORA: (*Reacting to his tone*) Because he is a Rajah. Because he was feeling generous. Because he hoped I'd go to bed with him. I don't know.

DURANCE: But how could he . . . feel himself in such intimacy with you? Had you met him before?

FLORA: No, David – it was a muddle –

DURANCE: But my dear girl, in accepting a gift like this don't you see – (*Pause.*) Well, it's your look-out, of course . . .

FLORA: Shall we go?

DURANCE: . . . but I'm in a frightfully difficult position now.

FLORA: Why?

DURANCE: Did he visit you?

FLORA: I visited him.

DURANCE: I know. Did he visit you?

FLORA: Mind your own business.

DURANCE: But it is my business.

FLORA: Because you think you love me?

DURANCE: No, I . . . Keeping tabs on what his Highness is up to is one of my . . . I mean I write reports to Delhi.

FLORA: (*Amused*) Oh, heavens!

DURANCE: You're a politically sensitive person, actually, by association with Chamberlain . . . I mean this sort of thing –

FLORA: Oh, darling policeman.

DURANCE: How can I ignore it?

FLORA: Don't ignore it. Report what you like. I don't mind, you see. *You* mind. But I don't. I have never minded. (*She steps on to the verandah.*)
(*In despair*) Oh – look at the sky! We're going to be too late!

DURANCE: (*To hell with it*) Come on! Our road is due west – if you know how to drive a car we'll make it.
(*They dash to the car, which roars into life and takes off at what sounds like a dangerous speed.*)

FLORA: 'My suitor came to say goodbye, and now I'm packed, portrait and all, and waiting for Mr Coomaraswami to take me to the station in his chariot. I'll post this in Jaipur as soon as I get there – I'm not going to post it here because I'm not. I feel fit as two lops this morning, and happy too, because something good happened here which made me feel half-way better about Modi and Gus and getting back to Paris too late – a sin which I'll carry to my grave.'

PIKE: This appears to be about the portrait. FC had arranged to return to France to sit for Modigliani in the autumn of 1919, but she delayed, arriving only on the morning of January 23rd, unaware that Modigliani had been taken to hospital. He died on the following evening without regaining consciousness, of tuberculosis, aged thirty-five. Thus, the frontispiece of this book shows the only known portrait of Flora Crewe, by an unknown Indian artist.

SCENE SEVENTEEN: ENGLAND

MRS SWAN *opens her front door from inside.*

MRS SWAN: Goodbye, Mr Das.

ANISH: Goodbye, Mrs Swan – thank you.

MRS SWAN: If you change your mind, I'm sure Flora wouldn't mind . . .

ANISH: No. Thank you, but it's my father I'm thinking of. He really wouldn't want it, not even in a footnote. So we'll say nothing to Mr Pike.

MRS SWAN: Well, don't put it away in a trunk either.

ANISH: Oh no! It will be on the wall at home, and I'll tell my children too. Thank you for tea – the Victoria sponge was best!

MRS SWAN: I'm baking again tomorrow. I still have raspberries left to pick and the plums to come, look. I always loved the fruit trees at home. (*Walking from front door to the gate. A quiet street.*)

ANISH: At home?

MRS SWAN: Orchards of apricot – almond – plum – I never cared for the southern fruits, mango, paw-paw and such like. But up in the North-West . . . I was quite unprepared for it when I first arrived. It was early summer. There was a wind blowing.

(*Cross-fading, wind.*)

And I have never seen such blossom, it blew everywhere, there were drifts of snow-white flowers piled up against the walls of the graveyard. I had to kneel on the ground and sweep the petals off her stone to read her name.

SCENE EIGHTEEN: INDIA

NELL: 'Florence Edith Crewe . . . Born March 21st 1895 . . .
   Died June 10th 1930. *Requiescat In Pacem.*'
FRANCIS: I'm afraid it's very simple. I hope that's all right.
NELL: Yes. It was good of you.
FRANCIS: Oh no, we look after our own. Of course.
NELL: I think she would have liked 'Poet' under her name. If I
   left some money here to pay for it . . . ?
FRANCIS: There are funds within my discretion. You may count
   on it, Miss Crewe. Poet. I should have thought of that. It is
   how *we* remember your sister.
NELL: Really?
FRANCIS: She read one evening. The Club has a habit of asking
   guests to sing for their supper and Miss Crewe read to us
   . . . from her work.
NELL: Oh dear.
FRANCIS: (*Laughs gently*) Yes. Well, we're a bit behind the
   times, I expect. But we all liked her very much. We didn't
   know what to expect because we understood she was a
   protégée of Mr Chamberlain, who had lectured in the town
   some years before. Perhaps you know him.
NELL: Yes. I'm not really in touch with him nowadays.
FRANCIS: Ah. It was just about this time of year when she
   was here, wasn't it? It was clear she wasn't well – these
   steps we just climbed, for instance, she could hardly
   manage them. Even so. Death in India is often more
   unexpected, despite being more common, if you
   understand me. I'm talking far too much. I'm so sorry.
   I'll wait at the gate. Please stay as long as you wish, I have
   no one waiting for me.
NELL: I won't be a moment. Flora didn't like mopers.
   (FRANCIS *leaves her.*)
   (*Quietly*) Bye bye, darling . . . oh – damn! (. . . *because she
   has burst into sobs. She weeps unrestrainedly.*)
FRANCIS: (*Returning*) Oh . . . oh, I say . . .

NELL: Oh, I'm sorry.

FRANCIS: No – please . . . can I . . . ?

(NELL *stops crying after a few moments.*)

NELL: I've messed up your coat. I've got a hanky somewhere.

FRANCIS: Would you like to . . . ? Here . . .

NELL: Yes. Thank you. (*She uses his handkerchief.*) I came too soon after all. I hated waiting a whole year but . . . well, anyway. Thank you, it's a bit wet. Should I keep it? Oh, look, I've found mine, we can swap.

FRANCIS: Don't you worry about anything. What a shame you had to come on your own. You have another sister, I believe. Or a brother?

NELL: No. Why?

FRANCIS: Oh. Flora was anxious to return to England to be an aunt, she said.

NELL: Yes. I had a baby in October. He only lived a little while, unfortunately. There was something wrong.

FRANCIS: Oh. I'm so sorry.

NELL: It's why I couldn't come before.

FRANCIS: Yes, I see. What rotten luck. What was his name?

NELL: Alexander. Sacha. Alexander Percival Crewe. How nice of you to ask. Nobody ever does. I say, how about that blossom!

(*They start to walk.*)

FRANCIS: Yes, it's quite a spot, isn't it? I hope you stay a while. First time in India?

NELL: Yes.

FRANCIS: Mind the loose stone here. May I . . . ?

NELL: Thank you. I'm sorry I blubbed, Mr Swan.

FRANCIS: I won't tell anyone. Do call me Francis, by the way. Nobody calls me Mr Swan.

NELL: Francis, then.

FRANCIS: Do you like cricket?

NELL: (*Laughs*) Well, I don't play a *lot*.

FRANCIS: There's a match tomorrow.

NELL: *Here?*

FRANCIS: Oh, yes. We're going to field a Test team next year, you know.

NELL: We?
FRANCIS: India.
NELL: Oh.

SCENE NINETEEN

EMILY EDEN: 'Simla, Saturday, May 25th, 1839. The Queen's
Ball "came off" yesterday with great success . . . Between
the two tents there was a boarded platform for dancing,
roped and arched in with flowers and then in different parts
of the valley, wherever the trees would allow of it, there
was "Victoria", "God Save The Queen" and "Candahar"
in immense letters twelve feet high. There was a very old
Hindu temple also prettily lit up. Vishnu, to whom I
believe it really belonged, must have been affronted. We
dined at six, then had fireworks, and coffee, and then they
all danced till twelve. It was the most beautiful evening;
such a moon, and the mountains looked so soft and *grave*,
after all the fireworks and glare. Twenty years ago no
European had ever been here, and there we were with a
band playing, and observing that St Cloup's Potage à la
Julienne was perhaps better than his other soups, and that
some of the ladies' sleeves were too tight according to the
overland fashions for March, and so on, and all this in the
face of those high hills, and we one hundred and five
Europeans being surrounded by at least three thousand
mountaineers, who, wrapped up in their hill blankets,
looked on at what we call our polite amusements, and
bowed to the ground if a European came near them. I
sometimes wonder they do not cut all our heads off and say
nothing more about it.'